BREAKING UP

JOSEPH TUROW

BREAKING UP AMERICA

ADVERTISERS AND THE NEW MEDIA WORLD

THE UNIVERSITY OF CHICAGO PRESS / CHICAGO AND LONDON

Joseph Turow is a professor in the University of Pennsylvania's Annenberg School for Communication. He is the author of five books, including *Media Systems in Society: Understanding Industries, Strategies and Power* and *Playing Doctor: Television, Storytelling and Medical Power*, and has written many articles for scholarly and popular periodicals. He is the 1997 chair of the Mass Communication Division of the International Communication Association.

The University of Chicago Press, Chicago 60637
The University of Chicago Press, Ltd., London
© 1997 by The University of Chicago
All rights reserved. Published 1997
Printed in the United States of America
06 05 04 03 02 01 00 99 98 97   1 2 3 4 5
ISBN: 0-226-81749-0

Turow, Joseph.
   Breaking up America : advertisers and the new media world / Joseph
Turow.
      p.   cm.
   Includes bibliographical references and index.
   ISBN 0-226-81749-0 (alk. paper)
   1. Advertising—Social aspects—United States.   2. Target
marketing—United States.   I. Title.
HF5813.U6T85   1997
659.1'042—dc20   96-9853
                                                                              CIP

⊗The paper used in this publication meets the
minimum requirements of the American National Standard
for Information Sciences—Permanence of Paper for
Printed Library Materials, ANSI Z39.48-1984.

For Jonathan, Marissa, and Rebecca

CONTENTS

PREFACE

THIS BOOK IS ABOUT the way advertisers have been breaking up America and about what that may mean for the media and society. The study came out of my long-standing interest in how media industries work and how they contribute to culture. I noticed that media were increasingly encouraging people to separate themselves into more and more specialized groups and to develop distinctive viewing, reading, and listening habits that stressed differences between their groups and others.

I believed initially that mass-media firms were the primary sources of this development, a result of executives' competition for audiences in the face of cable TV, home computers, the Internet, interactive television, CD-ROM, and other new technologies of the 1970s, 1980s, and 1990s. The more I looked at the issue, though, the more I suspected that the advertising industry, in its influential position as the major support system of U.S. media, was the key force behind this divisive message to America. Intrigued by the complexity of the situation and concerned about its social implications, I decided to study the contemporary relationship between advertisers, the media, and their approaches to America.

I began the examination with the late 1970s because my preliminary work suggested that this was when advertisers started to fundamentally reevaluate their views of America and the media. Three methods guided the investigation: in-depth reading of advertising and media trade magazines, attendance at industry conferences, and interviews with executives from a variety of industries. The methods complemented each other, and I emphasized different ones for different parts of the book.

The trade publications were particularly useful for chapters 3, 4, and

5, which track the development of advertisers' shared ideas about America over eighteen years. To the casual observer, magazines aimed at advertising practitioners may seem simply to be lists of who has won what account and who has been promoted to what position. Actually, though, advertising trade publications such as *Adweek, Direct Marketing,* and *Advertising Age* are filled with discussions of society. That is because ad people see understanding the U.S. population as one of their primary mandates. After all, they have to convince Americans to buy things.

Ad agencies and their clients generate materials that explore consumer trends in even more detail than the trade press does, but most such reports, memos, and computer printouts are proprietary. In the absence of access to large bodies of in-house marketing data, and because the memory of ad practitioners must be considered spotty when it comes to recalling attitudes about different types of Americans as those attitudes evolved over time, trade magazines represent the best vehicles for tracking the way advertising and media practitioners talked to each other about U.S. society from the late 1970s through the mid–1990s.

Debates about audience-measurement systems, critiques of the "best" ads of the month, interviews with executives, excerpts of speeches from conferences, suggestions for the most efficient ways to attract certain audiences to certain media: these and many other items in the trade press reveal advertisers' assumptions about consumers and their lifestyles. Often the presentation of consumers is blunt and explicit. Just as often, the picture ad people paint of consumers is implicit and must be teased out of their discussions.

In either case, advertising practitioners are not likely to disclose specific information to the "trades" that their firms consider especially valuable about consumers. The reason that they deal with the trade press at all probably relates to a belief that being quoted might give existing and potential clients the sense that they are dealing with executives and organizations at the cutting edge of trends. Such self-interest notwithstanding, what advertising practitioners say in the trade magazines contributes to a continuing discussion across their industry about what is happening in society, how marketers ought to respond to it, and how they *are* responding to it.

I started my investigation of this discussion by reading all articles that appeared in *Advertising Age* from 1977 through mid–1995, taking notes on the ones that mentioned consumers in any way. I chose Crain Communications' *Advertising Age* because for decades it has been the central journal of news and opinion for the advertising industry. Currently, Crain sends out eighty thousand copies a week that it estimates are read by 300,000 people. Through most of the eighteen years, issues ranged in length from thirty-five to seventy-five pages. During part of the 1980s, the magazine expanded to twice a week, often exceeding 100 pages.

Summaries of over twelve thousand *Advertising Age* articles made it into my computer. My database program allowed me to search for any word I had entered about any article. So, for example, I could chronologically organize summaries of all the writings that described particular consumers—men, women, Hispanic Americans, suburbanites, children, blacks, and others—and that discussed strategies for reaching them via media. To make sure that *Advertising Age* was not a peculiar place to draw data for chapters 3 and 4, I examined less systematically several other media and marketing trade magazines that appeared during the '70s, '80s, and '90s, most prominently *Marketing and Media Decisions, Variety, Broadcasting, Mediaweek, Adweek,* and *Direct Marketing.* I found that the basic themes about American consumers were the same across all the magazines.

My aim in chapters 5, 6, and 7 was to explore the way in which advertisers' considerations of the U.S. population have been shaping contemporary media. Here the interviews and conferences were most useful. I attended seven industry conferences on topics as varied as interactive television, broadcast network TV, cable TV, direct marketing, and the general entertainment business. They gave me an additional window on the way advertising and media practitioners discuss strategies to attract and hold audiences. In addition, the conferences, together with my reading, pointed me to decision makers involved with issues regarding advertising, audiences, and media that stood at the center of the chapters.

I spoke to eighty-six decision makers, mostly by telephone, for periods that ranged from fifteen minutes to an hour and a half, with most lasting about half an hour. Here are the names of the people who graciously let me interview them, with their title at the time of our talk: Mark Abellera, copywriter, Messner Vetere Berger McNamee Schmetterer/Euro RSCB; Doug Alligood, senior vice president/special markets, BBDO Worldwide; Robert Alter, vice chairman, Cable Television Advertising Bureau; Kevin Ampter, art director, Messner Vetere Berger McNamee Schmetterer/Euro RSCG; Robert Arix, president, Capital Sports; Tony Levitan, co-founder, Greet Street and Virtual Mall; Roger Baron, vice president, director of market research, Foot Cone Belding; Rena Bartos, president, the Rena Bartos Company; Bonnie Berest, executive director of media services, Publicis Bloom; Andy Besh, senior vice president of marketing, the Sci Fi Channel; Judy Black, senior partner and co-director of interactive development, Bozell; Eric Blum, account manager, Modem Media; Burt Boersma, former senior vice president, publishing director, Meredith Corporation; Ted Bolton, president, Bolton Research; Stu Budow, vice president, client services, Vitt Media Services; Gilda Bullon, account executive, Mendoza, Dillon & Asociados; Shelly Cagner, press relations, Arbitron; Ray Cave, former managing editor, *Time* magazine; Stanley Cohen, former Washington editor for *Advertising Age;* Jon Coleman, president, Coleman Research; Charlie Connard, vice president, Strubco; John Cummings, president, John Cummings and Partners.

Adam Curry, CEO, Onramp; Fred Danzig, former editor, *Advertising Age;* Doug Darfield, vice president, Univision; James Derosier, vice president, Mastercard; Steve Descheines, head of market development, *Time* magazine; John Dobbs, agency client services director, Hensley, Segal Rentschler; Barbara Dolan, client services director, Mowry Company; Scott Donaton, reporter, *Advertising Age;* Rich Dunray, interviewer, Irwin Research Services; Laura Eisman, art director, *Family Life;* Ann Elliot, director of information, Nielsen Audience Measurement; John Evans, executive vice president of development, News Corporation; Kate Fitzgerald, reporter, *Advertising Age;* Patricia Glick, senior research analyst, Magazine Publishers of America; Gordon Hughes, vice president in marketing, Outdoor Advertising Association; Alan Gottesmann, analyst, Paine Webber; Jay Guither, vice president in charge of new ventures, Arbitron; Tommy Hadges, president, Pollack Media Group; Dale Hopkins, marketing director, E!: Entertainment Television; Larry Hyans, vice president, audience analysis, ABC-TV; Marian Jacobson, brand manager, Gatorade division, Quaker Oats Company.

Alexandra Jaffe, manager of promotion/marketing, CBS Interactive; Dorothy Kalins, editor, *Garden Design;* Hal Katz, CEO, Katz Marketing and Media; Suzanne Kaufman, executive vice president, director of new technologies, Media Edge; Allen Klein, executive vice president, group creative director, Leo Burnett; Judith Langer, president, Langer Associates; Gary Langstaff, president, Retail Resolve; Anthony Lee, marketing development vice president, Spiegel Catalog; Byron Lewis, chair and CEO of Uniworld ad agency; Owen Lipstein, editorial director, Sussex Publishing; Kenneth Maley, president, Media Consultants; Lee Masters, president and CEO of E!: Entertainment Television; Jeff Milgram, president, Event Marketing Strategies; and Ross Mottla, program director, WDRE: The Underground Network; Jerry Ohlsten, director of marketing, Simmons Market Research; Joseph Ostrow, executive vice president, media director, Foote, Cone & Belding Worldwide; Barbara Paddock, event marketing, Bank of New York; Brad Pallas, art director, *Woman's Day;* Lance Primus, president, the *New York Times;* James Ramsey, senior vice president—exeuctive creative director, McCann-Erickson; Mark Rice, vice president, network—New York agencies, Nielsen Media Research.

Don Rogers, account executive, Modem Media; Charles Rutman, senior vice president, corporate media director, Backer Spielvogel Bates Worldwide; David Sandler, senior editor, *Time* magazine; Adrien Seixas, station sales, Bohbot Entertainment; Arnie Semsky, executive vice president, director of media and programming services, BBDO Worldwide; Raymond Serafin, writer-reporter, *Advertising Age;* Joe Silverman, corporate communication, Leo Burnett; Louis Slovinsky, senior vice president, corporate communications, HBO; Adam Smith, creative director, *Swing* magazine; Steve Sternberg, senior partner, BJK&E Media Group; Brad Surling, manager of Eastern region, Onramp; Emily Swartzentruber, senior vice president, media director, J. Walter Thompson, New York; Hans Tennsma, design director, *Family Fun* magazine; Jonathan Tuttle, design director, *Parenting* magazine; Lesa Ukman, president, International Events Group; Donna Warner, editor-in-chief, *Metropolitan Home;* Brook Wayne, writer, *Time* magazine's advertorial division; Mike Wilberding, senior vice president, director of client services, Ogilvy & Mather, Detroit; Thomas Wyman, former president, CBS Incorporated.

In the end the trade papers, conferences, and interviews yielded a rich soup of information about the way people from various parts of the advertising and media industries have worked together to understand America and to adjust their media materials to match that understanding. I could not have put my findings together into this book were it not for the enormous help of many people along the way. In addition to those I interviewed, a number of people and organizations helped me with resources and time to work on this book. I am grateful to the National Endowment for the Humanities for supporting an important segment of this research. The University of Pennsylvania Research Foundation and the Annenberg School for Communication at Penn, under the direction of Dean Kathleen Hall Jamieson, also funded portions of the research and writing. Student assistants over a number of years, Mimi Bartell, Karen Frazer, David Jarman, Melissa Jumper, George Nimeh, Vincenzo Petretti, Maggie Williams and Ben Wyche, pitched in with bibliographic searches and editorial comments. Thanks also to Larry Gross, Russ Neuman, Jan Radway, Dan Romer, Michael Schudson, Horst Stipp, and Susan Williamson for their helpful suggestions. John Tryneski and Jo Ann Kiser, my editors, offered insightful advice as the manuscript moved toward completion.

My wife, Judy, has followed all of this from beginning to end. Her genuine enthusiasm for the project has mixed with good critical insight, an ability to place the whole thing into perspective, and remarkable patience. I thank her most of all.

Joseph Turow
Philadelphia, 1996

ONE

TARGETING A NEW WORLD

"**ADVERTISERS WILL HAVE** their choice of horizontal demographic groups and vertical psychographic program types."[1]

"Our judgment as to the enhanced quality of our subscriber base has been confirmed by the advertisers."[2]

"Unfortunately, most media plans are based on exposure opportunities. This is particularly true for television because G.R.P. analysis is usually based on television ratings and ratings do not measure actual exposure."[3]

Most Americans would likely have a hard time conceiving the meaning of these quotations. The words would clearly be understood as English, but the jargon would seem quite mysterious. They might be surprised to learn that they have heard a specialized language that advertisers use about them. Rooted in various kinds of research, the language has a straightforward purpose. The aim is to package individuals, or groups of people, in ways that make them useful targets for the advertisers of certain products through certain types of media.

Clearly, the way the advertising industry talks about us is not the way we talk about ourselves. Yet when we look at the advertisements that emerge from the cauldron of marketing strategies and strange terminology, we see pictures of our surroundings that we can understand, even recognize. The pictures remind us that the advertising industry does far more than sell goods and services through the mass media. With budgets that add up to hundreds of billions of dollars, the industry exceeds the church and the school in its ability to promote images about our place in society—where we belong, why, and how we should act toward others.

This book is about a revolutionary shift that is taking place in the way advertisers talk about America and the way they create ads and shape media to reflect that talk. The shift has been influenced by, and has been influencing, major changes in the audiovisual options available to the home. But it most importantly has been driven by, and has been driving, a profound sense of division in American society.

The following pages argue that the era we are entering is one in which advertisers will work with media firms to create the electronic equivalents of gated communities. Marketers are aware that the U.S. population sees itself marked by enormous economic and cultural tensions. Marketers don't feel, though, that it benefits them to encourage Americans to deal with these tensions head-on through a media brew of discussion, entertainment, and argumentation aimed at broadly diverse audiences. Rather, new approaches to marketing make it increasingly worthwhile for even the largest media companies to separate audiences into different worlds according to distinctions that ad people feel make the audiences feel secure and comfortable. The impact of these activities on Americans' views of themselves and others will be profound, enduring, and often disturbing.

The changes have begun only recently. The hallmark is the way marketers and media practitioners have been approaching the development of new audiovisual technology. Before the late 1970s, most people in the United States could view without charge three commercial broadcast stations, a public (non-commercial) TV station, and possibly an independent commercial station (one not affiliated with a network). By the mid–1990s, several independent broadcast TV stations, scores of cable and satellite television channels, videocassettes, video games, home computer programs, online computer services, and the beginnings of two-way ("interactive") television had become available to major segments of the population with an interest and a budget to match.

As the following pages will show, people in the advertising industry are working to integrate the new media channels into the broader world of print and electronic media to maximize the entire system's potential for selling. They see these developments as signifying not just the breakup of the traditional broadcast network domain, but as indicating a breakdown in social cohesion, as well. Advertisers' most public talk about America—in trade magazine interviews, trade magazine ads, convention speeches, and interviews for this book—consistently features a nation that is breaking up. Their vision is of a fractured population of self-indulgent, frenetic, and suspicious individuals who increasingly reach out only to people like themselves.

Advertising practitioners do not view these distinctions along primarily racial or ethnic lines, though race and ethnicity certainly play a part, provoking turf battles among marketers. Rather, the new portraits of society that advertisers and media personnel invoke involve the blending of income, generation, marital status, and gender into a soup of geographical and psychological profiles they call "lifestyles."

Breaking Up America explains how this vision of America came to be and how advertisers developed it from the mid–1970s through the mid–1990s. The core argument is that the U.S. is experiencing a major shift in balance between society-making media and segment-making media. Segment-making media are those that encourage small slices of society to talk to themselves, while society-making media are those that have the potential to get all those segments to talk to each other. During most of the twentieth century, a huge number of ad-supported vehicles— mostly newspapers and magazines—have served as a way to reinforce, extend, even create, identities for an impressive array of segments that advertisers have cared about, from immigrant Czechs to luxury-car owners to Knights of Columbus and far more. At the same time, some ad-sponsored newspapers, radio networks, and television networks—especially the latter—have been able to reach across these groups. Through entertainment, news, and information, society-making media have acted out concerns and connections that people ought to share in a larger national community.

For those who hope for a caring society, each level of medium has had its problems. Segment-making media have sometimes offered their audiences narrow, prejudiced views of other social segments. Similarly, society-making media have marginalized certain groups, perpetuated stereotypes of many others, and generally presented a portrayal of the world that is more the ideal vision of the corporate establishment sponsoring them than a reflection of competing visions of various publics. Nevertheless, the existence of both forms of media has meant that the *potential* has existed for an equilibrium between healthy social segments and a healthy collectivity. In the ideal scenario segment-making media strengthen the identities of interest groups, while society-making media allow those groups to move out of their parochial scenes to talk with, argue against, and entertain one another. The result is a rich and diverse sense of overarching connectedness: what a vibrant society is about.

Breaking Up America argues that we are losing the potential to achieve that scenario because of a profound movement by advertisers away from society-making media. The fundamental changes taking place in the television industry have been leading national advertisers, along with their ad agencies and media firms, in unprecedented attempts to search out and exploit differences between consumers. These activities have centered on entering individuals' private spaces—their homes, their cars, their offices—with lifestyle-specific news, information, entertainment, and, especially, commercial messages. They also have involved tailoring public spaces—concerts, races, and other open-to-the-public events—so that they attract customers who fit narrow profiles demanded by particular sponsors.

At the business level, what is driving all this is a major shift in the balance between targeting and mass marketing in U.S. media. Mass marketing involves aiming a home-based medium or outdoor event at people irrespective of their background or patterns of activities (their lifestyles). Targeting, by contrast, involves the intentional pursuit of specific segments of society—groups and even individuals. The Underground [radio] Network, the Comedy Central cable channel, and *Details* magazine are far more targeted than the ABC Television Network, the Sony Jumbotron Screen on Times Square, and the Super Bowl. Yet even these examples of targeting are far from close to the pinpointing of audiences that many ad people expect is possible.

The ultimate aim of this new wave of marketing is to reach different groups with specific messages about how certain products tie into their lifestyles. Target-minded media firms are helping advertisers do that by building *primary media communities.* These are formed when viewers or readers feel that a magazine, TV channel, newspaper, radio station, or other medium reaches people like them, resonates with their personal beliefs, and helps them chart their position in the larger world. For advertisers, tying into those communities means gaining consumer loyalties that are nearly impossible to establish in today's mass market.

Nickelodeon and MTV were pioneer attempts to establish this sort of ad-sponsored communion on cable television. While they started as cable channels, they have become something more. Owned by media giant Viacom, they are lifestyle parades that invite their target audiences (relatively upscale children and young adults, respectively) into a sense of belonging that goes far beyond the coaxial wire into books, magazines, videotapes, and outdoor events that Viacom controls or licenses.

The idea of these sorts of "programming services" is to cultivate a must-see, must-read, must-share mentality that makes the audience feel part of a family, attached to the program hosts, other viewers, and sponsors. It is a strategy that extends across a wide spectrum of marketing vehicles, from cable TV to catalogs, from direct mailings to online computer services, from outdoor events to in-store clubs. In all these areas, national advertisers make it clear that they prefer to conduct their targeting with the huge media firms they had gotten to know in earlier years. But the giants don't always let their offspring operate on huge production budgets. To keep costs low enough to satisfy advertisers' demands for efficient targeting, much of ad-supported cable television is based on recycled materials created or distributed by media conglomerates. What makes MTV, ESPN, Nickelodeon, A&E, and other such "program services" distinctive is not the uniqueness of the programs but the special character created by their *formats:* the flow of their programs, packaged to attract the right audience at a price that will draw advertisers.

But, as later chapters will show, media firms have come to believe that simply attracting groups to specialized formats is often not enough. Urging people who do not fit the desired lifestyle profile *not* to be part of the audience is sometimes also an aim, since it makes the community more pure and thereby more efficient for advertisers. So in the highly competitive media environment of the 1980s and early 1990s, cable companies aiming to lure desirable types to specialized formats have felt the need to create "signature" materials that both drew the "right" people and signaled the "wrong" people that they ought to go away. It is no accident that the producers of certain signature programs on Nickelodeon (for example, *Ren and Stimpy*) and MTV (such as *Beavis and Butt-head*) in the early 1990s acknowledge that they chase away irrelevant viewers as much as they attract desirable ones.

An even more effective form of targeting, ad people believe, is a type that goes beyond chasing undesirables away. It simply excludes them in the first place. Using computer models based on zip codes and a variety of databases, it is economically feasible to tailor materials for small groups, even individuals. That is already taking place in the direct mail, telemarketing, and magazine industries. With certain forms of interactive television, it is technologically quite possible to send some TV programs and commercials only to neighborhoods, census blocks, and households that advertisers want to reach. Media firms are working toward a time when people will be able to choose the news, information, and entertainment they want when they want it. Advertisers who back these developments will be able to offer different product messages—and variable discounts—to individuals based on what they know about them.

Clearly, not all these technologies are widespread. Clearly, too, there is a lot of hype around them. Many companies that stand to benefit from the spread of target marketing have doubtless exaggerated the short time it will take to get there and the low costs that will confront advertisers once they do. Moreover, as will be seen, some marketers have been slower than others to buy into the usefulness of a media system that encourages the partitioning of people with different lifestyles.

Nevertheless, the trajectory is clear. A desire to label people so that they may be separated into primary media communities is transforming the way television is programmed, the way newspapers are "zoned," the way magazines are printed, and the way cultural events are produced and promoted. Most critically, advertisers' interest in exploiting lifestyle differences is woven into the basic assumptions about media models for the next century—the so-called 500 Channel Environment or the future Information Superhighway.

For me and you—individual readers and viewers—this segmentation and targeting can portend terrific things. If we can afford to pay, or if we're important to sponsors who will pick up the tab, we will be able to receive immediately the news, information, and entertainment we order. In a world pressing us with high-speed concerns, we will surely welcome media and sponsors that offer to surround us with exactly what we want when we want it.

As an entirety, though, society in the United States will lose out. The following chapters argue the dark side of the unrelenting slicing and dicing of America that advertisers are already beginning to orchestrate through all major media. The chapters show that marketers look for splits in the social fabric and then reinforce and extend the splits for their own ends. Wanting the marketers' money, media firms buy into these divisions, build formats around them, and work to attract the audiences they imply. The way they do it—urging consumers toward media designed for them and away from media designed for others—discourages people from coming into contact with news and entertainment that other parts of society find important.

One of the consequences of turning the U.S. into a pastiche of market-driven labels is that such a multitude of categories makes it impossible for a person to directly overlap with more than a tiny portion of them. If primary media communities continue to take hold, their large numbers will diminish the chance that individuals who identify with certain social categories will even have an opportunity to learn about others. Off-putting signature programs such as *Beavis and Butt-head* may make the situation worse, causing individuals annoyed by the shows or what they read about them to feel alienated from groups that appear to enjoy them. If you are told over and over again that different kinds of people are not part of your world, you will be less and less likely to want to deal with those people.

The creation of customized media materials will likely take this lifestyle segregation further. It will allow, even encourage, individuals to live in their own personally constructed worlds, separated from people and issues that they don't care about or don't want to be bothered with. The desire to do that may accelerate when, as is the case in the late-twentieth-century United States, seemingly intractable antagonisms based on age, income, ethnicity, geography, and more result from competition over jobs and political muscle. In these circumstances, market segmentation and targeting may accelerate an erosion of the tolerance and mutual dependence between diverse groups that enable a society to work. Ironically, the one common message across media will be that a common center for sharing ideas and feelings is more and more difficult to find—or even to care about.

The ideas explored in this book tie into a growing literature on the way we "imagine" the civilization that surrounds us. The writings spring from the basic realization that words such as *society, community,* and *na-*

tion do not stand for real "things"; you can't point to a society or nation as you can point to a zebra in a zoo. Rather, the words represent abstractions, conceptions on how people relate to others. We typically use the word society, for example, to refer to large numbers of individuals, groups, and organizations that see themselves linked politically and economically. We might think of the word community as indicating people who live in the same locality or, alternatively, as meaning people who hold similar interests.[4]

Saying that people generate versions of society implies that society is constructed; it is created through communication.[5] In a multitude of ways, people tell themselves and others about who belongs to society, what they are like and how they live, what is good about them, what distasteful. Every such construction involves selection. Accuracy, if it is considered important, may be only a small part of the challenge. Categories that may seem easy to gauge—for example, the number of people in the society who are literate—turn out upon closer inspection to reflect a lot of social deliberation, even argument. (Exactly how do we judge whether a person is "literate"? Why that way and not another way?)

Claiming the right to construct versions of society for large populations means claiming a lot of power. The military, education, government, medicine, religion, and the law are among the institutions that traditionally hold the prerogative to proclaim what the world looks like or ought to look like. In the U.S. and many other countries, media such as newspapers, magazines, movies, radio, musical recordings, and television also offer constructions of the world to millions of people. While medicine addresses health care concerns and the law sees the formal rules in society as its domain, the media institution takes as its territory the depiction of these and all other institutions. The media, in short, are the quintessential vehicles for portraying the life of society *to* society.[6]

Most people who write about the media's power to present notions of society emphasize that it takes place through the telling of stories in one form or another. Their point is that all forms of media performance, from *Beverly Hills 90210* to MTV videos to *Rush Limbaugh* to the *New York Times,* continually provide people with insights into parts of their society with which they have little direct contact. The power of stories is not that all people interpret media images in the same way, for they often do not. Rather, the tales direct attention toward certain concerns and away from others. Stories tell audiences what civilization out there is like, how they fit in, what others think of people like them, and what people "like themselves" think of others.

Because of their concern with storytelling, though, the writers ignore an even more blatant way in which media signal social similarities and differences to large populations. That is through the very structure of the media system: the number and distribution of different types of media outlets—different magazines, newspapers, radio stations, and so on. The idea that the structure of an institution promotes certain views of social life has been put forward convincingly by social historian Benedict Anderson. Using the concept of "nationhood" in Malaysia as a starting point, Anderson shows how the governing elite has inserted its ideas about society into the structures, or basic patterns, of daily life. The way citizenship is defined, who gets to go to school, when they go to school and where, who gets to be a civil servant—these and other laws have built into the fabric of public activities particular ideas about society and its boundaries.[7]

Anderson doesn't mention media, but his point would seem generalizable there, as well. *Format* is an especially relevant part of media structure. The term refers to the layout and general approach that TV networks, magazines, newspapers, and other media outlets take to their material, including advertising. It is the format that creates what people think of as the "personality" of those media. Radio stations may act out their particular formats through the songs they play, the commercials they air, and the banter of the on-air personalities. Magazines and newspapers have detectable formats, too. The *New York Times* is recognizably the *New York Times* every day, while *People* magazine has a very different, yet consistent, style. In television, *Nick at Nite,* a nightly cable service loaded with TV shows and movies chosen to attract people who grew up in the 1950s and 1960s, is but one example of a channel format.

With Benedict Anderson in mind, we should expect that the organizations involved in news and entertainment would build certain social values, priorities, and ideas about the audience into the formats they create. Tracking how they do that would seem particularly useful now, when the media system is changing drastically. Understanding the views of society that media practitioners are knowingly building into the new media structure can help us get a handle on what the new structure means in comparison to the one it is gradually displacing.

Exploring the new media system's structure also provides a new way to evaluate a growing literature that centers on the consequences of the new wave of television technologies for American life. There are those who feel that new gizmos will bring society together and others who believe they will push it apart. Nicholas Negroponte, director of the futuristic Media Lab at the Massachussetts Institute of Technology, is an unabashed utopian. In his 1995 book, *Being Digital,* he notes that organizations are at work creating intelligent computer-based menus, or "navigators," that will construct distinctive rosters of news and entertainment according to people's descriptions of their interests as well as continual analyses of what they choose from among the navigators' selections. Technology will encourage even the daily newspaper to be customized and delivered by wire to a flexible and portable paper-thin screen; Negroponte calls it *The Daily Me.*

Negroponte sees this development as a boon for both the individual and society, even though he is conscious of the tensions between the two. Despite his prediction that "true personalization" will be the order of the day, he insists that the technological setup will not deter people from looking outside their personal spheres.[8] Marketing consultants Don Peppers and Martha Rogers could hardly disagree more. They predict in their marketing guidebook *The One to One Future* that interactive media will inevitably lead people to belong to "image tribes"—their term for primary media communities made up of people who share lifestyles.

They picture a society linked by optical fibers, "with the information power of today's supercomputers at Everyman's fingertips." Individuals, they say, "will have the chance to restrict the flow of information to themselves, and to congregate into politically segregated factions, electronically connected only to other like-minded group members."[9] Marketers should realize, they say, that "an image tribe's common gathering places will include the electronic stores, electronic bulletin boards and video mail meetings of tomorrow's . . . media. If you have a business in the future . . . you'll turn your store into [that kind of] electronic gathering place."[10]

Like Negroponte, Peppers and Rogers attribute social consequences not to media firms—or any other organizations—but to the logic of media technologies. It will happen, they argue, because media technologies will make it happen. Such technological determinism is not total fantasy. After all, decisions to develop technologies such as interactive

TV and the Internet necessarily involve assumptions about what the world is like and how the world ought to be. Those values might well lend what might be called "social tendencies" to a new technology. Still, once technologies are introduced into the media system, government agencies, corporate competitors, and other forces shape them in ways their creators never considered. Executives develop formats and content that present perspectives on society. These may be quite different from the views that shaped the products in the first place.

The views of technological determinists, then, must only be a starting point. The best tack is to evaluate their predictions in view of the influences that are acting to shape the way the technologies are used. Answering three basic questions is crucial for getting a sense of the media system's trajectory for defining Americans to Americans: What considerations lead executives in media industries to hold certain views about society? To what extent, and how, do those views guide the way they create formats and content for the media system? And to what extent, and how, do these resulting formats and content encourage consumers toward separate primary communities ("image tribes") or toward a balanced concern for the personal and the collective?

The advertising industry provides a compelling place to answer these questions. A proposition at the core of this book is that what advertisers do gives them the power over the very structure of the media system. A corollary is that it is impossible to grasp the direction or implications of the emerging media world without looking at the ad industry's role in that world.

Advertising involves payment for attempts to persuade people to purchase or otherwise support a product or service. It is by itself a major producer of communication materials. Billboards, handbills, catalogs, audio cassettes, records, even video cassettes, are part of a blizzard of media that sometimes carries only sales messages. Often, though, advertisers (the companies that want to sell products or services) find it useful to be media clients, to pay media firms for placing commercial announcements alongside materials that don't seem to have any obvious persuasive intent—for example, newspaper and magazine articles, radio programs and television shows. The advertisers hope that the people using those media will attend to the commercial messages and respond favorably to them.

Media executives typically consider it part of their duties to think about how advertising can fit into their plans. Their motive is the same as it has been for over a hundred years: money. In the U.S., funding for the media through taxes is meager. Media firms have therefore developed two other streams of support: one from individual consumers and the other from companies that want to sell products or services to them. Purchases by individuals are most familiar in the book, newspaper, and magazine industries as well as in the recorded music and movie businesses. The approach has also gained ground in the electronic media. Pay-cable channels such as HBO, pay-per-view movie selections, and digital music services assess the public for discrete items (the viewing of a particular film, for example) or for unlimited use of a service for a specified period of time.

But charging individuals has always led many media executives to fear that after a certain point, and not too high a point, the public will simply not want to pay any more. Moreover, the technology of broadcasting in its early days did not allow individual stations to charge fees to listeners. (The begathons of public radio and television are vivid reminders that no hand reaches out of the electronic box to stop individuals from tuning in if they haven't paid.) The result was that media firms found themselves hoping that their cash flow would be augmented by advertisers wanting to reach their audiences.

Historically, the advertiser-media relationship developed differently in different media. Newspapers and magazines allowed ads early in their existence, while moviemakers and movie theaters have only recently invited advertisers into their operations on a national level. Book companies have always dabbled in advertising, mostly to announce their own books. Similarly, while recording firms have never placed advertising between music cuts, they have advertised their other albums within CD cases. Home video distributors have been following the record model, typically placing only film ads on their cassettes. At the same time, some video firms have been quite a bit more active than record companies in building revenues by using videos themselves to persuade people to buy products. So, for example, a marketer (McDonald's, Goody's) may advertise that consumers can get one or another of a company's video at a deep discount where they buy burgers or music CDs.

These examples suggest how widespread and varied advertiser support of the media has become. For a number of key industries, in fact, ad support makes the difference between life and death. For consumer magazine and newspaper publishers, advertiser sponsorship has come to equal at least 50 percent of their revenues. For broadcast radio and television, advertising has until recently represented virtually all of the cash intake.

If Wall Street estimates are anything near accurate, the amount of money advertisers shell out is impressive. According to the firm of Veronis, Suhler and Associates, which brokers the sale of media companies, in 1993 advertisers spent about $26.6 billion in support of network and local television broadcasting and about $9.4 billion to fund network and local radio broadcasting. In addition, the ad industry spent $46 billion on daily newspapers, compared to the $31.9 billion that consumers shelled out. Advertisers funded consumer magazines to the tune about $7.3 billion, while consumers dropped a smaller $6.7 billion into the periodicals' coffers.[11]

Cable television did not follow the pattern; there subscriptions to consumers accounted for $19 billion while advertising comprised a much smaller $2.5 billion. Yet advertisers' interest in cable developed only in the 1980s, and slowly at first. By the 1990s, though, advertising was growing in cable faster than in most other media. Veronis, Suhler predicted that cable advertising would increase nearly 11 percent a year through much of the decade, a rate that would be almost three times the growth of cable subscriptions from consumers.[12]

While these advertising numbers are imposing, they do not represent nearly the full presence of advertising in the media system. They do not, for example, reflect the monies that advertisers spent to sponsor relatively new vehicles such as CD-ROM, online services such as the Internet and America Online, supermarket-based radio stations, and informational kiosks at stores and shopping centers. Nor do they include promotions (sweepstakes, coupons, giveaways), direct marketing (e.g., catalogs, infomercials), and the placement of products in the plots of video games, TV shows, and movies. Industry estimates indicate that the amount spent for all advertising more than doubles if, following recent inclinations among ad people, we draw the boundaries of the industry to include these activities.

Expenditures of such magnitude begin to suggest why media executives consider the needs of advertisers when they consider starting a new magazine, cable channel, or Internet site. Which advertisers they think of depends at least partly on the medium.[13] It is hard for television executives to ignore Philip Morris, for example, which spent about $2 billion to advertise hundreds of products in 1989, 19 percent of it going to network TV and 2 percent going to local stations. Even more difficult to ignore are classes of advertisers—food firms, airlines, tobacco companies, and the like—that pack a lot of financial clout in certain media businesses. For example, only five department stores (May, R. H. Macy, Sears, Campeau, and Dayton Hudson) together contributed about $819 million to newspaper coffers in 1989.[14]

Less obvious, but even more concentrated in their ability to direct the flow of cash to media across the U.S., are the advertising agencies that serve national advertisers. In 1993 thirteen advertising agencies each paid over one billion dollars to various U.S. mass media firms for carrying their commercial announcements. The range of manufacturers whose cash the agencies controlled was quite broad. For example, Young and Rubicam, with $1.7 billion in ad placement billings (and $7.9 billion worldwide), operated in support of firms as diverse as AT&T, Bausch and Lomb, Colgate Palmolive, Dr. Pepper, Eastman Kodak, Holiday Inn, and Xerox.[15] Of that money, the agency allocated $645.8 million of its billings to network TV, $158.9 million to consumer magazines, $97.8 million to newspapers, and $22.9 million to outdoor advertising. Much of the rest went to cable TV, local ("spot") TV, network radio, Sunday newspaper-distributed magazines, and business publications. Other agency leaders doled out money in rather similar proportions.[16]

Popular books, movies, magazine articles, and television shows encourage most people to think of a large and powerful ad agency such as Young and Rubicam when they think about the advertising industry. Although not the only model for success in an increasingly complex marketing world, a "full service" agency such as Y&R does embody the three basic functions of adwork: creative persuasion, media planning and buying, and market research.

It may seem strange to list the creative persuasion function first after spending several paragraphs on the buying clout of the ad industry. Ultimately, though, advertising is about persuasion. Creative directors, copywriters, art directors, and illustrators work individually and in teams to come up with ideas that will move the chosen audience to try a product or service. No shrewdness in buying time or space can blur the primary importance of the ideas behind the message and the artistry of the execution.

Society is constructed in this meeting of ideas and artistry. Whether a magazine ad that details the joys of a Ford Mustang, a TV commercial that extols Pond's cold cream, or a video game that includes McDonald's Hamburglar in its cast, the creators' goal is to suggest a story that bespeaks the product's usefulness for the audience. Of course, to do that the ad people must have thoughts about the audience, particularly as it relates to the product they are selling. The goal is to imagine the product in a social environment that reflects the intended audience and its values. Armed with these imaginings, a creative team can concoct a sales pitch. Inevitably, it portrays a world of the intended audience, a problem in that world, and actions that show how the product can solve the problem.

The phrase "intended audience" leads us to a concern with media buying, the second agency function. Just as "creatives" must construct a version of society when they make commercial messages, so planners must work with an idea of the proposed audience's social world when buying time and space. The reason is that the planners have to choose the correct place for the ad to be seen by its intended market. They do that by learning as much as they can about the people and their interactions with media at home and out, at work and play. While planning involves the detailed imagining of this audience and its media use, sometimes in cooperation with creative personnel, buying involves the pragmatic acting out of this imagination. The aim is to choose the most efficient media vehicles that resonate with the lifestyles that planners visualize the audience to have.

The major stimulus for creatives and planners regarding the market is provided by the ad agency's research function. Research might involve compiling results of previous investigations, including those by the agency's clients. It might involve commissioning original surveys or experiments with potential customers to check on the persuasiveness of a new ad or the success of one that has already has been introduced to the marketplace. It might involve joining other firms in ongoing "syndicated" studies that inquire about social trends, general product use, media habits, or other characteristics of the American population. Through these and other approaches, researchers construct detailed portraits of the intended audience and its position within the society at large. Then creatives and planners mix those portraits with their own sensibilities and apply them to their work.

That work affects the media's construction of society in at least two ways. Most obviously, the advertisements that show up in magazines, radio stations, TV networks, and other media act out advertisers' notions of their audiences and their worlds. Less evident, but at least as important, media planners run the ads only on formats that they feel are in sync with their assumptions about society that are reflected in the ads. In view of the tens, even hundreds, of millions of dollars that national advertisers dole out to vehicles that match their expectations, it is not surprising that media firms create and revise formats in attempts to be in sync with client needs. Formats that do not attract the kinds or numbers of people advertisers care to reach will fade away.

When people read a magazine, watch a TV show, or use any other ad-sponsored medium, then, they are entering a world that was constructed as a result of close cooperation between advertisers and media firms. Designed with marketing goals in mind, the formats and commercials aim to signal to people whether and how they fit the proceedings. They also signal what people might buy or do to keep fitting in.

And yet, with all their traditional influence over media content and structure, advertising agencies have not been comfortable with the contemporary media scene. Since the early 1980s, in trade magazines and at conferences, agency executives have been warning that transformations in technology have been threatening their power over media and audiences. Some executives have argued that millions watching at home may abandon ad-sponsored programming entirely as pay-per-view presentations without commercials become increasingly popular. Others have pointed out that the explosion of new television choices, a product of the video and cable revolution, has complicated the business of media planning immensely, since people have been migrating away from the broadcast networks to other audiovisual channels.

The following chapters show how researchers, creatives, media planners, and their bosses have been nervously facing up to the sea of changes in their business, working furiously to make sure that the transformations that are taking place favor them. Targeting lifestyle segments through specialized formats has become their central solution. Chapter 2 sketches the history of target marketing, suggests why advertising executives and social analysts have played it down until recently, and notes how it began to gain attention in the 1960s and 1970s. Chapter 3 explores how the ideas about a profoundly divided American society developed among advertising and media practitioners in tandem with their increasing fascination with targeting in the 1970s and 1980s.

With this background in mind, Chapter 4 "maps" the different images of divided America that advertising and media practitioners have attempted to capture. It shows how they have constructed and deconstructed the activities and attitudes of women, men, homosexuals, African Americans, Hispanic Americans, Asian Americans, the affluent, the suburbs, families, children, seniors, and other familiar labels—all under the broad umbrella of disposable income. The goal has been to locate and label the most relevant consumers and then reach them via various media.

Chapters 5 and 6 track the approaches that marketers and media practitioners have been developing to attract certain desirable audiences, often while keeping undesirables away. Creating targeted formats that signal an interest in certain types of people, engaging in targeted publicity across formats, tailoring ads and media materials to individual consumer interests—these represent only the tip of a huge glacier of activities that have been reshaping the media landscape. Chapter 7 carries such developments into the future by showing how major marketers and media firms have been preparing themselves for an era that heightens signaling and tailoring with new technologies, building into them visions of of an ever-fragmenting America.

Chapter 8 evaluates all of this in terms of other cross-currents in American life and links it to the perspectives that were introduced in chapter 1. Among other points, it concludes that the spread of targeted, customized media ought to ignite concerned discussion across the American public. The hope is that this book can be a nudge in that direction.

TWO

IN MASS MARKETING'S SHADOW

IN JUNE 1980, in recognition of its fiftieth anniversary, the weekly trade newspaper *Advertising Age* joined with the American Enterprise Institute to sponsor a conference on the future of the industry that it covers. The speakers were luminaries from a variety of fields. Joining ad-agency leaders and academic economists were historian and Librarian of Congress Daniel J. Boorstin, pollster George Gallup, science writer Isaac Asimov, and Federal Trade Commissioner Michael Pertschuk. The diversity of topics was impressive. They ranged from technical papers on copy testing to opinions about industry mergers to prognostications (by Asimov) on advertising in the year 2000.

Casting a somber shadow over some of the celebration was the spectre of what people there called "the new media." The term emerged in several contexts, invariably causing concern. Speaking at one panel, the famous copywriter and agency head Jerry Della Femina verbalized his angst about the many channels that cable television was bringing to increasing numbers of U.S. homes. The "cable thing," he noted, offers "more possibilities, with more chances for agencies to be good." But, he added, "there's nothing more frightening, either, because it's a whole new ball game and I don't understand it, I know. And yet, we're going to start rushing into it."

Herbert Maneloveg, a well-respected media planner at Della Femina's agency, preferred to emphasize the potential for advertising that cable and other media could bring. In a keynote address, he framed the challenge historically. "Think," he urged,

> of the new technology. Cassettes, satellite transmissions, cable, facsimile printing, videodiscs, computer-based regionalization

and demographic segmentation, opportunities for in-home learning techniques through disc and tape, just to name a few, plus automated checkout counters to instantly know sales results . . .

For the past three decades we have oriented ourselves to communicating to the most mass; we now possess the capability to concentrate on the least waste, to speak to smaller segments of our population, one group at a time. In new, unique ways.[1]

Maneloveg's spin on these media reflected a perspective of his industry toward the start of an avalanche of new audiovisual media vehicles for ads. As the decade progressed, and as the segmentation and targeting of audiences became the buzz words of the advertising business, the historical frame that Maneloveg used to highlight what was different—and what challenges lay ahead—became the accepted line. The received view was that in the previous media era (the era of broadcasting) target marketing did not exist. The new multichannel world, by contrast, would require it. As Jayne Spittler, director of media research at the Leo Burnett advertising agency, said in 1994, "We used to think we could do everything. We'd use mass media . . . and be all things to all people. The new media world has diluted those kinds of efforts. And we deluded ourselves with that strategy."[2]

Actually, the situation is quite a bit more complicated than that. As the following pages will show, targeting has always been part of the advertiser-media relationship. What was different about the efforts of advertisers beginning in the late '70s was not so much the decision by advertisers and their agencies to aim at specialized audiences during the past decade and half. It was, rather, the emergence of target marketing as a hot, hip, even central, strategy after decades of being considered a relatively marginal part of the national ad industry's thinking.

Still, the comments of Maneloveg and Spittler do reflect accurately a sense of the importance of mass marketing compared to target marketing in the twentieth century. In fact, throughout almost all of the twentieth century, the advertising industry stressed its mass-marketing role so much that its market-segmentation activities and the forces guiding them went unnoticed by social analysts.

The history of target marketing and its relationship to media went unstudied, as well. While much literature exists on the genesis of the mass market, writings on the development of market segmentation and its relationship to advertising vehicles are sparse. When chroniclers of advertising or mass media do mention audience specialization, they invariably discuss it as a small part of their story about the growth of mass-market media that culminated in TV. The typical approach is to note that radio and magazines went after slices of the general population during the 1950s so they could compete with television, which aimed at the whole pie.

This analysis is not wrong, but it does leave an incorrect impression. Evidence indicates that what people now call target marketing goes back far earlier than the 1950s—at least to the first quarter of the twentieth century. Moreover, placing the development of advertising within the general development of U.S. business suggests that competition between television and radio did not fundamentally cause the rise of target margeting. The home tube is merely the latest advertising vehicle to accommodate marketers' long but inexorable movement through the twentieth century away from enormous, undifferentiated audiences.

But if market segmentation and targeting have had a steadily increasing presence among advertisers, why have advertising practitioners and social analysts played them down until recently? As the following pages suggest, the reason seems to lie in the fixation that the mass market has had on both the advertising industry and people who study it. Reaching "the masses" through a few key media has been efficient for advertisers and highly lucrative for ad agencies. Their high-profile work has drawn curiosity and concern from generations of academics, who have explored the logic of the mass market. Target marketing has simply gotten lost amid discussions of bigger deals.

Advertisers' stress on the mass market goes back to America's industrial revolution of the late nineteenth century and the mass production of goods and the messages that characterized it. Factory activity was based increasingly on the principles of "continuous process" or "flow" production. Conveyer systems, rollers, and gravity slides sent materials through the production process in an automatic, continuous stream. As a result, companies could transform massive batches of raw materials into finished goods.

The new approach changed American business. The manufacturing capacity of the United States increased sevenfold between 1865 and 1900.[3] Colossal industries were born. Many of the factories created products that had been made by hand, often by the user's family, only a few years before. Other plants turned out things—toothpaste, corn flakes, safety razors, cameras—that nobody had made previously. The volume of "things" produced seemed unlimited.

The large number of items encouraged competition between manufacturers of similar goods. One result was the creation of brands. With brand-name products, a company did not just make soap, it created "Ivory" or "Colgate." Still, to make money on a particular brand of soap or any other mass-produced item, a manufacturer had to make sure that hordes of people were quickly made aware of the products and persuaded to buy them.

The solution was to try to mass produce customers in the same way that the factories mass produced the merchandise. As it turned out, people were available in bulk, for with mechanization and industrialization at the end of the nineteenth century came the rise of the dense city population. As new factories drew workers from American farming communities and foreign countries, the areas around factories swelled. Census figures show that between 1870 and 1900 the U.S. doubled its population and tripled the number of urban residents. Manufacturing and transportation centers in the Northeast and Midwest saw the largest growth.[4]

Each metropolis was an enormous brew of people with all sorts of backgrounds and languages. The key to attracting customers, marketing executives reasoned, was to take advantage of the crowded city. Signs throughout neighborhoods, on walls as well as on streetcars and trucks, formed a popular way to trumpet the virtues of department stores and branded products. But the most important way to advertise consumer goods at the turn of the twentieth century was the city newspaper. The number of English-language, general-circulation dailies increased from 489 in 1870 to 1,967 in 1900. Circulation totals for all daily publications rose from 2.6 million copies in 1870 to 15 million in 1900.[5]

Newspaper publishers aimed at the large, diverse populations that major manufacturers and department stores eagerly sought. Advances in printing technology allowed publishers to mass produce their output in ways similar to those of their advertisers. The goal was to reach out to the growing numbers of readers concentrated in particular areas. With color comics, syndicated columnists, a hefty sports section, photograph-filled Sunday magazine, and more, the newspaper became a mosaic of features designed to attract as many different types of people as possible.

Underscoring the importance of bulk readership numbers, many publishers proudly alleged their daily circulation figures on the front pages. Being able to bring the most people to advertisers became virtually synonymous with business success. In fact, newspaper firms kept the price of their dailies at around a nickel even as the cost of printing technology and paper rose. Executives knew that the inevitable loss of readers caused by a price rise would alienate advertisers. A new business philosophy was developing. Newspapers were relying mostly on advertising instead of circulation revenues for their profits. The percentage of newspaper revenue coming from advertising rose from half in 1880 to 64 percent by 1910.[6]

Magazines were heading in the same direction, but on a national rather than local level. After the Civil War, responding to the pressures of the new economy and the rising population, many magazine publishers pursued much larger audiences. They were guided by the proposition that low subscriptions would lure readers and that production costs would be made up by advertisers interested in mass circulation. Major sponsors would be those manufacturers that wanted to go beyond local newspaper boundaries to reach readers in many big cities and those mail-order firms that wanted to act as department stores for consumers in rural areas. On the strength of this approach, in 1901 the *Ladies Home Journal* became the first magazine to pass a million in circulation. Two years later, the readership of the *Saturday Evening Post* was an unprecedented two million. The *Post* brought in ad revenues of $25 million.[7]

The modern ad agency developed in sync with the rise of the mass-market audience. The man who is thought to have started the first advertising agency in the 1840s, Volney Palmer, was essentially a newspaper space salesman. Palmer and those who imitated him made money by soliciting notices about products from merchants who wanted to sell to a wide territory. He would place the notices in a group of newspapers to which he often had exclusive space-selling rights. Though merchants were expected to write the ads, they saved time and energy by paying the ad agency one sum to reach far-flung audiences. The advertising agent typically received compensation from various newspapers in the form of commission (often 25 percent).

The ad agency's function changed as manufacturers began to market branded products nationally and as department stores reached out to huge urban populations with a broad spectrum of goods. Both the manufacturers and stores needed not so much space brokers but firms to help them create advertisements that would stand out among competition. Advertising agencies started copy and art departments, and by around 1910 the task of preparing advertisements had become their central responsibility.[8] Along with the agency's creation of the ad came its work on the ad "campaign," which included early forms of market research and media planning.[9] As part of their growing research concerns, agencies in 1914 helped establish an independent organization, the Audit Bureau of Circulation, to verify the size of a periodical's audience.

The Audit Bureau's emphasis on sheer audience size reflected the audience approach of the era. A sense that "men" or "women" or "children" could use a product was about as detailed as most national advertisers got in customizing their appeals. Daniel Pope has written that in the first quarter of the twentieth century, few advertisers "were prepared to recognize and fewer to accept the nation's heterogeneity."[10] At a time when people were coming to the U.S. from all over, one well-known advertising executive seemed proud that his business was knitting a whole country together. "We are making a homogenous people out of a nation of immigrants," ad-agency president Albert Lasker told his staff in the 1920s.[11]

This celebration of marketers' ability to reach the masses through the right kinds of broadly distributed persuasive messages became even stronger with the development of advertiser-supported radio in the 1920s. Using different methods, the major radio ratings services reported the number of people in a sample who had listened to a particular show, and extrapolated this figure to a national audience. Demographic categories such as gender, income, occupation, and geographical location—let alone reports of lifestyle differences—were not part of the standard way that sponsors and ad agencies thought about broadcasting at the time. The goal was to help brands grow as much as possible in the mass market.

The radio networks themselves did direct some programs—religious fare and special dramatic presentations, for example—at specialty audiences. These, however, were typically placed in time slots that were not sold to sponsors. As for commercial programming, advertisers acknowledged only the most obvious social divisions in the audience—women, children, and men. They pursued these groups at times when women, children, or men, but not the entire family, were most likely to be at home. Detergent companies went after women with daytime serials; cereal and beverage firms tried to get youngsters' attention through after-school adventure series; shaving firms used weekend sports programming to hook men. In the evening, when everyone was likely to be in the house, everyone was the target. Historians agree that during radio's reign as the primary domestic medium, from the 1920s through the 1940s, agencies and their national advertisers did not question the assumption that broadcasting was to provide them the opportunity to reach vast, generally undifferentiated audiences with their commercials.

In radio, shows were owned by the advertiser and often produced by the firm's ad agency. The networks sold time and gave up a lot of control over their formats; advertisers primarily shaped the nature and arrangement of material on the network schedules. A different model for selling air time took over as the commercial television industry grew in the 1950s, and it led to a new view of the audience. In television, power over the medium's programming flow and tone—the format—gradually was taken over by the three networks, ABC, CBS, and NBC.

Executives at ABC, CBS, and NBC urged the new approach on advertisers. As government criticism against television content began to pick up steam during the Kennedy era, network leaders concluded that controlling their own schedules was imperative if they were to respond credibly to government complaints. More important, they understood that they could increase the amount they charged for network time if program schedules could be created that maximized the flow of people from one program to another. This could be carried out only if advertisers moved away from full sponsorship to "participating" advertising, in which a network took the risk of creating or licensing a show and then sold time—typically thirty-second or sixty-second spots—during program breaks to a number of advertisers.

Many advertisers also favored buying slots on schedules that network programmers put together. By the early 1960s, television set ownership extended to more than 90 percent of U.S. homes. As the cost of television time began to skyrocket, marketers began to think that they could reach more people by scattering their commercials across a number of time periods than by putting it all of them into the expensive production and sponsorship of one weekly program. Networks made the new deals especially attractive by offering refunds if audience ratings were not met.

As competition between the networks over the sale of participating ad time heated up during the 1960s, advertisers' desires to learn more about the audiences for different shows grew. The dominant arbiter of ratings in network television was the Nielsen company. Nielsen ratings were based on mechanisms called audimeters. Audimeters were inserted in television sets of a sample of American households that the firm considered representative of the population. The audimeters kept a continuous record of the times the sets were on and the stations to which they were tuned. Their use in radio dated from 1935, but they became especially prestigious for evaluating national television-viewing behavior.

Like the radio ratings, the Nielsen system initially reported simply the raw number of households in the audience of a sponsored program. But Nielsen was cross-checking its TV audimeter information with data obtained from diaries kept by another sample of homes. Ratings computed from the diary sample gave information as to which family members watched each program. Since Nielsen gathered information about these family members, it could report that data with the audimeter results. Advertisers could obtain ratings of programs according to categories such as gender, age, educational status, urban or rural location, and other factors.

This demographic information began to guide the way the ad industry and the networks talked about programming even in prime time (evening periods), when most people were at home. Broadcast historian Erik Barnouw notes some of the consequences:

> Network executives now tended to survey their schedules in terms of demographic product demands. Negotiations resembled transactions to deliver blocs of people. An advertising agency would be telling a network, in effect, "For Shampoo Y, our client is ready to invest $18,000,000 in women 18–49. Other viewers are of no interest in this case; the client doesn't care to pay for irrelevant viewers. But for women 18–49 he is willing to pay Z dollars per thousand. What spots can you offer?"[12]

Advertising practitioners could have chosen to see these changes of the early 1970s as pointing away from their traditional mass-market em-

phasis. They could have started to devise even more particularistic methods for gauging narrow audiences in TV. That they did not do it at the
time underscores the strong traditional perspectives that the broadcast
networks had established with the national advertising industry. Neither
national advertisers nor the national networks were yet interested in
much audience differentiation in TV. In the late 1970s, Nielsen reported
that ABC, CBS, and NBC together reached more than 90 percent of all
American homes on a typical evening. That 90 percent, Nielsen said,
generally represented more than 50 percent of the entire U.S. population.[13] Those kinds of numbers attracted many wealthy sponsors. Despite the attraction of eighteen- to forty-nine-year-olds, their overall aim
was still to use the medium to reach the largest population possible—to
go after what many executives called the "tonnage" of the mass market.[14]

The mass market was so public and seemed so powerful that social
observers seized on it for examination. They linked advertisers' obsession
with the mass market to a more general issue that Western thinkers had
been exploring since the nineteenth century: the transformation from a
rural community where people trusted each other in face-to-face dealings into an urban civilization where anonymity and mass-produced culture made the contract rather than the handshake the norm. Advertising,
they felt sure, played an important role in the urban society. But exactly
what were the consequences of gathering large, diverse populations to
media in the interest of selling them goods?

Historian Daniel Boorstin was perhaps the most vigorous champion
of the view that advertisements were helping to create a nation out of a
collection of immigrants. Building on philosopher George Santayana's
comment that "American life is a powerful solvent," Boorstin placed the
advertising industry squarely in the center of the twentieth-century process through which millions of people of all incomes and backgrounds
were transmogrified into a shared sense of themselves as Americans.[15] He
believed that advertising taught an implicit lesson on the materialistic,
fluid, and ultimately democratic nature of contemporary U.S. society.
"Americans," he wrote, "were increasingly held to others not by a few
iron bonds [such as religious and political affiliations], but by countless
gossamer webs knitting together the trivia of their lives."[16]

Many writers, though, saw advertising's broad influence as problem-
atic economically, ethically, or both.[17] Often they reflected post—World
War II concerns about the corrosive effects of mass culture on indivi-

duals and society. Some stressed that advertising was a tool by which the capitalist establishment enforced its hold on citizens.[18] Others railed against what they saw as advertising's participation in the creation of "mass society," a cultural environment that debased traditional values and denigrated the kind of "high" culture that, they claimed, undergirds great civilizations.[19]

Yet no matter what the perspective, studies of advertising's role in American life took as their starting point the idea of media—network television, newspapers, magazines—with broad circulation.[20] The studies posed conclusions about advertising images—such as Michael Schudson's insight that they were a form of "capitalist realism"[21]—in terms that accepted the emphasis on undifferentiated audiences. Even streams of thought that challenged the very idea of mass society and emphasized that viewers and readers with different backgrounds experienced media images differently did not challenge the notion that media aimed at the largest, most diverse audiences possible. The creation of media images for people with different backgrounds was simply not part of their domain.[22]

Yet targeting was around and growing. One can find reports of audience segmentation and targeting by advertisers early in the twentieth century. There is ample evidence that even in the era of the mass magazine there were many executives in the national advertising industry who believed that they should reach different types of people in different ways, and who seem to have acted on that belief. On the agency side, knowledge of the magazine and newspaper business often went far beyond the mass-market periodicals to more specialized output.

In an influential 1915 textbook called *The Business of Advertising,* Earnest Elmo Calkins showed a clear awareness of the use of different periodicals to target various populations, including children, farmers, college students, and religious people, and of "trade" or "class" magazines such as those aimed at plumbers or Masons.[23] He appreciated the targeting value of a small-town newspaper, saying that it "gives local influence to the advertisements which it carries."[24] And he suggested "canvassing consumers" in different cities around the country in order to gather information for an ad campaign.[25]

Some media firms also noted social distinctions. In 1913, for example, the *Chicago Tribune's* research department began a massive house-to-house survey in residential districts throughout the Windy City. Its report, released in 1916, presented figures on rents, buying habits, and the number of dealers for different product lines for each district.[26]

Similarly, around 1915 the Eastern Advertising Company, which controlled nearly all of New England's streetcar advertising, published the *Advertisers Hand Book of New England.* The compilation offered data on literacy, school expenditures, manufacturing activity, population density, country of origin, occupations, and incomes in different areas. For every town served by streetcars, it listed numbers of passengers, estimated annual volume of retail sales, and numbers of dealers in fourteen leading lines of business. The preface to the *Hand Book* boasted that the work would allow an advertiser "to select the exact spots where he wishes to concentrate. . . . He can concentrate on the exact type of population he desires . . . and he can calculate the number of dealers he might sell, or the volume of trade in his line that he can hope to do in a given trolley system district."[27] It all sounds very much like what would today be called local market segmentation.

Then there was the introduction of Crisco Oil, carried out in 1912 by Proctor and Gamble with the help of the J. Walter Thompson ad agency. The campaign showed that both firms were well aware of the utility of markets, from railway chefs to immigrant Jewish kitchens to Southwest American kitchens, that reflected lifestyles relevant to their product. They even practiced what today would be called integrated marketing—encouraging a process that linked advertising activities with store promotions and public relations.[28]

These examples support social historian Susan Strasser's argument that the seeds of "market segmentation and targeted promotion" were sown in the first quarter of the twentieth century, as advertisers and their agencies looked for ways to expand their products' reach.[29] It is, however, difficult to determine how frequently such activities were carried out by national advertisers. Chroniclers of the ad industry stress that at this time the advertising trade was fixated on how it could sell to the largest number of people with the lowest cost in time and money. Books about the ad business that were written during the first quarter of the twentieth century reflect that fixation. Earnest Elmo Calkins, for example, discourages readers of his text from advertising in the magazines he mentions that aim at special audiences. They are often inadequate, he reasons, largely because they are not as efficient as mass-market periodicals in reaching large audiences.

The same underplaying of market segmentation by ad people took place during the 1930s and 1940s. During these decades, though, the use of media by national advertisers to target particular types of people, and even their presumed lifestyles, is easier to document. There were some targeting activities in radio; local stations that aimed at immigrants or farmers or blacks received sporadic national advertising money.[30] But ad agencies carried out targeting by lifestyle on a more consistent basis via the so-called "specialty" magazines of the twenties and thirties.

While the term specialty referred to narrower subject matter than was found in the mass-circulation periodicals, it also implied a more segmented audience. New periodicals such as *Time, Fortune,* the *New Yorker,* and *True Story* had no intention of competing with broad-based magazines such as the *Saturday Evening Post.* They created distinctive personalities for themselves that sought out smaller slices of the market. Their publishers expected to draw readers who identified with those personalities, and, in turn, to attract advertisers wanting to speak to people with those characteristics.

Consider, for example, the way the *New Yorker's* founding publisher described his periodical in his initial prospectus of the early 1920s:

> The *New Yorker* will be a reflection in word and pictures of metropolitan life. Its general tenor will be one of gaiety, wit and satire, but it will be more than a jester. It will not be what is commonly called sophisticated, in that it will assume a reasonable amount of enlightenment on the part of its readers. It will hate bunk. . . .
>
> The *New Yorker* will be the magazine which is not edited for the old lady in Dubuque. It will not be concerned with what she is thinking about. This is not meant in disrespect, but the *New Yorker* is a magazine avowedly published for a metropolitan audience and thereby will escape an influence which hampers most national publications. It expects a considerable national circulation, but this will come from persons who have a metropolitan interest.[31]

Paging through issues of the *New Yorker* from the 1930s, one certainly finds ads that reflect this perspective. Many of the advertisements seem tailored to the readership and especially aimed at out-of-towners considering a visit to New York. Partial-page plugs for upscale New York department stores such as Bloomingdale's and Best's mix with larger announcements for trendy night clubs such as the Rainbow Room and first-class Manhattan hotels such as the Mayflower, Essex House, and San Remo. Full-page ads for national liquors such as Courvoisier and Old Overholt seem also to reflect a specific sensitivity to the intended readers. On the other hand, advertisements for Plymouth, Coca-Cola, Goodyear, and other well-known brands mirror not at all the elite environment of the magazine and could well have been in the *Saturday Evening Post* or *Reader's Digest*. Those advertisers and their agencies clearly felt that while the *New Yorker* audience was one they wanted to speak to, the size of the readership (less than 500,000) did not warrant distinctly new work.

Magazine chronicler John Tebbel has noted that the increase in specialization that characterized magazine publishing during the 1920s and 1930s foreshadowed what he calls an even more "decisive" trend in that direction during the 1960s and 1970s.[32] His reference is to the death of the traditional mass-circulation magazine and the explosion of weekly and monthly journals aimed quite explicitly at readers in term of their demographics and lifestyles. Led by successful upstart magazines such as *Psychology Today* and *Rolling Stone,* most of the new periodicals were aimed at slices of the population whose incomes, buying habits, and strong interests in particular subjects attracted national advertisers.[33]

Media historians invariably posit that the shift toward targeting within the magazine industry had to do with the rise of network television as a commercial force during the 1950s. The general line is that major advertisers found they could reach the same kinds of large, diverse audiences they purchased through *Life, Look,* the *Saturday Evening Post,* and *Coronet* for comparable costs, but with the impact of moving pictures and sound. As general periodicals went down in flames, a new target-oriented magazine industry rose from the ashes. Publishers began to realize they could serve these distinctive needs and not compete head-on with network television if they could prove to certain advertisers and their agencies that they were delivering slices of the population that were particularly attractive to them.

Media historians point out that a similar development occurred in radio, which lost much of its broad-based network audiences in the 1950s in the face of TV. In a search for new ideas, broadcasters hit on the notion of a station format built around the flow of music organized by a "disc jockey." It was not a wholly new idea; programs with radio personalities playing records dated back to the 1930s. What was novel, however, was that now an entire station's schedule was dedicated to the DJ format. Moreover, and most important, the music the station played was aimed at particular audiences—typically age categories and listening preferences—rather than "everybody."

The problem with this version of the changes in magazines and radio is that it ignores forces in the broad business and marketing system that were emphasizing market specialization. The basic change at work was product differentiation. It involved systematic attempts by manufacturers to create slightly different versions of the same products in order to aim at different parts of the marketplace.

Historian Daniel Pope traces the activity back to the early 1920s.[34] By then, economies of scale had made it feasible for a manufacturer to differentiate its creations. General Motors, a troubled company with a confusing collection of car brands, was the leading edge of the change. Managed by Pierre Dupont and Alfred Sloan, the firm pulled out of its problems by reorganizing its marketing strategy based on price segments. The different GM cars (Chevrolet, Pontiac, Buick, Cadillac) would be priced differently and therefore be advertised to buyers with different incomes. Especially after World War II, they based their work on the dictum that appeal to everyone would likely turn out to be an appeal to nobody in particular. "Better, [the thinking went] . . . to divide up the broader market and design a campaign that could reach and attract a specific target audience with distinctive needs or desires."[35]

This sort of logic led manufacturers increasingly to support magazines and radio stations that reached the consumer segments that they coveted. Advertisers and their agencies also began to support research companies that allowed them to learn about the buying and leisure habits of listeners to particular stations and subscribers to particular periodicals. In retrospect, the work had important implications for the future of marketing. It began to create a model for audience segmentation in other media.

By the late 1970s, many signals indicated that it was television's turn to be transformed by market segmentation. In manufacturing, increased competition was pushing product differentiation along so that smaller and smaller numbers of a product could be made and marketed profitably to certain segments of society. In market research, competition among firms was leading to ways that differentiated groups in new, unusual, and profitable ways.

The changes ran the gamut from expensive to inexpensive products. At the relatively expensive end, auto manufacturers began to create cars not only for different income groups but for distinct social categories and the activities and attitudes—lifestyles—that were linked to them. Buick, for example, decided in the early '80s that its previous broad appeals "to everyone who might be interested in a car" would no longer work in an environment where imports were grabbing substantial shares of the U.S. market.[36] As a result, the company and its ad agency pegged three different models at three different, quite specific types of consumers. The Somerset Regal was pitched toward upscale, stylish working women in their thirties; the Century was aimed at an audience that was male, a bit older than Regal's, with a flair for wealthy things and winning at life; and the Skyhawk was positioned to entice a younger, collegiate market.[37]

At the relatively inexpensive end, producers of low-priced supermarket goods also found it useful to tie into lifestyle differentiations. Chronic shelf wars had long given marketers a strong reason for turning out variations in certain brands of soup, cereal, and baby foods. Variations that took up more shelf space would edge competitors out. Getting those "brand extensions" to sell meant investigating consumer preferences to find groups that might be interested in one or another concatenation of the product.

Items that seemed basic suddenly were changed to fit various lifestyles. "In the old days," a Proctor and Gamble executive noted, "Tide was one big brand. It stood for clean, white clothes and all women 18 to 49, whether they had kids, or didn't have kids, washed their clothes [with it]. But now, you have Tide with Bleach, Tide Ultra, Tide Unscented. And each of these brands are still targeted at women 18 to 49, but they are targeted at differences between segments of women 18 to 49."[38]

It was in this manufacturing and marketing environment that widespread talk grew among marketers about using television to reach different audiences in the same way they were doing with radio and magazines. Cable was the first technology to spur advertisers toward thinking about fundamental changes they would have to make in their approach to the home tube and its viewers. This conduit for the new marketing era had actually been around since the 1940s. Until the 1980s, though, its use in American homes was negligible. Early cable operations were called Community Antenna Television (CATV) systems. They served communities that did not have nearby TV stations and had a hard time using roof-top devices to catch signals from the nearest city.

In the 1950s and 1960s, broadcasters were quite happy to have cable companies relay their signals to out-of-the-way areas that couldn't get them. They recognized early, though, that cable companies could dilute the value of their stations if they started laying wires in and around cities. Residents of a Chicago suburb could, for example, enjoy the sports programming of Cincinnati, New York, or Atlanta channels. These could be relayed to the cable operator by microwave and distributed to the operator's customers via coaxial copper wire.

During the 1960s, the FCC agreed with broadcasters' arguments that the government had to protect "free" broadcasting in metropolitan areas from being damaged by competition from cable operators who demanded payment for their signals. As a result, the government agency formulated rules that made it nearly impossible for cable firms to expand their operations to the exurbs and suburbs of major cities. By the early 1970s, though, cable forces began to get the upper hand politically, FCC rules changed, and cable operators' long, difficult march into metropolitan areas, and major competition with broadcasters, began in earnest.

Another federal policy that opened the TV world to competition between technologies was the "free skies" entrepreneurial approach to satellite use in the 1970s. It allowed two developments that pointed to cable TV's future impact on national advertising. The first was Home Box Office. A subsidiary of Time, Incorporated, HBO began to deliver fairly recent films to cable systems around the United States in 1976 via the Satcom 1 satellite. Systems that purchased a satellite dish could carry HBO, charge subscribers an additional fee, and share the proceeds with

Home Box Office. Instantly, Home Box Office gave cable a national brand and a unique service: programming home viewers could not get from over-the-air stations.

Close on HBO's heels was Atlanta broadcaster and sports financier Ted Turner. Early in 1976, he announced that he was going to make the programming of his Atlanta UHF TV station available to cable systems via the same Satcom 1 satellite as HBO. Coining the term "superstation" to describe his concept, Turner reasoned that cable system owners and viewers would appreciate the mix of old movies with Atlanta Braves baseball and Hawks basketball. Turner would benefit by the transmission fee a subsidiary firm would charge cable firms picking up the signal, from the broad attention his teams would receive, and from the extended audience his advertisers would get. By the end of 1976, Turner's station was being carried by twenty cable systems in different parts of the country.

The rise of HBO and Turner's superstation received a lot of attention in the advertising trade press. Naysayers could argue correctly, though, that not much had really changed from the standpoint of national advertising. HBO didn't even carry ads. As for the broadcast channels that cable systems retransmitted to their subscribers' homes, they simply expanded the audience for standard commercials by a bit. Even the power of cable could be questioned. The number of new channels delivered to people's homes *was* relatively larger than before, but not astoundingly so. Most systems (75 percent of them) still carried fewer than twelve channels, including the three or more local channels homeowners received before they paid for cable. To top it off, the great portion of America still didn't have cable: Even by 1978 cable television was received in only about 17 percent of American homes.[39]

Nevertheless, some in the advertising industry began to take notice that major shifts were in the air. As early as 1976, a number of leaders in the advertising industry tried to determine the ramifications of an advertising world with satellites and new cable channels. Many already worried that future increases in competition from a variety of sources—not just cable—would diminish audiences for their commercials on any one channel. They also worried that, as HBO's appearance implied, the power of sponsorship over media firms would ultimately decrease as people would pay selectively for their own programming.

Richard Pinkham, chair of the influential Ted Bates agency's executive committee, was aware of the potential threats to advertising's hegemony, but he insisted that they could be defused. At a workshop session of the Association of National Advertisers (ANA), he allowed that the home audience would be more fragmented, that viewers would have more alternatives. But, he insisted, so would sponsors:

> Will there be opportunities . . . staring you in the face as CATV and satellite transmissions emerge?
> Will there be opportunities for your company to own programming, tailor-made to attract precisely your target audience no matter how small. . . .
> How much thought have you given to the marketing potential of two-way communication? What should your company do to get there first? At least one of our clients is already experimenting with techniques to exploit this kind of one-to-one contact with the consumer in her living room. Are you working on it?
> What will facsimile printout from the television set do for you? Should you start now to devise a sponsored woman's page or crossword puzzle or sports section? Will you be able to devise a TV commercial with printed recipes and perhaps a coupon? . . .
> Are sponsored videodiscs a possibility?
> Have you thought of using CATV's low rates to buy time for your sales force to demonstrate your product or show its possibilities on the counter or announce a special cents-off promotion? Should you start now to train them as television salesmen?[40]

Pinkham's words reflected a conviction within the ad community that television—delivered through cable, satellites, or other methods yet unknown—would be the next medium to be influenced by market segmentation. But, as chapter 3 will show, advertisers' interest in using new media for target marketing was propelled not only by developments in manufacturing, market research, and media technology that made targeting useful. The strength with which target marketing as a philosophy took hold in the ad industry during the '80s had a great deal to do with ad practitioners' belief that the technological changes were themselves symptoms of a more profound change in America. Marketers adopted the conviction that America was becoming a divided society, slowly but inexorably losing its ability to be persuaded collectively through even network TV. With this belief came a sense, often grudging and hesitant, that the media and advertising had to be transformed even more to take advantage of these changes.

THREE

THE ROOTS OF DIVISION

"*WE'RE NOT WIRED TO* the ghettos," Ted Turner declared to advertising executives in October 1978. He was talking about his self-styled "superstation." About two years earlier he had linked the Atlanta-based UHF station WTCG (Watch This Channel Grow) to Satcom 1 so that it could reach suburbs and exurbs around the United States via cable systems. This had thrust it into forty-two states and 2.5 million cable TV homes. Now he was trying to whip up national advertiser support for his activities.[1]

"Those of you that don't take advantage of us will be sorry," Turner warned about seventy potential customers he had invited to lunch in Chicago. Already, the millionaire billboard executive turned broadcast and sports-team owner claimed, his channel 17 from Atlanta had attracted national ad dollars from Miller Brewing, Panasonic, Toyota, and Union Oil. He said Mobil Oil would start sponsoring a WTCG theater hour at the start of 1979.[2]

Turner boasted that the station was being delivered via satellite to 106 of 213 so-called market areas of the nation. He hoped to reach an additional twenty areas by the end of the year, at which point it would reach 2.8 million homes. According to Turner, the superstation was a good buy not merely because of the audience size, but because of the "upscale quality" of the cable audience.[3]

He expanded this theme a year later while addressing the American Association of Advertising Agencies (the 4A). "Where you have idiots watching idiot shows, I guess you can sell them idiot products," he told the assemblage. "Not with us." His superstation, he suggested, was set up to deliver upscale men to discriminating sponsors. "Isn't a financial news show the best place for Merrill Lynch or Mercedes-Benz?"[4]

Turner continued with a sharp vision of the future of television, the TV industry, and the TV audience. By the mid–1980s, he pronounced, the three major networks would be eclipsed, their audience shares dropping sharply. Cable television, with a multiplicity of channels, would skyrocket in popularity from a less than 20 percent presence in U.S. homes as he spoke to a 50 percent presence in 1984. As a result, he said, "your TV sets will become something on which you can see anything you want to see whenever you want to see it. Not just what three nincompoops in New York decide for you."[5]

This wasn't a very kind way of speaking about the television networks or much of the American public, but then Ted Turner did not have a reputation for cordial phrasing. His irrepressible bravado had given him a reputation of a risk taker who would stand up to established interests. And he clearly saw it in his interest to admonish national advertisers that the world was changing and that they needed to start acting toward television and its audience in drastically new ways.

Just before his Chicago talk, Turner had shocked national advertisers who bought time on his station. He had taken the unprecedented step of saying that he would be charging them higher, "national" rates for their commercials. The extra fare, which would not apply to local Atlanta stores and products, was to take account of the extra viewers the station reached around the United States.

Until that time, sponsors had assumed that the superstation's additional audience was gravy, a kind of giveaway bonus for advertising with Turner. But Turner now wanted to position his station to the advertising industry as a growing national marketing tool. He suggested that the network "nincompoops" might well be reflecting the rather primitive outlook of many Americans who watch broadcast TV. And he argued that since cable homes were different—populated by people with affluent suburban lifestyles—their viewers were naturally demanding, and getting, higher-quality material on his superstation. Not coincidentally, Turner claimed it was the sort of environment that ought to lure advertisers interested in getting away from the unattractive masses.

"You'll be able to target your ads much better than you can today," Turner declared to the assembled ad executives about WTCG, which he would soon rename WTBS. "For example, we have a fishing show, a lot better place for rod and reel ads than *The Incredible Hulk*."[6]

Ted Turner, who soon became known as "the mouth from the South," often preferred to portray himself as a populist-entrepreneur tilting against the media powers. When talking to ad people, though, he became an elitist, emphasizing a group that was hard to reach efficiently on TV: adults (in this case, adult men) with lots of money and leisure time. He undoubtedly knew that stressing the ability of his station to deliver them played to the advertising industry's two areas of great angst: its growing anxiousness about broadcast TV and its rising interest in target marketing.

Turner was both a symbol and key actor in developments that were causing rumblings through the advertising industry during the early 1980s. New cable channels allegedly viewed in the wealthier neighborhoods of the U.S. were encouraging general discussions about the future of media. How should the advertising industry approach the new media and the people who use them, and why?

Agreement quickly took hold that advertisers needed audiovisual formats that could appeal to narrower, more targeted audiences than before because society had become more fractured than ever before. By the mid–1980s, advertising practitioners' sense of a divided and troubled America went beyond Turner's brash and existential attitude. Social divisions are becoming deeper than ever, they said, and marketers might as well try to exploit them. A panoply of research organizations supported this belief, underscoring it with historical and contemporary analysis about the roots of increased division.

The first five years of the 1980s saw an intense examination by marketers of the social forces guiding the changes in media that had Ted Turner crowing. Principals from major and minor ad agencies, research companies, and consultancy firms gave speeches on the subject. The issue came up at industry meetings. Trade publications printed articles on the subject.

There was much consensus on the basic outline. America, the story went, was undergoing a fundamental shift in its social fabric that was driving transformations in media. From the 1940s to the late 1960s, the nation had been united in purpose. The trauma of World War II had created a public that, to quote one ad executive, was "mentally wedded to mutual cooperation and togetherness brought on by [the] conflict."[7] Since people of all sorts could relate to broadly distributed norms and goals, mass marketing and a three-network universe were perfectly appropriate for reaching this kind of society.

About twenty years later, however, pressures such as the civil rights movement and the Vietnam War led the nation to become "less homogeneous, more splintered."[8] America seemed "split asunder into innumerable special interests—gray power, gay power, red power, black power, Sunbelt and frostbelt, environmentalists and industrialists . . . all more aware of their claims on society."[9] In addition, the success of the economic system of the '50s and '60s freed people to experiment with a variety of lifestyles.[10] The generation of the post—World War II era, the famous "baby boomers," grew up much more individualistic than their parents. Questioning traditional values and ways of life, they privileged the search for their own identities and new types of communities.[11] They were also involved in transforming the industrial economy in which they worked toward a more participatory, decentralized, and entrepreneurial environment.[12]

According to this tale, while the ideological left played its part in unleashing forces of social division, the political right did so, too. Many marketing trend watchers claimed that Ronald Reagan's election to the presidency in 1980 was evidence of an increasingly divided America. Reagan's victory, they said, reflected a substantial movement of national attitudes toward more self-reliance, attention to market forces, and less federal regulation as ways to address problems of national competitiveness, economic stagnation, and growing poverty.[13] In 1984, when Reagan beat Walter Mondale to win a second term, pollster Daniel Yankelovich pointed out that Mondale personified the core image of self-sacrifice. To the publisher of *Advertising Age,* the election showed that Americans "are tired of making sacrifices."[14]

It also seemed clear to marketers that liberals of varied tones were exposing deep social divisions in their fights with conservative groups such as the Moral Majority. Battles over the regulation of advertising content, cable television, and other media issues flared increasingly away from Washington, D.C., since liberals found the capital inhospitable.[15] Sensing this climate not long after Reagan's election, *Advertising Age* columnist Stanley Cohen opined that the nation was divided on key cultural issues and "full of anger."[16]

The word in the ad industry was that the increase in media fragmentation was a direct response to this social fractionalization. Advertising practitioners did not see this as bad. As U.S. society became more divided, it needed more outlets to reflect those divisions. People no longer wanted to be treated in "batches," as mass markets.[17] As early as the 1960s, specialized periodicals had begun to replace mass-circulation magazines. Now the three-network universe was beginning to erode in favor of a multichannel world. To many ad executives such changes reflected a society with increasingly divided interests, "a public moving to its own drumbeat."[18]

Related to the sense that the U.S. as a nation had growing divisions was the conviction that the society was developing starker distinctions between those who could afford to live nicely and those who could not. The American middle class was fading. Marketing researchers traced the beginning of the slide to the 1970s. By the early 1980s, speakers at ad industry meetings considered it a truism that the number of U.S. families in the center of the middle class (which meant bringing in roughly $25,000 in annual pretax income) was becoming smaller.[19] *American Demographics,* a magazine read carefully by marketing practitioners, noted that the percentage of U.S. families with middle-class incomes fell from 62.4 percent in 1969 to 55.9 percent in 1983.[20]

No one questioned the prediction, heard often, that the middle-class population would continue to decrease relative to the rest of the nation. A variety of economic, governmental, and social factors, it seemed clear, was imposing downward pressure on many middle-income families, forcing them into the lower-middle-income stratum (which in 1983 was tagged at between $14,748 and $24,700 a year) and even below.[21] At the same time, a substantial number of dual-career couples were making enough money to catapult them, through marriage, into salary ranges far beyond the upper-middle-income edge of $39,000. In other words, U.S. society was becoming more polarized than before; a substantial number of people was moving down and a substantial number was moving up. The majority class was getting smaller by the year.

Speakers and writers went even further with generalizations about the new social world confronting marketers. In addition to being increasingly more fractured and income-polarized than in the past, they said, American society was becoming more self-indulgent than before. They saw self-indulgence as a logical partner to the emphasis on individualism. At the start of the '80s executives forecast that the decade would mark, in the words of one, "a continuing trend away from the Protestant ethic . . . and toward self-fulfillment." The nation would see the proliferation of a "me-first" mentality.[22] There would be greater concern with pleasure and money as a "tool for pleasure."[23]

Linked to this self-involvement, many marketers contended, was a growing suspicion of institutions, a desire to decentralize authority, and a search for narrower communities in which to find friendship and loyalty.[24] By the 1990s, ad people were likely to connect this general suspicion, even cynicism, to their finding that Americans were living in a world of diminished expectations, "where economic, educational and other types of resources play much more important roles in how consumers act."[25]

Of special concern in all this was the credibility of advertising. One study released in 1980 found that despite a general anti-regulatory sentiment, seven in ten Americans believed advertising should be regulated more strongly.[26] Such stinging indictments were heard in one form or another throughout the decade.[27] Concerns about the public's skepticism of traditional advertising would weigh on marketing executives into the '90s as they planned target marketing strategies and tactics.

To the notions that America was increasingly segmented, self-involved, and suspicious, ad executives and trade magazine writers added yet another general tag: that many of the social segments were characterized by a pace that was increasingly frenetic. Ad people described increasingly mobile populations with changing habits and frenzied lifestyles.[28] The large percentage of people in their twenties who moved every four years, the increase of women who worked outside the home, and the growth of single-parent homes (up 49 percent in 1982 compared to 1970) were just three developments that had implications for marketers.[29]

Media executives were most concerned when harried lives broke people away from what had been predictable habits with the media, as they increasingly seemed to do.[30] Of particular concern was that their speeded-up way of dealing with the world made them hard to pin down for messages. Both the circulation director of *TV Guide* and the president of CBS Magazines asserted in 1988 that the dramatic drop of news-stand sales in the magazine industry could be blamed at least partly on the fact that women did not visit the supermarket as often as previously because they were working.[31] Many advertisers were also startled to learn in 1983 that viewers with many cable channels "are volatile, unpredictable and prone to channel switching, especially during commercials."[32] By the late '80s, the problem had been traced not just to the remote control and increased channel capacity but to the "limited attention spans and itchy remote control trigger fingers" of the TV generation grown to adulthood.[33]

Advertising executives drew their basic view of U.S. society from popular writings by a small set of social observers—especially Daniel Yankelovich (his book *New Rules*), John Naisbitt (*Megatrends*), Alvin Toffler (*The Third Wave*), and Peter Drucker (articles in the *Harvard Business Review*). To etch in specifics of this world, advertisers, their agencies, and media firms turned to the research industry that had grown around marketers' attempts to probe the hearts and minds of consumers. Not surprisingly, this industry centered on the segmentation of Americans by lifestyles and the beliefs thought to be connected to the lifestyles.

By the 1980s the research business had moved away from its long-standing concern with understanding people mainly in terms of such traditional "demographic" categories as gender, race, and income.[34] Heightened competition in the general economy led marketers to look for new approaches.[35] Competition among research firms led them to a "market research arms race" that continually pushed new methods.[36] The emphasis, increasingly, was on exploring in detail the activities and interests—the lifestyles—that could be associated with people exhibiting certain demographics.

Marketers' reckoned that lifestyles emerged as the hot new partitioning of society for at least three reasons. One had to do with researchers' awareness of high-profile alternative living options—the "hippies," "yippies," and others—that made news during the late 1960s. These developments led marketers to the idea that people with similar demographics might have particular personality profiles and ways of acting in the world. A second reason was the increased sophistication in researchers' statistical tools. It allowed them to find clusters of relationships among demographic, attitudinal, behavioral, and geographical features of a population that marketers hadn't noticed before. A third explanation for the exploration of lifestyles was the rise of the computer as a standard business research tool. By the late 1970s, the plunging cost of computer power made it economically feasible to merge large databases for marketing purposes and perform new kinds of number-crunching analyses on the newly merged files.

The analyses segmented the population and located those segments in geographical areas with previously unheard-of specificity. Drawing from credit card records and other unobtrusive ways of getting information, analysts learned what individual consumers bought, what else they read, how they played and drank, where they vacationed and where they lived. Statisticians developed new ways of making sense of how these data related to one another across broad populations.

By the mid–1980s, the information-gathering power of U.S. market research firms had far surpassed anything in previous decades. As part of what a trade magazine columnist called their "awesome capacity to gather data," the thirty-five largest companies had central telephone facilities with about 2,500 interviewing stations, most equipped for computer-assisted interviewing. They regularly mailed questionnaires to a panel of 640,000 households. They tracked the purchases of 50,000 households through special diaries and 27,500 households through special product scanner systems. Moreover, the firms had permanent test market data collection sites in 50 cities, including 22 malls.[37]

Three of the most widely used of the new breed of market research tools during the 1980s and into the 1990s were SRI International's VALS (Values and Life Styles), Claritas Corporation's PRIZM (Potential Rating Index For Zip Markets), and the Yankelovich Monitor. The Yankelovich Monitor was the oldest and least quantitative of the three. Launched in 1970, it claimed to track the strength of various trends and relate the social changes to consumer behavior in the marketplace. Developments that the Monitor highlighted to its corporate clients in the years after Ronald Reagan's 1980 election to the presidency included strategies that consumers were using to reconcile so-called "Me Decade" values of the 1970s with difficult economic realities. The firm's researchers broke consumers into three groups (*successful adapters, resistant adapters,* and *traditional adapters*) that, they said, adjusted in different ways to the new world of the 1980s. They noted that the findings would be useful to the credit card industry, among others, for it highlighted why and how certain kinds of people were likely to use credit during the coming years.

A very different way to think about consumers was provided by PRIZM beginning in 1974. The proposition guiding it was that "throughout the nation, Americans live in distinctive community types, refusing to blend into the mythical melting pot."[38] A related proposition was that people with similar cultural backgrounds and circumstances naturally gravitate toward one another geographically. Reaching them was physically possible because in 1962 the U.S. Postal Service had created a Zone Improvement Plan that gave neighborhoods numbers (zip codes) to speed mail delivery. The corollary was that individuals living in the same postal zip codes would exhibit similar patterns of consumer behavior.

Taking off from there, PRIZM's creators used cluster analysis on the U.S. census and databases from other research firms (including those from such major database houses as Simmons Market Research Bureau, Mediamark Research, and R. L. Polk) to classify every zip code into forty lifestyle groups. Among the classifications were such colorful titles as *Bohemian Mix, Blue-Blood Estates,* and *Shotguns and Pickups. Shotguns and Pickups* referred to small rural towns with more mobile homes than the norm, more large families with school-age children, and more blue-collar workers with only a high school education.

To the demographic categories were added descriptions of lifestyles. One supporter enthused that "with PRIZM and a zip code, [Claritas] can draw on thousands of census and consumer statistics to produce accurate portraits of any neighborhood, right down to the cereal in the cupboard and the antacid in the medicine cabinet."[39] Zip 85254 in northeast Phoenix, Arizona, for instance, was part of the *Furs and Station Wagons* cluster. Surveys indicated that people with the characteristics of northeast Phoenix residents tended to buy more vermouth than the U.S. average as well as to be more likely to belong to a country club, read *Gourmet* magazine and vote the GOP ticket. Zip 46772 in Molalla, Oregon, and Zip 43701 in Monroe, Indiana, were part of the *Shotguns and Pickups* circuit, with its very different way of life:

In *Shotguns & Pickups,* even the smallest home can come equipped with a giant-sized TV, wood stove, a ceramic bird collection and a dusty pickup in the driveway. . . . With their large families and modest means, Shotguns and Pickups residents like to stretch their budgets with frozen pizzas, dry soups, TV dinners and powdered soft drinks. They also install their own mufflers and repair their brakes on their Mercury, AMC and Subaru cars. For leisure, women enjoy needlepoint, men enjoy woodworking and hunting, and the family likes gardening; residents buy canning jars 79 percent more often than average Americans. In Shotguns and Pickups, no one has to pretend a fondness for outdoor living: deer season ranks up there with Christmas for favorite holidays.[40]

Claritas researchers contended that their clusters described real lifestyles that marketers could identify and target, if they wanted them. They also claimed that such a "geodemographic" approach to populations allowed marketers to pay greater attention to changing tendencies in purchasing behavior than could otherwise be the case. One example they trotted out in 1982 to pique interest in their program showed that consumers in white-collar, upscale communities were cutting back on purchases of U.S.-made cars faster than were members of middle- and lower-class communities. Another study, linking PRIZM data with information on consumer confidence, suggested that as the economy softened, the upscale suburban components of the market experienced a much more rapid erosion in confidence about the future than did upscale urban areas.[41]

A still different approach to sizing and slicing up consumers was the VALS program, first offered commercially by SRI in 1978.[42] It was based on the idea that it is possible to classify consumers into lifestyle-relevant psychological categories that affect their buying habits. The initial tack, used throughout the '80s, combined information about values and lifestyles with demographic data such as age, sex, and income to classify each individual in terms of one of the four VALS categories: *need-driven consumers* (supposedly found in about 11 percent of the U.S. population), *outer-directed consumers* (about 66 percent), *inner-directed consumers* (about 21 percent), and *integrateds* (only 2 percent of the population). The latter they considered were true leaders who have combined into their personalities the Achiever quality of inner-directedness with the Socially Conscious quality of outer-directedness.[43]

Through subcategories such as *survivors, sustainers, belongers, emulators,* and *achievers* the population was further fragmented. VALS developers contended that such categories could predict people's buying styles as well as suggest the appeals that advertisers should use to persuade consumers with different VALS. Using VALS data, for example, the Merrill Lynch investment firm found that its ad slogan "Merrill Lynch is bullish on America" appealed to belongers rather than to the achievers who were its true target market. As a result, the slogan was changed to "Merrill Lynch: a breed apart."[44]

But while marketers paid a lot of attention to PRIZM, Monitor, and VALS, these were merely the tip of the huge iceberg of research activities designed to help advertisers and their agencies understand their environment. The largest firm was A. C. Nielsen, with hundreds of millions of dollars in U.S. revenues. Most famous for its virtual monopoly on network television ratings through audimeters and diaries, its major cash engine was actually a division that helped manufacturers keep track of the movement of their competitors' goods out of warehouses and into stores.

Nielsen's size and quantitative approach contrasted with tiny firms such as Planmetrics. Planmetrics used methods and perspectives from anthropology to provide clients with information about how people thought about and used their products. One Planmetrics study of dishwashing, for example, provided the marketing insight that when people do it themselves (as opposed to using machines) the vast majority don't follow the pattern their mothers used. "They squirt the dish-washing liquid directly onto the dirty dishes," instead of filling the sink with soapy water.[45]

Between Nielsen and Planmetrics firms lay research companies with a wide array of techniques and perspectives. All offered to show consumer-goods advertisers the most lucrative ways to think about society and its constituent parts. They also proposed to help media firms find ways to plumb their audiences for attributes that could make the audiences attractive to advertisers.

Some companies were even pushed into it. A. C. Nielsen, for example, was forced by the advertising and cable TV industries to come up with a new way to measure viewers. Both groups were deeply suspicious of Nielsen's diaries, which they believed were riddled with errors owing to viewer tendencies to list only the more prominent channels that they watched. While they considered Nielsen's audimeter more reliable, its problem was that it reported only on the channel to which each TV set in the sampled home was tuned—not on who was watching. Advertising agencies and the cable industry demanded a quantitative ratings device that reflected the emerging target marketing era where the individual "viewer" was becoming much more important than the "household," which had been the major measure of concern to the Big 3 networks.

The result, Nielsen's People Meter, required family members and their guests to push buttons designated for them on a meter when they sat down to watch. It offered the potential for breaking the individual viewing behaviors of family members by demographics, geodemographics, and lifestyle characteristics such as buying patterns and hobbies. The technology caused fireworks when it showed the Big 3 receiving far fewer viewers for certain shows than the audimeters had noted. In their defense, the broadcasters claimed that many people, especially children, were simply not pushing their buttons.

Advertisers accepted the device as a correct accounting of viewership, however, and the People Meter became the accepted basic ratings technology into the 1990s. At the same time, Nielsen felt compelled to continue the research arms race. Even while perfecting the People Meter to audit the use of VCR tapes and other home video technologies, it competed with a number of other firms in an expensive search for a "passive people meter." The gizmo would recognize the faces of particular individuals and chart the different viewing patterns of each without the need to press buttons.[46]

Market researchers were aware that the cumulative result of all their studies was an image of a fragmented nation that was changing frenetically. Most agreed that these data jibed with trend-spotting guru Alvin Toffler that things were simply happening faster than in previous decades. Everyone would have to learn to live with the new speeded-up world.

An alternative view is that this warp-drive picture of America might be a reflection of the warp-drive competition among researchers to find ever more profitable ways of slicing up society. Yet this understanding of market researchers' constructions of society never came up in the trade press, if it came up at all. Even market researchers who offered the most angry challenges to SRI, Claritas, and the rest of the research field did not question the overall message, at least in public.[47] The notion that Americans were increasingly divided from one another, self-indulgent, suspicious, and frenetic seemed to be accepted by respected and moderate social observers such as Yankelovich and Naisbitt. They saw it rooted in long-term trends nurtured by the left that celebrated difference. They saw it upheld by the right-leaning political and economic tendencies evident in the election of Ronald Reagan. And, finally, they found it supported through their own quantitative and qualitative research.

And yet, during the 1980s many national advertisers were hesitant to dive into the new electronic media that many of them were heralding as the newest way to reach this divided society. Much of their interest in Turner's channels in the late '70s and early '80s had less to do with general enthusiasm over the cable medium's potential for marketers than with specific complaints about the broadcast networks. These years were marked by the price for network time soaring beyond even the high rate of inflation. Ad agencies did not protest too much at the start. Their commissions were typically based on what they spent of their clients' money, so they got rich on their share of the super-inflated TV take. As the economy slowed in the new decade, though, clients began to ask tough questions about efficient expenditures. Along with these questions came outrage about network "clutter"—the bunching of commercials so close to each other that ad people worried viewers would not remember their expensive spots.

Compounding the problems of high network prices and advertising clutter was the belief that ABC, CBS, and NBC were forfeiting their audiences. Nielsen reports indicated that the Big 3 had lost five rating points–5 percent of total national TV households—in prime time between 1976 and 1981. In fact, in highly cabled cities such as Tulsa, network prime time shares were dipping as low as 56 percent in 1983.[48]

Agency buyers believed that the decrease resulted primarily from increased viewership of pay cable channels that did not accept commercials, especially HBO and the Movie Channel. The rest of the drop could have resulted from a combination of ad-supported cable, the growing number of independent broadcast stations, and the small but rising number of VCRs in American homes. The amount of advertising on cable networks was still laughable compared to their over-the-air counterparts. In 1981, overall network cable billings were expected be around $100 million. It would be a healthy gain over 1980's $35 to $45 million billings, but nowhere near the $5.5 billion that advertisers expected to pay ABC, CBS, and NBC that year.[49]

In the mid–1980s major national advertisers still featured mostly mass-market plans of action. Marketers were quite aware that their traditional mainstays, the three major broadcast television networks, could no longer present them with over half of all households in the nation during a typical minute in a typical evening, as they had done through much of the 1960s and 1970s. Far from leaping to cable TV, videocassettes, computers, and other potential new ad vehicles, though, they treated the new media as "ancillary" to advertising on the Big 3 networks. They were not about to leave ABC, CBS, and NBC abruptly in order to place most of their marketing billions into magazines, radio networks, cable programs, home video, and other avenues that, they felt, reached minute fractions of their desired audiences. They believed that in many cases they could not find alternative dependable media that would be targeted to reach the particular slices of the audience that they wanted. That was particularly true if they wanted to make their case on television.

To media folk who questioned their slowness in shifting money from broadcast to cable, ad-agency executives replied that they had a responsibility to stake out the territory and decide how a medium ought to be judged before pouring a large amount of their clients' cash into it.[50] A deeper reason for their caution was that the advertising industry had invested forty years in thinking about television as a mass-market medium. Decades before, they had readily accepted changes from mass marketing to target marketing in the magazine and radio industries because those media were giving way to what they saw as a better mass-market replacement, television. Advertisers knew they could rely on television to reach nearly everybody at once with words and pictures.

To many media planners of the '80s, the new developments were fundamentally different from that earlier media shift. It seemed clear that if television went the fractionalized way of magazines and radio, there would no replacement. That would mean a loss not just of numbers but of the unparalleled efficiencies in money, time, and employees that came from bargaining with just a few networks.

In the media-buying business, the key to pleasing clients meant proving that their money was being used efficiently. When it came to television, that traditionally meant buying time that would provide the same accumulation of viewers of different shows (even if they were counted more than once) more cheaply than another agency could; it was called getting the best price for gross rating points, or GRPs. Despite all the talk about smaller network ratings, the mandate to accumulate the lowest-price GRPs possible continued through the '80s. Media planners reasoned that to match the GRP number of a few years earlier for a particular broad audience (say, women aged 18 to 49), they would simply have to buy more time on the networks than they did back then. Though expensive, that was still easier than accumulating audiences across a panoply of "niche" audiovisual technologies, from targeted cable channels to CD-ROMs to online services. Not only did these technologies involve more money to reach fewer people than network TV, it was difficult for marketers to understand how to advertise on some of those media, how to determine the most money-saving approaches to purchasing, and how to measure results reliably.

The efficiencies of TV could be especially large for packaged-goods firms that wanted to reach huge numbers of potential customers. As the director of market research for a major ad agency noted, agency media buyers could save lots of time by gathering all their money together for a network deal. "Rather than having one buyer go to the marketplace for a million and a half dollars for barbecue sauce and another buyer spending two million for salad dressing, and rather than have eighty-five different—that's about [the number of brands] the client's got— negotiations, you lump them into a single multi-hundred million dollar negotiation. And the networks give you a very good rate."[51]

In reply, magazines, radio, and new-media executives urged ad people to consider that while targeting through them might cost more, it could also establish better and more enduring relationships with consumers than ABC, CBS, and NBC ever could. Not everyone in the ad world bought these arguments. Many, however, did seem to agree with the new-media executives' fallback position, that in the coming years media technology would be developed that would combine fine-tuned targeting with high efficiency. "That's where everyone wants to end up," said one media planner. "The question is, when can the [media] technology be there to make it cost-efficient?"[52]

Not wanting to be left behind, agencies and their clients tried to experiment with advertising on new media, especially cable. At the start, media buyers' preference would have been to place commercials on HBO and other pay-movie channels, since that was where most of the really desirable viewers seemed to be going from the networks in the early 1980s. Despite pay-cable executives' public stance against any such intrusions, advertising executives kept raising the subject. The Arbitron research firm even conducted a study that found 45 percent of pay-cable viewers wouldn't object to seeing commercials between movies on pay TV.[53]

Lacking an entry to the pay-TV arena, though, advertisers experimented with ad-supported networks that viewers received at no extra cost with their cable subscriptions. The legitimacy of moving some over-the-air TV dollars into cable was bolstered by marketers' awareness that in late 1981 cable had reached 30 percent of U.S. homes; the rate of cable's penetration into American homes was climbing fast.[54] Further enhancing cable's reputation were major media firms such as Hearst, Warner, Westinghouse, Time, Paramount, MCA—even ABC, CBS, and NBC—organizing ad-supported channels or buying into them. USA Network, purchased in 1981 by Time, Paramount, and MCA, claimed to reach a variety of well-off audiences with shows oriented toward men, children, or women at different times of the day.

Other formats claimed to concentrate on upscale portions of specific audiences in the manner of magazines. Examples were women (the Health Channel and Hearst-ABC's Daytime), teens and young adults (Warner's Music Television), culture-lovers (ABC's ARTS and CBS's unsuccessful culture channel), men (ESPN, now partly owned by ABC), news freaks (Turner's Cable News Network and Westinghouse's Satellite NewsChannels), blacks (Black Entertainment Television), Hispanic Americans (Spanish International Network), Christians (Christian Broadcasting Network), travelers (the Weather Channel), and game-show addicts (UTV). Not quite part of that bunch was the Modern Satellite Network, which sold time to marketers wanting to air long commercials (sometimes called infomercials) or public relations films.[55]

As the fragmentation of media channels received growing coverage in the trade press, and as cable's penetration continued to erode the network affiliates' TV ratings,[56] the agency climate changed perceptibly in favor of heralding the potential of targeted advertising in future media. In 1981, the trade newspaper *Advertising Age* commented that "ad agency competition for leadership status in establishing their TV superstation and cable TV expertise" was "intense." The result, it said, was that agencies were "showering down position papers, research and reorganization plans" on ways to tie marketing aims to changes in the media world.[57]

Not everyone was convinced that the time for drastic shifts to targeting via television had come. Many marketers seemed to agree, though, with the president of the Ford Motor Company, who remarked in 1981 that cable was the tip of a long-term trend away from a broad, "shotgun" approach to consumers that was network TV's hallmark. The future, he said, belonged to "such rifles as cable TV, VCRs and discs, regional and special interest publications, and local radio and TV." For over thirty years, "network TV has dominated our thinking in this area. Over the next thirty, this will likely change."[58]

Media futurists ignited further anxiousness about the coming targeting options. They argued that advertisers' attention should not be focused only on the entertainment and news services that cable delivered. In the coming years, they predicted, expanded channel capabilities would be linked with computer technology to deliver information services such as electronic newspapers, banking, and shop-at-home services.[59] These and other possibilities pointed to new marketing strategies in cable as well as in other emerging media that could feed to cable, such as satellites, VCRs, and teletext (the sending of written news and other information over the air). The new-media prophets also predicted that innovations would take place on the creative side of advertising. That would range, they said, from interactive ads to ads of many lengths, to entertainment programs created by marketers which would, in effect, be commercials.

Richard Gilbert, an advertising consultant, production-house owner, and formerly the head of a mid-size New York agency, exhorted his colleagues in 1981 to catch the wave of futuristic excitement. He bemoaned that most ad agencies seemed not to understand that the coming cable world would not be merely a refinement of broadcast television. Rather, he insisted, it would require ad agencies to see themselves in broader creative and marketing roles. He urged that "restless trendsetters break from the pack." Advertisers "are anticipating this new complex video culture and question how it can be made to advance their own marketing needs," he wrote. "Ad budgets for 1983 and 1984 are not that far away. If cable is at a 30% household penetration now, who knows where it will be in the near future. Can anyone afford to wait?"[60]

The 1980s marked an odd period, then, when marketers' use of media to reach Americans did not match their own sense of the fragmenting of American life or their methods for searching out the fragments. Ad people talked to one another about U.S. society in ways that they could not actualize in their own media plans. Print and electronic competitors to the Big 3 networks joined the discussion, urging ad people that they could in fact use them to divide the nation for advertising purposes in efficient and effective ways. They offered and discussed these trends publicly in existential tones that offered no moral judgments. A quick-changing America that was divided into a nearly infinite variety of self-seeking slices, depending on the product or issue, was a reality that might make business sense—perhaps not now, but surely in the future, when the media could be shaped to fit marketers' needs.

And as marketers pushed the vision, people throughout the media and advertising industries picked it up, elaborated upon descriptions of fractured, self-indulgent, suspicious, and frenetic people to suit their needs, and announced their conclusions to the rest of the trade for their own aggrandizement. The result was a cacophonous and often amoral competition over ways to slice up U.S. society. As it progressed, the slices made ad people more and more inclined to support media that would help them home in separately on the many groups that they were sure lived very differently from one another.

FOUR

MAPPING A FRACTURED SOCIETY

LIFESTYLE HAS ALWAYS BEEN a key consideration in the media business. *Vogue* magazine has for decades been edited for "women" who want to know about high clothing fashion. Monday night football on network television has for many years been aimed at people—mostly "men"—who care about the sport. Outdoor highway advertising for hotels has long been predicated on the basic idea that "travelers" in their cars are likely to want to find a place to sleep.

The difference between these examples and the lifestyles that ad people discussed frequently beginning in the late 1970s lies mainly in the passion for detail—the desire to get more specific about consumers' activities and attitudes through a cannonade of research. Practitioners at the time were sure that the U.S. was going through what Peter Franchese, the editor of *American Demographics* magazine, called a "symphony of demographic change." "The trick," he suggested, "is to find a faster growing segment before everyone else does or build market share [in a segment] faster than anyone else."[1]

No longer was it enough to talk about "homemaker" or "woman" or "black." Marketers subjected these and other labels to new research and came up with several groups within them—different kinds of women, several kinds of homemakers. Their counterparts in the media used advertisers' differentiation of audiences by lifestyle as a guide to segments of society that they ought to target.

The media executives built their appeals to advertisers around one or both of two claims: the *claim of efficient separation* and the *claim of a special relationship*. The first was a media firm's assertion that it could deliver a desired group to advertisers without making them pay for audiences they did not want. The second was the claim that the target audience felt such an extraordinary tie to the media firm's outlet—the magazine, cable network, newspaper—that it paid attention to everything about the outlet, including the ads. The overall idea was that by speaking to the particular needs and lifestyles of identifiable consumers, the firm had been able to make itself part of the small set of magazines, newspapers, radio stations, cable channels, and other media outlets that those consumers considered most meaningful to their ways of looking at the world. People might well enjoy reading or viewing other materials, but would find the greatest relevance and credibility in that, their primary media community.

Both new and "traditional" media executives frequently backed up these contentions with facts from surveys that they had purchased from research firms or found in government reports. Because of the proprietary nature of much commercial research, certain audience data that media firms and their advertisers used in negotiations over space and time did not appear in any public forum. Moreover, many of the assertions were blatant self-promotions. Nevertheless, as people interviewed for this book noted, the trade press did reflect a feverish conversation about America that was taking place throughout the industry. Trend analyses, interviews, leaks of company strategies, and reports of conference addresses by key industry figures reflected the contemporary arguments about the relationship between U.S. media and the U.S. audience—and about how much advertisers' media strategies should change as a result of it.

The bulk of distinctions that people from the marketing and media worlds grappled with during the '80s and early '90s revolved around five categories: income, gender, age, race, and ethnicity. The seeming ordinariness of these labels belies the energy that characterized discussions of them. Marketers and their agencies piled differences in the five categories onto each other in their efforts to locate slices of America that were most useful to them. Media firms picked up on those slices and created new ones as they tried to attract advertising support through claims of efficient separation and special relationship.

Curiously, advertising and media practitioners' way of complimenting a group was to further divide it. Generally, the more attractive a population segment was to marketers, the more they segmented it. An implicit theme running through the trade press was that to make best use of different segments of American consumers, marketers and media would best see them living in different worlds.

Consider the way advertising and media practitioners talked about portions of the U.S. population with different incomes. Historically, advertisers had gone after members of the broad middle class because of their large numbers and their ability to buy goods beyond basics.[2] Discussions of lower-middle-income Americans, people with marginal "disposable incomes," were always rare in advertising trade magazines. Interest in lower-class people verged on the nonexistent.

By the late 1970s, marketers and media practitioners were de-emphasizing their interest in the broad middle class. They saw it shrinking in size as many of its members sank into lower-middle-class status and many others climbed into the upper-middle-income stratum. Consequently, they shifted their attention to those who were getting the most money, the upper and upper-middle classes.

Even descriptions of the "mass market," historically centered on the broad middle, took on a new slant. Executives from McDonald's, Hallmark, K-Mart, Proctor and Gamble, and other traditional sellers to "everyone" let the advertising trade know that their goal as mass marketers was not to reach everyone in the same way or at the same time. They noted that they were talking differently to different types of customers for the same products, since the reasons for purchasing might be different. And they stressed that the term mass market included customers from the growing upper income brackets in addition to those from the allegedly declining middle.

In the rare occasions that the advertising trade press noted the life options of the middle class, it portrayed them as relatively narrow—having cookouts, watching soap operas, fixing old homes.[3] By contrast, articles and advertisements in the trade press depicted the upper-middle and upper classes as multifaceted and continually open to new experiences. Conferences, meetings, press releases, and special trade magazine sections speculated about the characteristics and habits of people on the "fast track."[4] The guiding proposition was the one *Time* magazine used for its trade campaign of the early and mid '80s: "More than ever, real consumers are concentrated at the top."[5]

Actual numbers that advertisers used to denote "top" incomes changed through the 1980s and 1990s, not only because inflation pushed both salaries and prices higher but because different judges had different criteria. In the excitement over high-income earners, analysts competed with one another to define and differentiate them.[7] American Express analysts were smitten with what they claimed was an especially desirous and growing segment, people whose business activities and travel made them truly affluent spenders.[8] Another group of researchers noted that the wealthy could be divided into various personality segments—for example, discriminating, trendy, sophisticated, conservative, or adventurous.[9] Still a third way of cutting up the rich was to distinguish them according to how they got their money. "Today," a consultant said, "we have an affluent market that is so heterogeneous you may have dual paycheck families, inherited wealth, and retired wealth—all part of the affluent market."[10] The dual-paycheck rich, he noted, was especially self-indulgent, busy, and hard for marketers to reach.

A small group of print media tried to take advantage of this idea that the wealthy were becoming increasingly differentiated by lifestyle. They insisted in trade ads that their unique editorial slants would attract parts of the affluent population that would be hard to duplicate elsewhere without wasting it on people not in the target audience. So, for example, *Club Living* said it was "edited exclusively for the expensive tastes [and] opulent lifestyles of the member families of the country's finest private clubs."[11] *Newsweek* argued that because it now used two "screens"—job title and income—for its Executive edition, it could reach exclusively people who "have money *and* clout. Money to buy luxury items for themselves, and clout to make purchase decisions for their business."[12]

As the '80s turned into the '90s, many periodicals added claims of special relationship to these assertions of efficient audience separation. The reason was that an ability to reach key subgroups efficiently no longer seemed enough. Overlap between lifestyle magazines for the affluent required media firms to acknowledge that their audience could also be reached in other places. They insisted, though, that their readers held unique attachments to them that virtually ensured attention to ads.

Barron's portrayed itself as not only reaching the cream of key executives but cultivating a must-read bond with them. A trade ad showed a chief executive at his desk. A barbed-wire fence blocked the outside world from entering. Behind it the wealthy man was rapt, reading his issue of *Barron's*.

But while an increasing array of magazines and newspapers made claims of efficient separation and special relationship for subgroups of the rich, most print and electronic media firms argued that affluent segments were part of larger slices of society that combined the wealthy with the upper-middle class. Lifestyles could be just as usefully fragmented at those income levels, they contended.

"It's not a matter of simple demographics anymore," agreed an N.W. Ayer ad-agency researcher in 1994. "You can make $50,000 and be quite affluent," added a Claritas marketing executive that year, when the median income was about $35,000.[13] Both were referring to marketers' consensus that unmarried people with upper-middle-class incomes might have as much disposable income as many upper-class households with several children. Marketers also showed a growing awareness that upper-middle-class consumers might concentrate certain parts of their disposable income into particular lifestyle areas, acting as rich people within those niches.

As a result, "upscale"—a combination of the selectively affluent with the genuinely affluent—became one of the hot-button advertising terms of the '80s and '90s.[14] The word suggested a large and growing portion of society with a disposable income that represented a marketers' dream. At the same time, ambiguity surrounded the actual income one needed to be upscale. That vagueness, and especially the idea of selective affluence, encouraged media firms to call a fairly wide spectrum of their audiences upscale.

Particularly during the '70s and '80s, "upscale" was a mantra that ad-supported cable networks, a new phenomenon, used in their attempts to lure sponsors. In their arguments to advertisers they pitted upscale families against middle- and lower-class ones. "It's becoming more and more evident," said the head of the USA cable network in 1983, "that there are now two TV universes—those with cable and those without." She added that with the well-off forming attachments to cable networks, "more than just the broadcast networks' gross numbers are declining. But it's the kind of [people] they'll be left with that is striking. Cable TV is attracting the upscale suburban viewer."[15]

Denigration of middle- and lower-income segments was common when new-media executives were trying to get advertisers' cash. Alvin Eicoff, a prominent direct-marketing consultant, was representative in claiming that the upscale "social stratum . . . tends to be motivated by a multitude of facts, not [the] snappy 30 second jingles" that sway the lower parts of society.[16] *Information Week,* echoing this notion, called its readers "affluent and demographically correct customers."[17] Similarly, a new-media executive emphasized to advertisers that new-media users were the antithesis of blurry, hard-to-understand mass markets. They represented, instead, an opportunity for "very focused, very potent micromarketing" to people who could afford the best.[18]

Yet a divisive corollary of this approach was that if upscale social segments held the key to marketing, downscale social segments were liabilities. That was the view of an executive of a major corporation involved in planning a futuristic interactive cable experiment. When asked in 1992 about the people who couldn't afford the paraphernalia necessary to join the marketing test, he said simply, "Fuck 'em. We don't care about them."[19]

It was well accepted among media and marketing practitioners that the great proportion of online and CD-ROM users were men. Firms that were urging marketers to promote themselves on the "information highway" drew pictures of upscale, educated males who were making computers and the media connected to them the center of their business and leisure activities.[20]

Through the 1980s and beyond, advertisers often added considerations of gender to their interest in income as a way to define desirable consumers. Men were important, yet they did not receive nearly as much attention as women in the trade press. Marketers had long considered women to be in control of their family's income and therefore more important consumers than males. They believed that men tended to buy a narrow collection of items instead of being "broad-range consumers."[21] And they held the view that male consumers weren't as changeable—as "volatile"—as women in their activities and attitudes.[22]

As a result, questions about how much men were changing in the era of social fragmentation were not asked nearly as often as questions about how much women were changing. Marketers' attention to changes among women was enormous. And much more than with men, they posited fragmentations within gender that continued and extended the divisions they were seeing in income.

Women took center stage even when the topic was men. Ad people agreed that what few substantial changes were occurring among males in the most attractive income levels had come about because of fundamental changes in the social situation of women. The major issue confronting the advertising industry when it came to females was stated well in a 1985 *Advertising Age* article titled "Graphic Changes Charted in the Middle Class." It linked the increasing distance between the vigorous upper-middle and the struggling rest of the middle class to rapidly growing differences in the jobs that women of working age were finding outside the home. Consensus among marketers was that two-career families had created sharp divisions in U.S. society. Release of data from the 1980 U.S. Census furthered marketers' belief that major changes had transpired in women's experiences.

"Ten to twenty years ago," a radio industry consultant stated in 1983, "women played a very minor part in the workforce." By contrast, she said, the 1980 U.S. Census data showed that the number of female lawyers increased by 188 percent from 1970 to 1980. Similarly, the number of female computer operators increased by 12 percent and female physicians by 44 percent.[23]

She acknowledged that in the early '80s there were still more women in the clerical ranks than in any other area. It was true, another consultant noted, that "very few women make big bucks." But nearly 60 percent were married,[24] and because many of those salaries were combined with husbands' salaries, "more families and women are upper middle class." The downside was that two-income families had become a necessity. As a result, "because more families are fatherless, more women are poor."[25]

Advertising and media practitioners concerned with selling to men struggled to make sense of how these developments affected men. Focusing on the upscale segments of the social equation, they concluded that men were becoming more dissimilar from one another because their women were changing. "Thirty years ago," said an Ogilvy and Mather agency executive, "we knew what men wanted because they all wanted the same things—a Chevy, apple pie, and to send their kids to college. But the changes in society have fragmented that, and we're not making many generalizations anymore."[26]

Actually, ad people *were* making generalizations about the new man and his role as a consumer. For example:

• In 1983, marketing consultant Judith Langer reported on interviews with the fast-growing group of men aged twenty-one to fifty-five who were living "without female partners." Many of the men were "pup tenters," with little desire for a nice-looking home. But Langer said she also found many "settlers" with "a surprising interest in furnishing, cooking and cleaning, tasks for which men have received little training."[27]

• In 1980, the Cunningham and Walsh ad agency announced that it had discovered "a new breed" of husband, which comprised 32 percent of all men. Like "the bachelor," these husbands "look for new and different products and buy on impulse."[28]

• The Benton and Bowles ad agency surveyed 452 husbands in 1980 and classified 13 percent as "progressive"—more comfortable with changing male and female roles than other men. B&B reported that the progressives practiced what they preached: they watched their sick children and recognized their wives' careers as equal in importance to their own. In addition, 71 percent cooked an entire family meal in a given two-week period, 61 percent did the laundry, and 53 percent cleaned the bathroom. (Cleaning the bathroom was evidently a big deal because it implied a say in soap purchases; a Doyle Dane Bernbach study also asked men about cleaning the bathroom.)[29]

• In 1985, studies found that many more men were doing the shopping and spending less time than women in stores. The researchers also stated that men were not as careful as women about what they bought and that single men were less careful than married ones.[30] A year later, researchers found that men who did most of the shopping for their families had greater self-esteem than those who did not.[31]

Jann Wenner, founder of *Rolling Stone,* put the changes squarely in marketing terms. "The evolution of the male shopper is a new phenomenon," he contended.[32] The *Ladies Home Journal* heralded the New Man's cultural as well as economical importance. "I don't have to play God anymore," it had a thirtyish man say in a 1981 trade ad. "If I'm not sure, I can say so. It sure beats the old macho bluster." The magazine's point to advertisers was that it was "exploring the problems men face to help women come to grips with their own."[33] That, the *Journal* argued, was helping it cultivate special relationships with its female readers.

Yet uncertainty about the extent of these changes came from a variety of quarters. A 1984 *Advertising Age* article allowed that the majority of men *are* changing, "taking a step here, two steps there, away from the old masculine stereotypes" but concluded that the truly "new man" "is hard to define but definitely in the minority."[34] An *Ad Age* piece four years later was less optimistic about being able to find new segments of men that would excite marketers. "So far," it said, getting to the bottom line, "publishers have been unable to slice the male reading audience into as many splinter categories as there are for women's magazines."[35]

Women, it was clear to all ad and media practitioners, were being buffeted by tides of change that were making splintering them more useful than ever. The traditional target, the middle-class female, seemed to have separated in a broad gamut of directions. "Tracking [middle-class working women] isn't as easy as it used to be," an *Ad Age* writer concluded, "because the middle class isn't what it used to be. It's richer, poorer, smarter and smaller—all at once." He pointed out that marketers were most interested in following females in the upscale portion of the middle class, since they were in charge of their family's large disposable income. Even K-Mart, which traditionally aimed at "the middle mass of American women," had determined to take on an "upwardly mobile" look, "weeding out low-end items and adding to the high end."[36]

But simply going after relatively well-off women was not enough for most marketers. With the realization that 52 percent of the work force was female, an armory of qualitative and quantitative tools were brought to bear on women of working age to see what more there was to be found.[37] Their investigations often pitted "working" women against "nonworking" women (or "homemakers") in a variety of ways. Comparisons between working women and homemakers generally worked to the detriment of the latter. J. Walter Thompson researchers found that "in almost every product category the working women were better consumers, bought more, spent more, or did whatever."[38] A Yankelovich study stated that compared to homemakers, working women were generally younger, more affluent, and better educated.[39] The Young and Rubicam agency added that working women "have completely different outlooks" on financial budgets and household needs than nonworkers and that these differences show up in their buying habits. Y&R concluded that working women were "now more attractive" than their nonworking counterparts.[40]

The reasons for the differences, ad people agreed, were time and mobility. It was clear to marketers that upscale working women were caught in a frenetic "time crunch" of momentous proportions.[41] Among other things, it was reshaping their shopping habits: moving them to catalogs, discouraging them from buying cosmetics in department stores (they went to drug stores instead) and leading them to skip buying greeting cards in Hallmark Stores (the drug stores and Wal-Mart won out again).

Some marketers in the early '80s became concerned that in the frenzy over the working woman society was condemning homemakers, who were consequently "miserable."[42] The issue was of such interest that the BBDO ad agency commissioned a special study of the subject in 1981. It pronounced homemakers quite content with their lot, much different from a stereotype of neurotic domesticity.[43] Still, *Advertising Age,* in its headline about the BBDO study, called homemakers a "happy breed."[44] The word "breed" underscored a belief that fundamental differences separated the lifestyles of female workers and nonworkers.

In the meantime, the division of women, particularly working women, proceeded apace. One J. Walter Thompson researcher suggested in a 1982 book about advertising to women that agency planners should recognize four types: the stay-at-home housewife, the plan-to-work housewife, the just-a-job working woman, and the career-oriented working woman.[45] Three years later, a consulting firm divided female America into eight classes, ranging from "Good Life" (which it characterized as working, married, no children) to "The Challenge" (working, married, children) to "Dependent" (not working, unmarried, children). Each segment, the firm contended, had its own specific lifestyle cluster—its own living situation, values and attitudes.[46]

Other researchers found different ways to divide women. How to exploit those categories was an issue that preoccupied media as well as marketing firms. Especially excited were companies that specialized in carrying ads outdoors (billboards, bus kiosks), in-store, or "on site" (in doctors' offices and hair salons). The pitch of all these firms centered on the new-found out-of-home mobility of working women. Now that women were on the move, the logic went, marketers would have to track them, and persuade them, away from home during much of the day.

Executives agreed that work was leading women to different primary media relationships. While they noted differences between media uses of female executives and those of other distaff employees, a theme of polarization particularly came out in discussions of working women and homemakers. Compared to "housewives," they reported, working women watched TV less, read more and different magazines and newspapers, and listened to radio more often. As early as 1983, radio stations leveraged this logic, marshaling statistics that focused on full-time working women. The Radio Advertising Bureau (RAB) prepared a brochure, "Radio: It's Red Hot to Sell Working Women," to highlight the subject.[47]

Media executives who aimed at the working female often used the "stay-at-home mother" as a code word for the relatively undesirable female. Daytime television viewers slowly became synonymous with "the unemployed, housewives, youngsters," as talk-show host Geraldo Rivera called them in 1989.[48] The head of the Lifetime cable network argued in 1988 that a new separation was taking place between women. Women's "lifestyle changes" has "resulted in the decline of daytime on broadcast networks." Where once daytime network television had been the place for marketers to reach women of all sorts, now only a small proportion was watching, he said. "The irony was that it became tough to find women as an ad target at a time when they became a more attractive market."[49]

There was disagreement among media executives aiming at working women about whether they were interested in material that homemakers or men also found interesting.[50] The Lifetime cable network was vociferous regarding its stand. Lifetime executives made sure to position the programming service as aimed at working women, not men or homemakers. "The bulk of what we do is demographically pure," asserted its president-CEO in 1988. "We want to reach upscale working women without diluting the audience."[51]

The tensions involved in trying to separate working women from homemakers, and different sorts of working women from each other, found a special cauldron in the magazine industry during most of this period. At its essence, the struggle was over how to claim understanding of, and special relationship with, different sorts of upscale women. The fighting especially took place between what were called "new lifestyle magazines" and "women's service magazines."

In the parlance of the magazine industry, "service" magazines were those books that cover the wide spectrum of a person's life—from personal problems to clothes to baby care to contemporary issues. By far the most popular service titles were the so-called Seven Sisters—the periodicals *Good Housekeeping, McCall's, Redbook, Family Circle, Ladies Home Journal, Woman's Day,* and *Better Homes and Gardens*—that had historically associated themselves with the values of the American housewife.

The new lifestyle magazines, by contrast, claimed to deal principally with the career issues confronting the working females who read them. *Working Woman, Working Mother, Self, Vital,* and *Savvy* were among the most recognizable of these. *Savvy* told advertisers that it aimed at the top 5 percent of the female work force when it came out in 1980.[52] *Working Woman* was not quite so picky, but its editor did state in 1985 that "cashiers in supermarket checkout lines . . . should not be a part of our . . . audience."[53]

The new magazines posed a philosophical as well as monetary challenge to the service magazines over how to most usefully construct and assert their hold on the best upscale women for advertisers. The new working-women's periodicals offered both the claim of efficient separation as well as the claim of special relationship. They contended that despite the smaller circulation than any of the traditional women's "books," they were reaching desirable females in a print environment the women considered their own, dedicated to their issues.[54]

For their part, the service magazines denied that there were fundamental differences between the needs of relatively upscale working women and homemakers.[55] But while they united against periodicals for working women, in the late '80s they found themselves fiercely fighting among themselves for unique identities to advertisers. "They are [seen as] general service . . ." a agency's media director said of the group. "But in an era of specialization, general is considered negative."[56]

Hearst Magazines provides a good example of how magazine publishers tried to construct distinctive audiences. Hearst owned both *Redbook* and *Good Housekeeping* and wanted to make sure that they wouldn't lose ads to each other. In previous decades, both *Redbook* and *Good Housekeeping* executives felt it was enough to tell ad people that their periodicals aimed broadly at young women with families. It was this family link, primarily, that distinguished them from Hearst's *Cosmopolitan,* which aimed at unmarried women.

In the late '80s, though, Hearst executives (along with their counterparts in all the Sister firms) worked to position each periodical as a targeted publication, to claim its efficient separation from those of other periodicals and, especially, its cultivation of a special relationship with readers. They asserted that they were moving to connect in unique ways with distinctive lifestyle slices of the relatively well-to-do female population, working or not. "The big thing for [*Redbook*] or any magazine that's going to lead in the '90s is you've got to . . . narrow in on a niche and be able to define it and address it editorially," said Hearst's publishing director in 1991.[57]

To build new notions about the magazines' audiences, Hearst accentuated small age differences that it had found when comparing samples of *Redbook* and *Good Housekeeping* readers. *Redbook,* which had a median reader age of thirty-nine, would aim to lower it to thirty-seven. That, said Hearst, would allow it to hold a "bridge" position between Hearst's rather racy *Cosmopolitan,* aimed at single women in their twenties, and *Good Housekeeping,* which targeted a median age of forty-one.

But to appear realistic as a bridge, the audience-and-magazine makeovers had to include lifestyle redefinitions. So, in trade magazine publicity announcing its makeover, *Redbook* told advertisers it was reshaping the image of its reader. During much of the 1980s it had been that of a "juggler" who managed to combine the roles of wife, mother, and worker and still remain sane—with the help of *Redbook.* According to the editor-in-chief, simply helping women juggle the realities of work and home was no longer so necessary or distinctive because working mothers were more experienced in 1991 than in 1981, when *Redbook*'s ad department came up with the term "the juggler" for an ad campaign.[58] *Redbook*'s new tilt, she suggested, would be toward women who wanted psychic self-indulgence in the midst of freneticism.[59]

This would include a strong dose of titillation, unique for a Seven Sister. Trade ads promised advertisers that the "new" *Redbook* would be "about her deepest thoughts . . . more sexy than servicy. More provocative than pedantic."[60] The editor-in-chief averred that its readers would appreciate "you-and-your-child" advice at the same time that they would relish a celebrity column and racy articles such as "Why I Date Your Husband." The bridge from *Cosmopolitan* was clearly on her mind. "If that [article] was in *Cosmo,*" she quipped, "the title would be "How to Date Someone Else's Husband."[61]

The audience Hearst carved out for *Good Housekeeping* came from a very different slice of social reality. Starting with the admission that dur-

ing the '80s "we were not considered very contemporary," *Good Housekeeping* management argued that the country was returning to their
magazine's view of the world as the Reagan era ended. Women, they
said, had had enough of the blatant careerism of the '80s and the sense
that they should do it all. To bolster their case, they released research
they had commissioned from Yankelovich Clancy Shulman and the
Good Housekeeping Institute's Consumer Research Panel. The studies
"revealed a rediscovery by women, whether they worked or not, of the
appeal of traditional roles as wife and mother."[62]

Good Housekeeping decided to capitalize on the change, especially as
it related to the mother who was becoming settled in her life roles. Trade
ads constructed a women who was older than the juggler. Her self-
indulgence was now focused on activities and products inside the home
rather than outside of it. She was the New Traditionalist—"a new kind
of woman with deep rooted values [who] is changing the way we live."[63]

The ads portrayed a mom, a boy, and a girl standing handsomely in
lush grass in front of a substantial home.[64] That the family was clearly
affluent reflected a new claim of efficient separation in its pitches. Recognizing the desire of some advertisers to reach only its more well-to-do
readers, *Good Housekeeping* used proprietary databases to create a "best
in the house" edition. It would ensure that certain ads would reach only
20 percent of its nearly four million subscribers. They would include
only those women whose family income suggested consumption activities not just of traditionalists but of upscale traditionalists.[65]

The *Good Housekeeping* portrait of a mother and her young children
raises the point that marketing and media practitioners of the 1980s and
beyond saw age as yet another key tool with which to create useful consumer segments. Ad people and media people saw the family, comprised
of one or two parents and one or more members of a younger generation, as the core unit of high-volume consumption in U.S. society. Yet
the approach that they took to the family and the different generations
that tied into it was exceedingly conflicted.

On the one hand, they believed that there was a large number of
adult consumers who held the kind of "pro-family" beliefs articulated
by members of the Reagan administration.[66] On the other hand, what
they discussed most was a fractured and frenetic family system marked

by working parents—or single or divorced parents—and hobbled by increasing distance between adults and children. So, while media firms and advertisers used slogans such as "basic family values" and "integrity, family security, and longevity," the strategies that they adopted to profit from the various generations often served to flow with, and exploit, social distances between the generations.[67] At the same time, they continued to take advantage of splits *within* generations based on income, gender, and other social fault lines. The result: targeting activities that aimed to reinforce splits in the family and the larger society at the same time.

The meanings of age to marketing and media practitioners can be found by examining the groupings they used, the changing character of the groupings, and the projected lifestyles. The most important age bracket of the post—World War II decades was eighteen to forty-nine. This was the group that the Big 3 networks and their advertisers lusted after as the primary spenders of society.[68]

The eighteen to forty-nine mass market also became a yardstick for media executives trying to carve out viable audience niches in the presence of the network TV behemoths. A relatively small number of print and electronic outlets chose to cultivate niches in the less competitive age areas of teens, children, or older adults. More often, other media tried to compete with television by emphasizing income or gender slices of the eighteen to forty-nine chunk—for example, rich eighteen- to forty-nine-year-olds or female eighteen- to forty-nine-year-olds. Increasingly, too, they focused on slices of ages within the eighteen to forty-nine frame. A radio network, for example, might go after eighteen- to thirty-four-year-old men by broadcasting heavy-metal concerts.

A good deal of the deliberations over age in the trade press and at conventions during the '80s and early '90s had to do with the competition over these sorts of narrowed labels. But more and more frequently executives' most energetic discussions of age—and the ones that had far-reaching implications—did not revolve around mere clusters of numbers. Rather, they saw an age cluster as indicating common cultural attributes shared by people of a generation. And they envisioned the connections (or absence of connections) between generations as pointing to new understandings of the American family and their implications for markets and media.

When it came to marketers' concerns with generations and families, baby boomers and their offspring received by far the greatest attention in the '80s and early '90s. It was a fixation that turned on the size of the parental cohort and its significance in consumption. The seventy-six million babies born from 1947 to 1964 resulted in a bulge of people that by the mid–1980s represented over 40 percent of all adults.[69] From a selling standpoint, their volumes of purchase were so high that the consumers who passed between the ages of twenty and thirty-nine in 1984 were seen as the collective force that powered the economic engine of the economy, earning about half of U.S. personal income.[70]

Always the generation that society had made room for, the leading edge of the boomers shared the angry, utopian years of the late 1960s. Now, they had become the collectivity that was setting occupational and domestic trends for the rest of society—the leading proponents of the self-indulgent and frenetic lifestyle that advertisers saw sweeping America in the 1980s.[71] At the same time, marketing commentators said, strong competition for good jobs and disappointments from the economy of the early 1980s were encouraging boomers toward a jaundiced, suspicious view of the society's institutions.[72]

Not surprisingly, as this "most desired market in America" reached its prime, advertisers and their consultants increasingly divided it.[73] One analyst cautioned that the boomer generation was "not a monolith. Within those seventy-six million are widely disparate subgroups; those born after 1957, for example, are markedly different from their predecessors."[74] But age splits were only the beginning of advertisers' dissection of boomers. Consultants offered likely segments that visualized different income levels onto different boomer lifestyles. They spoke, for example, of self-starters, materialists, and nesters, and recommended marketing efforts tailored to each. In fact, the centrality of baby boomers as consumers meant that all the income and gender divisions described earlier applied more directly to them than to any other group.

Publishers argued that upscale boomers' confessed ignorance about ways to manage life was an attribute that would help their magazines establish primary media relationships with the segment. Boomer ignorance was caused, editors and consultants asserted, by the unique social changes that the generation had experienced growing up in the 1960s and 1970s. "You have a whole group of people who are living a lifestyle that large numbers of people had never lived before," said one professional observer, who gave an example about women. "Women today have tremendous career opportunities and are living professional lives, but their mothers were housekeepers and don't have any advice for them."[75]

Boomer lifestyle issues changed from the late 1970s through the 1980s and into the 1990s as large clusters of the generation went from being single to getting married to moving into different stages of family consumption. As the '80s progressed, it was the boomers' consumption in families that most grabbed media and marketers. Executives believed that as boomers passed thirty-five, their fixation on careers began to mellow. Some said it was a kind of exhaustion after the high-climbing Reagan era, others that it was due to shocked reevaluation in the aftermath of the "Black Monday" stock plunge of 1987, still others that it was a natural part of the life cycle.[76] The result, they expected, would be a shift from indulgences outside the home—fancy cars, clothes, trips —to indulgences inside the home. Some dubbed the tendency "cocooning."[77] "[A] generation whose lives once revolved around 9-to–5 now looks forward to 5-to–9," contended an ad in 1993 for *Family Life* magazine, a new periodical aimed at upscale boomers.[78]

Ironically, though, the image of domesticity that came through in the discussions of marketing and media executives very much reflected the same fractured, frenetic image that advertisers had of boomers' lives outside the home. The big difference was that now offspring and their consumption habits made up a large part of the picture. What was unusual in the '80s, marketers felt, was how powerful children and teens had become as primary consumers and influence makers. The reason was not just that boomers, who had tended to be late in getting married in the '70s, were finally beginning to procreate in numbers that mattered to marketers. Boomers also suffered from the frantic schedules of two-career or single-parent households.

Thus, ad people concluded, teens and children older than five years had more primary buying autonomy than ever. They were given much more leeway in purchasing, advertisers believed, partly because parents felt guilty of ignoring them. Too, an increasing number of parents were asking teens and preteens to go to the store and buy food and clothes for themselves and others.[79] According to researchers for the supermarket industry, in fact, half of all teens were saying they had "a great deal of freedom" in selecting foods and brands.[80] Moreover, the amount they were said to spend directly was impressive. The Teen Research Unlimited consulting firm estimated that teenagers (twelve- to nineteen-year-olds) would spend $36 billion in 1987.[81] Children were not pikers either. In 1995, kids between six and twelve years old were projected to have direct disposable income of $7.5 billion. Marketers considered children "early adopters" who spent one billion dollars of their own money on various electronics products, including video games, TVs, stereos, CDs, and computer games.[82]

By the late 1980s, a growing number of marketers and media were beginning to take advantage of the new financial power of children and teens by treating them in the same way they approached adults: as multidimensional consumers who were worth segmenting. Marketers were separating boys and girls who could buy things into young (aged four to six), school age (seven to nine), and tweens (ten to twelve).[83] To these there were added divisions according to income, geography, the lifestyles connected to those categories, and even the benefits they hoped to derive from different products.[84]

By doing so, marketers were partitioning the youngsters according to the family's cultural capital—the social distinctions of the parents "whose own lifestyles cause the children to want to consume in ways consistent with theirs," according to one consultant. He went on to point out that these demographic segments may be current or future markets that distinguish lifestyles related to income and gender: "[F]or example, girls may be viewed as a future market for fur coats, boys as a future market for motorcycles."[85]

The Nickelodeon children's cable channel offers an example of this new lifestyle-segmentation in action. From its beginning as an ad vehicle in 1984, Nickelodeon's management appeared to understand advertisers' dual desire to reach children in an environment that spoke to them apart from their parents and yet also chose them for, and tried to reinforce in them, the attractive income and lifestyle characteristics of those parents. Through the 1980s and into the '90s, the network underwrote the Yankelovich Youth Monitor and Simmons research that showed children making a strong impact on purchases ranging from cereals, toys, and soft drinks to such major parental purchases as cars, VCRs, and CD players. Nickelodeon executives continually characterized the households they reached as upscale—"upper-income, multi-person and high in concentration of children and parents," to quote a 1994 sales sheet.[86] The Yankelovich Youth Monitor had found, Nickelodeon confided, that its upscale audience was being groomed by yuppie parents to make "a lot of money" and be "the ultimate consumers."[87]

The presence of Nickelodeon for children and the Music Television (MTV) cable network for teens reinforced for advertisers the image of boomer family members going in different directions. Studies on the increasingly separate use of media by different age groups further encouraged marketers to exploit the generational dispersal. Researchers were finding a growing number of children and teens viewing TV sets in their homes that were separate from those of their siblings and their parents. In 1983, 55 percent of American homes already were said to have more than one television set. By 1994, the number had risen to 66 percent; 28 percent of homes had three or more sets. Moreover, 79 percent had a VCR, 63 percent received basic cable, and 28 percent received pay cable.[88] Ad people saw the number of VCRs, video games, even computers, commanded by the youngsters of a house growing precipitously by the mid–1990s. They believed that children and teens watched broadcast, cable, or VCR programs—or played games—through their own TV sets in playrooms or bedrooms while their parents retreated to do the same in dens or *their* bedrooms.

When the People Meter replaced the household meter as the primary ratings tool in the late 1980s, the switchover was a final declaration by the TV industry that the U.S. had moved into an era where the "household" was no longer a realistic viewing unit. Much more than before, ad practitioners acknowledged different members of the family as separate from one another, involved in setting their own viewing patterns. They also saw youngsters increasingly as estranged from their parents in the cognitive realm, as the new electronic media split generations. "Adults, frequently boondoggled by tasks such as setting the clock on the VCR or loading computer software, often don't realize that, in general, kids are hip to technology as early as age 2," contended an *Ad Age* roundup of marketers' views. The director of consumer insights in the strategic planning department of a major ad agency's public relations subsidiary suggested that her firm was investigating, among other subjects, the tensions caused by what she called "the family dynamics of different learning curves."[89]

While advertisers of the 1990s saw widening gulfs between youngsters and their parents in boomer families, they saw an even greater gulf between mainstream families and two other groups: people older than forty-nine and the twenty-something cohort many dubbed Generation X. Marketers treated both populations as living in different worlds from children and their boomer moms and dads. The notion of connections across generations had little meaning. If anything, many ad people wanted to reach only certain age brackets. That meant using media that separated the desirable age groups from the undesirable ones. The upshot were media firms that hawked their ability to add a specific generational filter to the distinctions in gender, income, and other categories that they could deliver efficiently.

Consider the generations of Americans who were older than forty-nine years of age in the 1980s. Traditionally, when an age group passed forty-nine—or, some would say, fifty-five—its members began to suffer a remarkable decline of interest in them by general advertisers. The 1980s census, though, revealed that people fifty-five and older were substantially better off economically "than any other older generation in history," as *Advertising Age* put it.[90] Moreover, while high interest rates and inflation in the early '80s hampered economic growth among young adults, people over fifty-five tended to weather the environment sturdily, meeting mid-decade with a real boost in income and the highest disposable income of any age group measured, including the boomers.[91]

Arguing that a burst of enthusiasm for seniors was taking place among general marketers, *Advertising Age* declared that "the mature market is coming of age."[92] The enthusiasm, however, clearly had its nervous sides. One related to people sixty-five years and older. Advertisers considered them to be more homebound, less well-off—in general, more like traditional notions of senior citizens than people aged fifty to sixty-four. Advertisers made clear distinctions between what they called "mature adults"—those aged fifty to sixty-four—and people sixty-five and older.

It was therefore only the younger set of mature buyers that media looking to share in the newfound marketing enthusiasm for older folk hyped to potential sponsors. Magazines such as *Modern Maturity* and *Mature Outlook* emphasized the monetary attractiveness of the cohort, making the case that marketers should target it for mainstream products separately from other generations. They claimed that oldsters were not financially reliant on other generations of their family. To the contrary, these "maturity media" insisted, such people were happily adrift in a lake of self-indulgence and decreased responsibility. "The sense of familial obligation has changed and it's now acceptable to take from the family savings and spend," said an executive from the influential Yankelovich, Skelly, and White consulting firm in 1981.[93] In 1987, *Advertising Age*, repeating the theme, reported that a new car bumper sticker popular among vacationing seniors was "I'm spending my children's inheritance."[94]

Ironically, this generational hard sell by maturity media reinforced the nervousness that advertisers had about dealing with them. Many national marketers believed that maturity media were not worth pursuing in a big way except with products specifically designed for the mature audience. The drumbeat of vigor and financial independence had worked all too well. Marketers who wanted to reach "mature adults" decided that this was an age cohort that did not like to be reminded of its age and so would not consider maturity media part of their primary media relationships. Consequently, marketers aiming at older Americans often preferred media that focused not on aging per se but on leisure and business associated with upscale people between their late forties and early sixties. Ad vehicles known to reach a preponderance of that crowd included magazines on travel, golf, and interior design as well as radio stations that played classical and "beautiful" music.[95]

At the same time, it was clear to most involved with the mature market that as late as the mid–1990s, fifty- to sixty-five-year-olds had really not become as hot for the marketers of ordinary products as champions of that age group had hoped. Marketers with goods and services that could be tailored to, or created for, the mature market may well have bought the notion that the mature generation had a high disposable income that it increasingly was using on itself. But when it came to more ordinary fare—the soups, soaps, and clothes of everyday life—marketers and their agencies hesitated to target them.

One reason was that marketers tended to believe that people fifty years of age and older were more set in their consuming ways than younger ones and so less likely to try new products or be swayed by ads. A more important part of their hesitation stemmed, ironically, from their conviction that seniors had separated their daily lives from those of their children and grandchildren. Because financially attractive older people did not live in an extended family, they were unattractive from a "volumetrics" standpoint. That is, their self-sufficiency and lack of responsibility for other family members meant that they were not involved in choosing products for many people in high volume. The packaged-goods marketers that media coveted were interested in reaching people who bought stuff in large amounts and would be doing that for years to come. They were confident that the thirty-something moms who were *Ladies Home Journal* readers fit the volumetrics bill. They believed that the mature adults who read *Modern Maturity* and listened to classical music stations did not.[96]

Consequently, while national advertisers did not mind a small percentage of mature adults in the audience for ads for most of their products, they would get nervous if "fifty plus" appeared among the largest age categories. Limiting the number of older adults therefore became the preoccupation of some media firms. The hesitancy regarding the mature generation applied even to such mass-market activities as broadcast network television. Certain types of programs such as golf and news became standard niches for advertisers targeting the mature population and older. Beyond those compartments, however, older Americans were not nearly as welcome. CBS-TV executives found out to their chagrin that although older Americans were watching broadcast TV in large numbers, many advertisers shied away from programs with a substantial proportion of those viewers.[97]

But going after younger people raised another set of issues for advertisers and media practitioners in the mid–1990s. The long-attractive baby boomers were growing older, pushing inexorably toward the half-century mark. By the year 2000, demographers agreed, the numbers of Americans ages forty-five to sixty-four would jump substantially, while those ages twenty-five to thirty-four would diminish 4.9 million, to 38.2 million.[98] Marketers and media began to face up to the inevitable population shift with trepidation.

Some observers speculated that because of the huge size of the boomer population, the traditional age ceiling of fifty that separated valuable from less valuable customers would change. ("Old will be cool," predicted one writer, "and marketers will need a modified approach."[99]) A greater number of marketing executives seemed to believe that with boomers' high-consumption, family-buying years spent, and with their consumption habits set, they would no longer be the most valuable targets for advertising. The executives turned an increasing amount of their attention to the age cluster that demographers said was following the boomers and had reached its twenties and early thirties. What they saw was yet another social division, a cohort they called Generation X, that they evaluated as oppositional to the boomers and their families.

During the 1980s, a few marketers characterized this generation of consumers as a genuinely different one from boomers that would cause ad people headaches.[100] By the early 1990s, the popular press was giving marketers additional concerns about the cohort. A summer 1990 *Time* magazine cover story dubbed "America's next generation" a diffident bunch.

> They have trouble making decisions. They would rather hike in the Himalayas than climb a corporate ladder. They have few heroes, no anthems, no style to call their own. They crave entertainment, but their attention span is as short as one zap of a TV dial. They hate yuppies, hippies, and druggies. They postpone marriage because they dread divorce. They sneer at Range Rovers, Rolexes and red suspenders. What they hold dear are family life, local activism, national parks, penny loafers and mountain bikes. They possess only a hazy sense of their own identity but a monumental preoccupation with all the problems the preceding generation will leave them to fix.[101]

In a flurry of articles, probably sparked by the *Time* piece, writers tried to pin their own labels on the twenty-somethings. The offerings—Baby Busters, Slackers, The MTV Generation, The Forgotten Generation, The Latch-Key Kids, The Sesame Street Generation, the Nintendo Generation, the Whiny Generation, among many others—suggested both a negativism about the group and/or its estrangement from the boomer generation in rather stark terms.[102] Generation X was the one that stuck. It had received its identification with the under-thirty crowd of the '90s through a 1991 book titled *Generation X: Tales for an Accelerated Culture* by Canadian writer Douglas Coupland.[103] People in the know began to tout Coupland as the voice of the newly adult cohort that, as the *Toronto Star* put it, "came after the baby boomers snapped up all the good jobs and low-priced real estate."[104]

The nerve-racking picture burst into full view in 1992 through an address that Karen Ritchie, a senior vice president of the McCann-

Erickson Worldwide ad agency, presented to the Magazine Publishers Association. Ritchie argued that the forty-six million people between the ages of eighteen and twenty-nine years already had an annual collective spending power of $125 billion. This Generation X, she advised, represented a lucrative target that corporate America had "largely ignored" and was only beginning to come to terms with.[105] Her talk was excerpted in *Advertising Age,* and a few months later the trade magazine claimed in a front-page story that the media had begun to "wake up" to Generation X.[106]

Consulting firms such as X Communications joined Ritchie and others to enshrine the notion of a generational gulf. Marketers or media executives who publicly challenged the existence of that divide found themselves derided or ignored.[107] A growing number of industries began to face up to the need to cultivate the group they believed would soon overtake the boomers as their primary market. The major issue was how to persuade a group that was by most accounts "cynical" and "media savvy."[108] A number of agencies, claiming expertise in the issue, asserted that using the right language it was possible to persuade Xers.[109] Self-styled specialists in the cohort loved to cite Xer ads that they considered disastrously inept.[110]

Gradually, ad people began to work with clients to create new products for Xers. In a growing number of cases, they pitched these products as if they were created by new, small companies. The Miller Beer company distanced the company name from its Red Dog beer, calling its manufacturer Plank Road Brewery. Coca-Cola tried to let OK Cola work on its own, and General Motors did the same with Saturn. The consensus was that Xers would rather buy a small "David" brand over its Goliath competitor.[111]

Seeing marketers' interest in the upcoming generation, media outlets from radio stations to magazines to television networks argued that they had become part of Xers' primary media relationships. In broadcast TV, the Fox, UPN, and Warner networks; in cable the MTV, E!, Comedy Central, ESPN2, and Sci Fi Channel programming services; and in print, magazines such as *Details, Spin,* and *Vibe* emphasized how they fit with the group's video orientation and skepticism. Tying into Xers' alleged comfort with computers, *Vibe* had an early "home page" on the Internet, as well.

As consultants and agencies scrambled to display expertise, and as

Xers wrote indignantly to trade and general magazines that they did not want to be stereotyped, marketers voiced a belief that it was important to begin dividing up GenX and notice the unprecedented lifestyle "diversity" that income, gender, ethnic, and racial differences were bringing to the age group.[112] In 1995, for example, the Viacom-owned VH1 music cable network shucked off its boomer-oriented format for a slice of the Xer market. These "MTV graduates"—the twenty-five- to thirty-four-year-old targets of VH1—would be upscale and hip. They would, he said, be individuals "who have an ear for contemporary, if not cutting-edge, music—and the jobs and credit cards to fuel discretionary buying."[113]

Sometimes broadcasters hoped to draw both boomers and Xers. That happened when the Fox network won the right to broadcast professional football because the National Football League feared its broadcasts on CBS were skewing too old. The word circulated that the network would try to make the broadcast more interesting for Generation Xers by adding features that they were sure would attract young adults and probably not drive away the thirty-four to forty-nine crowd.[114] Mostly, though, marketers of the early 1990s tended to focus on the psychological and social distance, even alienation, that the twentysomethings felt from the thirty-four- to forty-nine-year-olds—the boomers–who had preceded them as the apples of marketers' eyes. New syndication programs were tilted to one group or another—such as when *Daily Variety* called *Rikki!* the "*Oprah* for Generation X," rather than assuming it to be attractive to both.[115] And while Big 3 broadcast network executives claimed to want younger viewers, they sometimes worried that airing programs too heavy with Generation X references would alienate their older, twenty-nine- to forty-nine-year-old targets.[116]

The acute sense of social division that marked discussion of Generation X by ad and media executives reverberated even more strongly in talk about groups that didn't make it into their typical discussions of age, income, and gender. Chief among these were blacks, Latinos (marketers tended to call them Hispanics), and homosexuals. National advertisers saw all three categories raising special issues. In the case of homosexuals the difficulty was a fear of boycotts from consumers who considered any association with homosexual lifestyles reprehensible. The challenge in

the case of Hispanic Americans was to exploit the group's huge population growth in the face of foreign language and generally low disposable
income. The quandary in the case of blacks was whether to see them as
a separate cultural entity, like Hispanic Americans, or to target them with
the white population according to distinctions in income, gender, age,
and other characteristics.

To ad agencies dedicated to these populations the issue was control
over images. The agencies argued that they held special knowledge of
the groups as separate cultural entities with their own advertiser-friendly
slices. They also claimed the right to shape the words and pictures that
national marketers used to speak to and about their constituencies. In
the mid–1990s, homosexual and Hispanic American advertising practitioners were beginning to acknowlege strong progress in exercising that
right. African American ad people, on the other hand, were arguing angrily that they were being denied it.

Of the three, the case of homosexuals was perhaps most different
from that of African Americans. Media consultants with an allegiance to
the homosexual market were gradually able to shape national advertisers'
understanding of homosexual consumers. They did it by convincing
marketers that the gay market contained a large segment with extraordinary disposable income: "young, single, urban males; higher than average education level; higher than average income level; usually no depen-
dents; usually high level of discretionary income; generally recognized as
taste-makers and trend-setters."[117]

During much of the 1980s, fear of being associated with homosexuals kept national advertisers away from gay media even while they accepted the gay market's value.[118] In the '90s, marketers such as Ikea,
AT&T, and Continental Airlines began to work with gay media consultants to find ways around the problem.[119] The advertisers' desire to do
that was fueled by an increased determination to explore new consumer
niches in the face of growing competition. Advertisers also believed that
increased tolerance of gay lifestyles had reduced the chance of damaging
backlash from other consumers. In addition, they found that direct-
marketing lists from gay consultancies offered the opportunity to advertise with a great deal of discretion to valuable slices of the population.[120]

When mainstream advertisers did decide to address homosexuals,
they treated it as a gender market. Following the custom of the day, gay-
media consultants encouraged them to break the market into pieces. Be-

cause gay men allegedly made more money than lesbians, the consultants privileged men over women. They also privileged upscale gays over others and young adults over older ones. In general, the consultants promised marketers that if they shucked off their hangups about advertising to gays they would find a kind of nirvana: wealthy markets of intensely loyal consumers reachable efficiently through media that had earned their audiences' special allegiance.[121]

The momentum of national advertisers to target gays was strong enough by the mid–1990s to sustain a questioning of the claim that homosexual men as a group were wealthier than the rest of America.[122] Homosexual media still found it an uphill battle to corral national ads, but it was far easier than in past years.[123] The reason the market held its value was that the consultants now claimed to be able to reach the gays who *were* wealthy, with the specific lifestyles advertisers wanted.[124]

Some homosexual commentators believed that gay marketers' consumption-driven take on the world marginalized important parts of the homosexual community, especially older men, men of modest means, and lesbians.[125] Nevertheless, gay activists generally lauded national advertisers' construction of homosexual markets on terms acceptable to both sides. In their fight against social conservatives, many from the National Gay and Lesbian Task Force saw their interests fused with those of advertisers. They considered marketers' premise that homosexuals made up a spectrum of markets linked to a gamut of specialized media as a badge marking their separate and legitimate standing in U.S. society. In the words of Robert Bray of the National Gay and Lesbian Task Force's "Fight the Right" project, "American business, whether or not it likes it, is a powerful force for cultural change."[126]

African American media consultants and ad agencies would probably have been a good deal less enthusiastic than their gay counterparts when considering American business trends and advertising to blacks in 1995. They held a suspicion of national advertisers because of their failure for decades to support black media or to hire black ad executives.[127] In the 1990s, the problem wasn't that advertisers were snubbing African Americans. With a total yearly spending by the blacks of $300 billion and the existence of a black middle class with substantial disposable income, and predictions that the population would reach thirty-nine million by 2010, this was a population that national advertisers could not ignore. Marketers were spending more than ever to reach black consumers.[128]

Still, African American ad executives were concerned. The problem they saw was that most national advertisers were content to have main- stream agencies and media consultants target African Americans along with whites of similar gender, income, age, or other characteristics. That, they argued, was not allowing black ad agencies to speak to and for black people.

To be sure, the issue meant dollars for the agencies that specifically targeted African Americans. They had worked for decades to construct images of black consumers as attractive targets for advertisers. Paralleling the growth of segmentation in general-market advertising, black adver- tising and media executives had labored to divide black consumers into the kind of slices that mainstream advertisers could understand. Instead of the white yuppie, for example, they offered the "buppie."[129]

What they found now, they said, was that executives at general adver- tising agencies often steered their clients away from black agencies or even black media. Numbers suggested they were right about not getting their share of the increasing pie. According to *Target Market News,* a newsletter tracking minority marketing trends, marketers spent $834 million targeting blacks in 1994, up 12.2 percent from 1990. But only $297 million, or 35.6 percent, was handled by black-owned agencies, compared with 33.3 percent in 1990. Part of the problem, *Advertis- ing Age* reported, was that even minority-owned agencies that were receiv- ing work from national advertisers were getting "creative" projects to reach their constituencies, not the lucrative media-planning and buying parts of the accounts. These were staying with the marketers' general agencies.[130]

As black-agency executives saw it, general ad agencies were derailing their chances. The general agencies were concerned that as their clients became increasingly interested in African American consumers they would consider switching more and more of their budgets, especially coveted TV buying money, to black-oriented shops. To head that off, the black executives contended, general-agency executives were describing African American consumers to their clients "as dark-skinned white people."[131]

It certainly appeared that black and general agencies were ap- proaching African Americans with very different lenses. General-agency practitioners sometimes even questioned whether race was an important marketing variable. In 1982, an executive at a mid-size agency cited research to show that lifestyle differences *among* black consumers—between the better educated, more affluent and the poorer, less educated—were greater than the differences between middle-class whites and middle-class blacks.[132] In the mid-'90s, general agency personnel made the same argument when it came to reaching blacks and whites in the up-and-coming age group of choice for advertisers, the Xers. With twenty-somethings of both races viewing the same Fox network programs, reading *Vibe,* following MTV, and warming up to the same black athletes, general market ad people asked rhetorically why commercials and ads that were populated with a mix of colors were not as effective as anything out of black agencies.

Black agencies responded with two propositions. One was that black-run agencies could best find the ways to communicate with blacks in truly effective ways. They insisted that black agencies knew best what media blacks use. And they argued that these media had special relationships with their target audiences: they filled "emotional and informational needs that make [them] attractive to the black buying public." Consequently, any advertising placed by black agencies would invariably get "better-than-average attention."[133]

But black-agency executives went beyond asserting expertise in media planning. Their second proposition was that their agencies, which were the only concentrated location of black ad talent, were crucial for creating ads that could truly move African Americans, whether in black media or in mainstream venues such as network television. The reason, they told potential clients, was that blacks had to be approached as a separate culture in U.S. society, even when they were viewing one of the Big 3 networks. "The truth is that the black community marches to different drummers," contended Byron Lewis, chairman of the largest agency owned by African Americans. "It fundamentally is moving from a position that is different from the white consumer. So, for example—and our clients love this—black people still tend to want to buy the more expensive products. You buy your sneakers and you buy your car not because it may be the best product in the world but it's what your neighbor, your peer, feels about the product. The purchase for us is more important than it is to the general market customer."[134]

Black-agency executives and media people suggested that justification by general agencies for playing down the need to segment and target African Americans was a smoke screen for not wanting blacks around as employees or competitors. They pointed to the huge growth of general advertisers' concern for the Hispanic market as a example of what should have happened. General marketers, they said, were using Hispanic American agencies in ways and numbers that put their use of black agencies to shame.

There was no arguing the skyrocketing interest in the U.S. Spanish-speaking market. The 1980 census had underscored the phenomenal growth of the Hispanic American population in Florida, Texas, and California.[135] The 1990 census showed this was no fluke, and demographers were predicting that Hispanic Americans would overtake blacks as the second-largest racial/ethnic group in the nation. Media firms and agencies that reached the huge, unassimilated Spanish-speaking audience began to look interesting to mainstream advertisers.[136]

Everyone knew that Hispanic American agencies had been struggling for several years to make their case. As awareness of Hispanic Americans grew among mainstream marketers in the 1980s, so did their belief that the market was fraught with many problems: a low average income; a diversity of backgrounds (Puerto Rican, Mexican, Cuban, and others) that, early on, led some national advertisers to back away out of confusion; and media firms, including TV and radio networks, that did not offer audience measurements that met the standards of general agencies.[137] For all the negatives, major national advertisers determined in the '80s that they had to latch on to the Spanish-speaking market because it was becoming a force to be reckoned with. Research firms confirmed Hispanic American media claims that in addition to a soaring population in the U.S., Spanish-speaking residents in this country were high on "volumetrics." That is, they were said to purchase a higher percentage of basic goods and services such as baby food, eyeliner, and long-distance phone calls than their counterparts in the general population because of their large families and foreign background.[138] In an era when niches were becoming popular, such people represented a real opportunity for firms to expand their market shares.

National marketers' comfort with targeting Hispanic Americans was heightened by three developments. One was a muting of the fierce debate between regional and national Spanish-language broadcasters over cultural variations that worried and confused English-speaking ad executives. Regional radio stations and magazines seeking national sponsors sometimes still insisted to advertisers that they had to take into account

Puerto Rican, Cuban, Mexican, and other communities when targeting Spanish speakers. But aware that the marketers did not want to take Hispanic segmentation too far, the two national television networks, Univision and Telemundo, succeeded in convincing them and their agencies that all the groups shared commonalties that could be parlayed into broadly successful Hispanic programming. The networks and some radio stations even insisted they had come up with a dialect that was accepted by all. To underscore the point, and with a nod to a long popular CBS news anchor, they called it "Walter Cronkite Spanish." [139]

Hispanic Americans as a separate market became an easier idea to push after the mid–1980s because of the second major development: greater acceptance of research on Hispanic American media by national marketers. In the radio area, Arbitron's commitment to a vigorous sampling of Hispanic American households led them, beginning in 1989, to offer studies that sampled a representative portion of the Hispanic American population in selected "high-density market areas"—areas that had 25 percent or more Hispanic Americans. [140] When it came to television, in 1992 Nielsen Audience Measurement embarked on a national survey of Hispanic American TV audiences that was separate from its general Television Index. It polled eight hundred households chosen according to the census definition of a Hispanic American household as one in which its "head" declared a Hispanic heritage. Encouraged by the reception, Nielsen also began a local Hispanic American TV ratings service. [141]

The Nielsen Hispanic Index was instigated, and to a large extent supported, by the Univision and Telemundo Spanish-language television networks in their effort to gain credibility with national advertisers. One feature of the survey's design was a new way to divide Hispanic Americans: by the issue of language dominance. Viewers were classified according to whether at home they considered themselves Spanish-only speakers, mostly-Spanish speakers, bilinguals, or English-only speakers. Nielsen found that fully half of the survey respondents belonged to the first two groups—precisely the audience that the two commercial networks, Univision and Telemundo, were trying to sell to advertisers. [142] In addition to giving credible quantitative support to the important size of this audience, the central place of language dominance in the Index and the absence of questions about country of origin (Puerto Rican, Mexican, and so on) indicated a victory for the idea of a national Spanish-speaking culture that national advertisers could understand. Using this start, the advertisers could segment Hispanic Americans along more traditional lines of gender, income, age, and other characteristics they used when they divided the general population. In fact, the Simmons Market Research Bureau, picking up on the idea that information about Hispanic American lifestyles had become a profitable commodity for many advertisers and agencies, had begun a study tracking TV, radio, and print media usage with purchasing tendencies. The resulting report was similar to the one Simmons created for the American population as a whole.[143]

The third major development that encouraged Hispanic Americans' popularity with marketers was the rise of advertising agencies with credibility adequate to convincing mainstream advertisers that Spanish-speaking residents of the U.S. could be most efficiently reached through a panoply of Hispanic American-centered activities—not just media but events and mailings that would speak directly to marketers' interests in them. One factor the agencies had on their side to lure marketers from mainstream agencies was obviously the language difference. But Hispanic American-agency and -media executives could not want to use language alone to assert special knowledge of the audience. They had their eyes on the growing population of second-generation Hispanic American youths who were "comfortable with—if not fluent in—English."[144] To claim this market segment, and even the approximately 50 percent of Hispanic Americans who primarily spoke English, Hispanic American-agency executives argued that Hispanic meant more than association with a language. Hispanics were, they argued, a particular race, "defined as Spanish-speaking and by a combination of cultural, national, geographic and even physical characteristics" that separated them as a group from English-speaking America.[145]

Much of the cultural difference, they said, came from a strong family consciousness. "The oldest chestnut [agencies use]," noted a media executive, "is that Anglos are motivated by personal gratification and Hispanics are motivated by family gratification."[146] *Advertising Age* reported, for example, that Hispanic Americans have unique shopping needs. "They tend to shop as a family, they eat out less often than Anglo families, they are very brand-conscious, and they are major consumers of fresh fruits and vegetables."[147] Understanding the nuances of such generalizations and implementing them in persuasive campaigns became the claim of Hispanic ad practitioners.

The claims were generally successful. By the mid–1990s, this construction of The Hispanic had become part of mainstream marketing.[148] Marketers waxed enthusiastic about the growing number of legal and illegal Spanish-speaking immigrants that Univision and Telemundo would help them reach. Long-range planning was aided by a belief that Hispanic Americans were assimilating more slowly than other ethnic groups. The sense of growth and stability in the market, in fact, led several huge general agencies to either start Hispanic divisions or buy top Spanish-language ad shops.

African American advertising and media executives viewed this energy in Hispanic American marketing with dismay. They pointed out that while the revenues of Hispanic American media were skyrocketing and the number of Hispanic American agencies was growing, and growing stronger under the protection of the major firms, the achievement of blacks in the advertising industry had essentially stalled. The quickly rising population of Asian Americans had also begun to grab the attention of major companies. Debate about how to define Asian Americans and how to speak to them, spurred on by the diversity of nationalities behind the word, recalled the issues advertisers had grappled with regarding Hispanic Americans in the early 1980s. Despite the complexities, marketers such as Sears announced they were dedicating substantial resources to understanding and reaching this increasingly wealthy part of the U.S. population.[149]

In this context, agency executives who were black believed they were getting too little attention. It was not merely that in 1994 only 1 percent of the creative professionals at large agencies—the copywriters and art directors who create ads—were black. They were used to being marginalized in general agencies even as they condemned it. They argued that they wanted to be treated the same way the ad industry was beginning to treat Hispanic Americans: as ethnics whose culture counted as a primary category for analysis in an age of segmentation.

African American practitioners saw a black complement to the Nielsen Hispanic Index as one way to address the problem. In both the late '50s and the early '90s, advocates for the black community and black business had yielded admissions from Nielsen that its system for achieving a sample of homes for the TV ratings did not include enough black Americans and so underplayed their presence in the American commercial TV audience. Yet even after correcting their sampling difficulties, Nielsen officials acknowledged that the nationally representative (11.3 percent) number of blacks in the firm's four thousand to five thousand household sample was too small to give accurate information about black viewing habits within specific demographic groups, such as upscale college-educated blacks with young children.

Because of their separate index, Hispanic American media firms were now able to offer advertisers such data, and black marketing executives were pushing Nielsen to create a counterpart index strictly for blacks. Privately, media executives played down the need for such an index, arguing that Hispanic Americans had been separated from other consumers by the natural divider of language. Moreover, they doubted that enough agencies, media, and marketers would pay for the separate service. Black-agency leaders seemed determined to push for more ways to segment their audience, however.

In view of the history of race in America, and in the ad industry in particular, it is ironic that black-agency executives pressed for the fractionalization of the black population by income, gender, age, and other categories in order to make a case for its ethnic importance. Clearly, they understood a key principle of the new media world: the more a population in U.S. society could be shown as distinctive, and the more it could be divided against itself and others, the more likely marketers were to consider it important. Chapters 3 and 4 have explored this principle as it has developed over the past few decades and as it has been embodied in the interactions of marketing and media executives. Both competing and cooperating, the executives searched for ways to exploit social rifts they perceived in the nation at large.

Consultants and agency researchers searched continually for new lifestyle pictures that they could link to new mixtures of income, geographic location, gender, sexual preference, age, generational position, ethnicity, race, and more. Media firms jumped at the opportunity to prove to potential sponsors that they could provide efficient access to one or more of these attractive slices of the population. Growing competition, though, meant that efficiency was not enough to make a sale. As a result, touting the utility of special relationships that particular magazines, radio stations, cable channels, or online services had with particular audiences became a prominent pitch. Ad people believed that people were spending growing amounts of time with media outlets that spoke particularly to their sense of community even while they turned (though less frequently) to other outlets, including the major TV networks, for portions of their news and entertainment.

For the swelling number of electronic channels that were aiming to take advantage of advertisers' interest in market segmentation and targeting, the notion of a wide array of special media relationships was crucial for survival. National advertisers and their agencies were more cautious. They worried about the cost of dealing with so many different media. They realized, though, that with proper attention to the efficient attraction of the right audience segments, media niches that cultivated special audience allegiances could go far in supporting their attempts to gain a share of the market in what they saw as an increasingly splintered U.S. society. As chapter 5 will show, marketers and media understood the challenge: to efficiently create materials that would attract the right people to the right places for the right ads, or to discover ways to follow the right people with ads wherever they wanted to go.

FIVE

SIGNALING DIVISIONS

*FRAGMENTATION, FRACTIONALIZATION, REGIONALIZATION, DECENTRAL-
IZATION:* These were the buzzwords at the 1980 meeting of the Association of National Advertisers, as executives who controlled the country's
major advertising funds searched for ways to understand the enormous
social and technological changes that they believed were upon them.
"There doesn't seem to be any question that the arrival of these new
means of receiving information and entertainment in the home is going
to cause a fractionating of viewing audiences," said Thomas Ryan, vice
president of advertising services for Gillette North America. For Penny
Hawkey, the head of the McCann-Erickson ad agency's creative group,
that increasing audience fragmentation suggested a formidable challenge. "The audience—the mass mind as we know it—is breaking up,"
she said at a panel on creative advertising. "It has options. It doesn't have
to watch the programming that the networks put in front of it. And it
doesn't have to watch our commercials."[1]

She was sure, however, that the audience breakup was a good thing
for marketers. Advertising copywriters and art directors would be much
more potent at persuasion, she contended, when "forced to address . . .
these splintered segments." The two other members of the panel agreed,
suggesting that the mass-market perspective of the past had stood in
the way of advertising's maximum effectiveness. "A lot of people now are
missing the boat as they embark upon the '80s," said Ed Scali, the creative force behind of a major ad agency bearing his name. "Of what
possible relevance is it to talk to a consumer as though he or she were
an entire nation? It's about as personal as being addressed as Dear Oc-
cupant."

Chapters 3 and 4 have already established media executives' growing interest in dividing American audiences to satisfy marketers. This chapter and the next explore the way media splintering played into advertising executives' desire to address increasingly specific slices of U.S. society. The following sections examine how media and advertising worked to "signal" particular social segments to their side. Signaling involves the creation of media materials in ways that indicate to certain types of people that they ought to be part of the audience and to other populations that they do not belong. Chapter 6 shows how marketing and media executives increasingly attempted during the 1980s and early 1990s to get even more specific than signaling in going after audiences. They did that by improving their "tailoring" abilities—that is, their capacity to customize ads to the backgrounds and lifestyles of particular individuals who are members of attractive groups.

In the 1980s and early 1990s, signaling was more established than tailoring in advertising and media firms. Using a variety of signaling tactics, media outlets and marketers routinely

• split their customers into different categories so as to reach them differently and speak differently to them;

• gestured that they were establishing different emotional as well as commercial relationships with different types of consumers;

• showed that they cared about certain types of consumers in certain ways by calling out to them across a wide variety of media that reflected those ways; and

• established alliances of compatible marketers and media vehicles that signaled to target consumers that they were linked to each other, to those marketers, and to those media by distinctive lifestyles—that is, by shared values, activities, and interests.

Guiding these approaches were industry ideas about media "formats" and "brands." A media format comprises the layout and general approach to content (including advertising) that a specific vehicle—a TV network, magazine, newspaper—takes to its material. It is the format that creates what people think of as the "personality" of a network, magazine, newspaper. When a company touts the distinctive identity of its format, that identity is known as a "brand." So, for example, CNN is a branded cable news format and *Ladies Home Journal* is a branded woman's service magazine.

Creating a "branded format," then, means arranging materials—songs, articles, programs—into a package that people in a target audience would see as reflecting their identity. Of course, in a typical day individuals might choose formats that reflected different, even conflicting, identities; a person might buy the *National Enquirer* as well as the *New York Times*. To media practitioners of the 1980s and early 1990s, however, that was increasingly irrelevant. They emphasized divisions rather than overlap in preferences and styles. They built those divisions into formats by choosing certain people, scenes, and sounds over others. The result was an elaborate picture of a fragmented society in which consumers were urged to decide where they most belonged.

Some of these developments were only beginning. Many media firms and marketers were more subtle than others about who should come to them and who should not. Too, targeting was often not as narrow as some marketing futurists asserted, particularly in cable. What's more, plans for the arena that marketers liked to believe had the potential to cultivate communities of consumers better than any other media—online services—were just getting off the ground amid an enormous amount of hype. Still, a model for marketing in a fractured media world was clearly emerging. As the 1990s progressed, it was hard to miss that electronic as well as print media formats were getting more selective. Calling out to people by innnovative concatenations of income, age, gender, ethnicity, race, consumption habits, personality, and more marked the vanguard of marketing.

Pushed across media by target-oriented conglomerates, the signaling of distinctiveness acted out images of an America that was becoming more and more fragmented in its attitudes toward the desirable tone, pace, and topics of daily life. The advertisers and outlets simply hoped that these activities would encourage their targets to consider themselves part of activities, values, and interests—lifestyles—which connected to their products. Clearly, though, the market-driven strategies of division tended to encourage more than that.

In urging the allegiance of target audiences to narrow clusters of media, the strategies discouraged the creation of central media-meeting places where all sorts of people could congregate to sample each other's views, news, and entertainment. The strategies also discouraged audiences from visiting media clusters not designed for them, thereby lessening an opportunity for them to get a feel for social diversity and ask how they and others fitted together in the larger society. And the strategies encouraged community-building tactics by ad agencies and media firms that, in the name of marketing efficiency, could not help but incite anger and alienation among at least some of those who were signaled away from certain formats.

The idea of signaling audiences through formats is not at all new. In the nineteenth century, the publishers of daily newspapers wanted to ensure that a paper could communicate its relevance to potential readers separate from the shouting sales pitches of street-corner newsboys. Screaming headlines and sensational photographs indicated one set of perspectives—and one type of customer—while restrained headlines and photographs, even on the same stories, implied quite a different approach and audience.

Magazines did the same thing. As chapter 2 noted, competition from television and other pressures encouraged the consumer magazine business to accelerate audience segmentation before it caught on in other ad-supported consumer vehicles. One result of the industry's success in making the transition was that it became the metaphor of choice for other areas of the media system. In the early years of ad-supported cable TV, ad-sponsored "home pages" on the Internet, and several other new-media experiments, executives from those firms often invoked the consumer periodical as their model. To understand the signaling of divisions by media and marketers in the 1990s, it is therefore important to begin with magazines.

The consumer magazine industry certainly contained a blizzard of choices at mid-decade; titles numbered in the thousands. Even the top two hundred consumer magazines in early 1995 covered an enormous number of subjects, from news to opinion, hobbies to commerce, science to fashion. The largest magazines, such as *Modern Maturity* and *Reader's Digest,* had paid circulations of twenty-two million and fifteen million, respectively. Magazines in the middle of the list, such as *American Health* and *True Story,* hovered around the 800,000 level, while magazines toward the bottom (*National Parks, Runner's World*) still managed to be above 400,000.[2]

This enormous competition encouraged art directors and other magazine executives to prove to advertisers that they could offer efficient sales platforms. When several magazine executives were interviewed for this study, they were typically eager to list the ways in which they distinguished their audience from others. Their market-driven prejudices started with basic demographics—income, gender, age, and family status are the ones magazine executives most quickly listed. Then they described such background experiences as education and type of job as well as consumption patterns such as vacation habits and shopping routines. They often made further distinctions by linking psychological profiles to demographic and lifestyle descriptions.

When questions in the interviews turned to the readers' race and ethnicity, though, the recitation of audience details tended to turn awkward, defensive, and evasive. Of course, a wide range of periodicals existed that aimed squarely at slices of the ethnic and racial markets. The evasion took place, though, in cases where consumer magazines were not explicitly racially or ethnically targeted. Reading between the lines of executives' comments, it seems that they sometimes worried that by highlighting members of particular minority racial or ethnic groups, especially through photographs, they might be alienating their traditional, non-minority audience.

Minority status was not always a problem. Writing that a person celebrates Saint Patrick's Day or Hanukkah might not offend anyone, and might even be positive. Other times, a person's religion or ethnic background need not be considered. Race was a more consistent matter, and often a tension-filled one. Sports, news, and entertainment magazines typically tried to signal a desire for black and white readers by profiling African Americans popular with target readers of both races. At different times, Michael Jordan, O. J. Simpson, and Whitney Houston were well known as "crossover" celebrities. The issue was touchier for magazines dedicated to fashion and hobbies as well as for service magazines. The non-celebrities on their covers and around their articles were often employed to signal readers about the people who have strong relationships with the magazine.

A look at major fashion and service periodicals in the mid–1990s suggests that they acted out a mixed and conflicted message about belonging from a racial standpoint. Inside the magazines, images of racial diversity did pop up—mostly of African Americans, but increasingly of

Asian Americans and Hispanic Americans. In many magazines, advertisements that featured upscale-looking blacks were prominent elements of a diversified look implying that lifestyle transcends race and ethnicity. But outside, on the covers that invite people into the magazines, the situation was far less polyglot.

A trip to any newsstand would support the point, but a bit of research clinched it. Of five service and fashion magazines chosen at random from 1994—*Parents, Money, Cosmopolitan, Self, and Redbook*—only one of the sixty covers had a non-white person on it. The non-white was a celebrity, black TV-talk-show host Oprah Winfrey, widely regarded in the entertainment community as a major crossover celebrity. It would seem that when it comes to the magazine cover, publishers of fashion and service titles in 1994 were afraid that racial diversity might give the wrong signal about the format's vision and drive away relevant readers.

A magazine cover is a touchstone for signaling points of distinction about the preferred audience. The discrimination goes far beyond race. Publishers, editors, design directors, and art directors consider the cover an invitation to the magazine. Their challenge is to communicate its purpose and audience to consumers passing quickly by the welter of competing covers on magazine racks. The general feeling within the industry is that a cover must make the most of a very short instance of opportunity by telegraphing the right prejudices to the right targets.

"A magazine has three seconds" to grab the interest of a customer in a store, a design director for *Family Fun* asserted. He pointed out, however, that *Family Fun* derived a high percentage of its circulation from yearly subscriptions rather than from single-copy sales in stores.[3] A large proportion of consumer magazines are subscriber-driven, since subscriptions add stability to a periodical's circulation numbers. One might think that the pressures to create an instantly sellable cover would therefore be weak for those titles. Not so. Across the board, people from the magazine industry as well as the advertising industry who were interviewed for this book noted that creating a cover as if single-copy sales were key to survival had become a media truism.

One reason was that single-copy purchasers could replenish and augment the subscription rolls. A second was a sense that even subscribers needed reinforcement in their decisions to keep paying for the magazine. A third was a belief that intriguing covers might lead the reader to establish a more enduring relationship with the magazine—to "keep it on the coffee table" longer than most titles, as one art director put it.⁴ This, in turn, would reward the magazine, since advertisers cared about the relationship readers enjoyed with magazines. Ad people believed that the longer a magazine would hang around the house, the more it would indicate that people cared about it and the more likely that people would read the articles and the ads.

Woman's Day, a once-every-three-weeks publication, used its cover in the mid–1990s to reach out to an unusually wide audience for a magazine—women aged eighteen to fifty-four who had families, according to art director Brad Pallas. The periodical's management proudly hyped it to advertisers as the largest-selling women's magazine in terms of single-copy sales. Single copies comprised 75 percent of its total circulation of 4.7 million units, and it affected the way editorial personnel did their work.

"The inside is not important at all when you're selling in the newsstand," said Pallas. He added that "for moral and marketing reasons, you have to make sure the inside [story material] matches [what was said on] the cover," because people would stop buying the magazine if it did not. Nevertheless, he noted that during the 1980s he and his editor came to the conclusion that cover lines—the come-on phrases on the cover that signaled readers to an issue—were so important that it paid to write them first and plan the issue around them.⁵

Along with a belief in the crucial importance of cover lines, Pallas said that he and his editor followed a number of principles regarding the construction of its covers that carried out their desire to quickly signal members of its target audience that *Woman's Day* was for them. Here are a number of paraphrased examples:

• On the newsstand, the top 50 percent of the cover is the most visible. Consequently, it is important to place at least four to five cover lines above that 50 percent. The most important cover line can go on a banner above the logo.

• Most of the other cover lines should begin on the left side of the cover, because people read from left to right.

• Cover lines should be placed in descending order to the priority that readers would place on the subject.

• Numbers attract readers. Consequently, the cover should emphasize lines such as "100 ways to cut 100 calories" and "46 meals in under 4 hours." The numbers should be printed within an inch or so of the left binding to take into account that on store racks the right sides of magazines are often covered by other periodicals.

- Cover lines on stories likely to be popular with a segment of the target audience can be added on the cover's right side. They also reinforce to the consumer that she will be getting a lot for her money.

- The picture on the cover should help the magazine stand out. It should also connect quickly with the audience the magazine is trying to reach.

- The cover should be different enough from issue to issue so shoppers will not worry that they have already bought that week's version.[6]

People in charge of covers for various magazines agreed that the basic propositions mentioned by Pallas were recognized throughout the industry. Yet they insisted what Pallas himself admitted—that most magazines differed from *Woman's Day* in choosing cover lines after they select articles. Moreover, they described the objective of most magazine editors as hailing audiences that were typically much less varied than *Woman's Day* readers. They insisted that by following certain traditional cover rules and departing from others, they could telegraph information about the people they wanted as readers.

To get an idea of how magazine creators were working to communicate both blatant and nuanced audience distinctions through their covers, consider *Family Fun* and *Family Life* in 1995. The art director of each magazine noted that its purpose was to attract mothers of school-age children with advice about doing things as a family. Both magazines signaled their difference from other periodicals through the title, with its emphasis on family; the cover lines, which were emphasizing activities between parents and children; and the cover photo, which always pictured a child. To distinguish the magazines from parenting magazines that revolved mostly around babies and toddlers, the art directors said they always chose photos of a six- to ten-year-old boy or girl, alone or with one parent.[7] They agreed that these basic features of their covers would give people glancing at the magazine a strong sense of the family-oriented lifestyle to which they said readers of the magazine had committed themselves. These features, they suggested, were meant to encourage browsers to make a quick decision about whether this type of magazine would be for them.

At the same time, each art director explained how she or he was incorporating subtle cues into the cover to signal the differences between the audience for the two titles. *Family Life*'s art director said her mandate was to lure upscale mothers of the baby boomer generation—"pretty much career parents"—who would be turned off by the emphasis on problems in traditional parents' magazines and would want an atmosphere of optimism. To signal the upscale approach, she said that she used an unusually flowing logo in sans serif type; photographs that were often borrowed approaches (such as the use of saturated light) from fashion magazines; and cover lines that proclaimed a certain "classic and poetic" creativity by not using capital letters, by positioning them not quite at the left border, and by making them short. To emphasize that the magazine aimed for the parent who wanted parenting periodicals to be calm and positive, she placed the magazine's motto—"celebrates the joy of childhood"—above the logo. She made sure that the individuals on the cover, and virtually all the people inside, were smiling. And she, her editor, and the marketing director took care that the short, creatively arranged cover lines ("best bikes," "being a good sports parent") suggested the happiest possibilities of parenting.[8]

Family Fun's design director said he used his cover to signal a perspective that was subtly but significantly different than *Family Life*'s. He said he thought *Family Life* was "excessively stylish . . . esoteric, pie in the sky." It reached out, he felt, to a small, wealthy population with rarefied interests.[9] In contrast, he wanted to show through his cover that *Family Fun* was aimed at a broader, though still prosperous, audience.

The design director said that *Family Fun*'s cover communicated an upscale tenor to its readers by highlighting activities such as travel to national parks that implied high disposable income. At the same time, he argued, his cover signaled to a broader audience than *Family Life* by being "less assuming, more in-your-face, simpler, a bit looser." For further evidence of his attempt at broader appeal than *Family Life*, *Family Fun*'s design director said that every now and then he and his editor would try to place a child of color on the cover; he noted an Asian American girl on the April 1995 issue. (*Family Life*'s art director acknowledged that her magazine cover had not had photographs of non-whites.) In addition, he said he had no qualms about using cover closeups of children's faces since they seem to draw people's attention on magazine racks. (*Family Life*'s art director said that she refused cover closeups of children's faces to maintain a stylistic distance from other parenting magazines.)

Moreover, whereas the art director of *Family Life* said that she privileged design over specifics in her cover lines to keep a classy, happy, and upscale look, her *Family Fun* counterpart used long cover lines in bold type and bright colors to draw attention to specifics about how relatively well-off parents could entertain school-age kids. In fact, a decision by *Family Fun*'s management to step up their push for single-copy sales in addition to subscriptions would, he said, mean getting even "closer" with the faces, "wackier, more playful" with the cover lines, and "nuttier" with the type. It was an approach that *Family Life*'s art director said she would not follow.

Though these sorts of distinctions can seem quite slender, even esoteric, magazine cover planners were adamant that even the smallest touches contribute to a magazine's ability to raise a mirror to its desired audience. In the 1990s, this "holistic" attitude toward signaling ever-narrower differences could also be found in radio, cable television, and other electronic media. Using sound, moving pictures, or both, media people worked with ad people to make clear whom their formats were for, whom they weren't for, and what that meant.

The radio industry's interest in targeting audiences was high in the 1990s. The number of radio stations in the U.S. reached about twelve thousand. In large and medium-sized cities, programming from more than thirty stations often filled the airwaves. The fractionalization of the radio dial spurred an expansion of formats, as radio executives struggled to home in on audiences that were large and desirable enough for local and national advertisers. One industry expert described a radio format as "the combination of on-air elements that a station uses—music, news, personality, the presentation."[10]

The audience slices for formats got quite thin. By the mid–1990s, stations that media planners considered successful in major markets such as Philadelphia and Chicago were reaching only 3 percent of the area's population. Even lower ratings could prove profitable if the station's format drew especially attractive audiences.[11] The competition was so furious that industry consultants were crisscrossing the country, using a variety of research methods to help generate more focused variations on old formats or to create new ones. One well-known station doctor estimated in 1995 that a good deal more than thirty formats were being used in the radio industry.[12] Most of the formats were based on music, and critics of the commercial radio scene were quick to point out that the range of music played on the nation's stations was far more restricted than the number of formats—or that the kinds of records released—would suggest.[13] To radio consultants, though, the bottom-line issue was not the aesthetics or diversity in a station's sound, but its ability to gather a distinct audience for sponsors when many stations reached similarly small numbers of people. "As the pie gets thinner and thinner," noted one consultant, "it's not so much whether you have ten thousand listeners at any given time . . . [but] what's the difference between [stations] A, B, C, and D."[14]

Radio industry executives who were interviewed for this study offered five propositions about listening patterns that guided the division of audiences into smaller and smaller pieces. First, individuals tend to listen to only three radio stations at any particular period in their lives, with the most "preferred" of those stations taking up 65 percent to 70 percent of their listening time. Second, music preferences in the U.S. tend to be characterized by a large and widening divide between blacks, whites, and Hispanic Americans. Third, men and women often have separate musical interests. Fourth, people ten years apart in age tend to belong to different "music generations" with different tastes. Fifth, these music preferences can be tools to separate into different audiences people with different styles of living and buying.[15]

Radio practitioners said, for example, that they could construct formats that would separate the black audience by age and lifestyle. Similarly, some consultants argued that recent statistical data regarding music preferences could help them program differently for people who shared the same demographics but different personality profiles or psychographics. One insisted that statistical analysis convinced him that he could create three formats to separate white women aged twenty-five to thirty-four into three groups—unmarried rock concert goers, unmarried stay-at-homes, and married parents. He suggested that such differences were viable in some markets and might indicate the future of audience fragmentation in radio.[16]

Consultants and programmers tended to describe formats by men-
tioning radio stations or particular artists that stood for the sounds.[17]
The trick in radio, one said, is to let a person know within two records
what personality the musical menu exudes. He and others noted that it
was the combination of a radio station's cues—the kind of music or talk,
the presence of announcers and their speech patterns, the presence or
absence of jingles and other identifiers ("interstitials")—that, crafted in
particular ways, kept listeners of a particular gender, age, race, and ethnicity coming back. According to him, that was key to establishing a
primary radio relationship with them.[18]

The segmentation of radio by race, age, gender, income, and lifestyle
became so taken for granted that it was even built into research on formats. If the exploration focused on ways to successfully vary a particular
format aimed at women aged twenty-five to thirty-four, women outside
that age group as well as men would not be invited to respond. Similarly,
when designing a sample for phone research on white formats, consultants would avoid phone numbers in what researchers call HDBAs, or
"high density black areas." Such distinctions were also part of a standard
instruction for the callers: if people gave the "wrong" age, gender, race,
or ethnicity (for example, Hispanic) at the start of an interview, the interview would be terminated. At least one research firm told its callers that
if the person on the other end appeared offended about the abrupt end
of the call (as individuals sometimes did) the interviewer should say that
the quota for the person's gender, age, racial, or ethnic category had already been filled. If the respondent's anger persisted, the call should be
transferred to a supervisor, who had been trained in further mollifi-
cation techniques.[19]

The preferences that underlay such indignities were built into the
formats. Creating an ambiance that would clearly convey the characteristics of the radio station's desired listeners was quite purposeful. Apart
from the musical sound, the DJs, ads, and contests that constituted a
format's sound made it clear who belonged and who didn't. One consultant said that a restaurant is a common analogy radio people use for a
format, since "when you walk in the restaurant you want sights and
sounds and you want a waiter with a certain type of attitude."[20] In radio,
as in the restaurant, people who don't know immediately whether the
place is for them will find out after a few minutes inside.

The idea could easily carry over to other media, and it did. Some-

times, executives struggling to bring together audiences that would excite advertisers went beyond merely implying who belonged and who
didn't. They underscored the invitation by building into the format material designed to alienate the wrong people while attracting the right
ones. That helped the media executives built an efficiently pure group of
intended consumers. It may also have encouraged anger and alienation
among those heckled away.

Consider the pressures on cable television programming services
that moved some people in the industry to act that way. In the mid–
1990s, the number of cable networks airing in different parts of the nation had reached about 150.[21] Limited cable channel capacity meant,
though, that most of the networks did not get a chance to be seen in the
approximately sixty million homes that were wired for cable. Morever,
the number of major owners was small. A handful of huge multiple systems operators (MSOs) such as TCI, Comcast, and Time Warner served
as gatekeepers to millions of homes and were virtual monopolies in their
areas. These MSOs often required cable networks to give them equity in
their businesses in order to be carried.

Like magazines, most cable networks typically derived income from
two sources, consumer payments and advertising support. In cable's
case, the consumer's portion was in the form of a per-subscriber contribution (usually about fifteen cents) that the cable operator built into
each monthly bill. Fortunately for the cable networks, the aims of the
MSOs and the aims of advertisers were basically compatible. In theory,
at least, advertisers interested in reaching narrow audiences would be
satisfied when subscribers believed they had greater choice with cable
than with broadcast television. One problem cable networks had, however, was passing muster with advertising agency media buyers. The reason was their loyalty to the Nielsen Cable Activity Report as the key
arbiter of cable network ratings. To be listed in the Report, a channel
had to be available in 3.3 percent of U.S. TV households (about 3.2
million homes) and generate at least a .1 rating in those households.[22]

In fact, of the 150-odd ad-supported networks available, only thirty-
one regularly made the grade.[23] Still, the ratings of even stalwart members of the club, such as CNN, ESPN, and A&E, typically hovered
around 1 percent of the cable audience, and often substantially lower.
Observers predicted that competition for audiences and advertising
would grow. Joe Mandese of *Advertising Age* put the issue starkly in

1995: "Increasingly, emerging cable networks are fighting established channels for access and share of viewers' minds—if not rating points. Conversely, veteran [cable] networks are facing cannibalization from within as . . . newer niche services threaten to fragment the audience even further."[24]

All these considerations increased the urgency that programmers felt regarding the need to develop a relationship with—to get "share of mind" among—a definable and marketable population of viewers. "There will be some ninety new channels in the next few years and launching a channel is not easy," said the CEO of Golf Channel. "You must have a clearly defined niche and programmers that are prepared will benefit. If you think this is a sprint, with only enough financing for a year or two and [are] undercapitalized, that's not healthy. You have to build a brand and identity."[25]

In the mid-'90s, branding had become the word that summed up the urgency of targeting through formats. "The time is now—or past—to build your brand," said a vice president at the Cartoon Network. "Two years from now, the viewing options are going to be so great that we're going to have a hell of a time getting people to watch."[26] "The most important thing for a young cable network," agreed Michael Cascio, vice president for the A&E network, "is for people to get a handle on who you are."[27]

Cascio was talking about his own programming service, which, as one of the fortunate thirty-one, had started over a decade before. His remarks underscore that even programmers for larger cable services such as his own realized the importance of establishing an identity that called out to as specific an audience as possible. Yet many of the cable firms that had Nielsen numbers and cared about large national advertisers were in a difficult position. They couldn't afford to see themselves as so targeted as to fall below Nielsen's radar. On the other hand, they were aware that with the proliferation of offerings they needed advertisers and viewers to go to their format because it had a distinct personality. The president of E! Entertainment Television summed up the tightrope that cable programmers were trying to walk. "The trick," he said, "is to be narrow enough to stand for something but to be large enough to make a business of it."[28]

One common solution was to call out to two overlapping audiences. The first audience encompassed a wide demographic that advertisers were pursuing in broadcast network TV, narrowed to encompass individuals drawn to the cable programming service's subject matter—documentaries, arts, entertainment, music. (An example might be upscale men eighteen to thirty-four years old.) The second audience—called the "super core" by some cable executives—retained the emphasis on subject interests, but added a more targeted sense of the age, gender, income, even race than the broadcast networks would claim.

The first approach aimed to gather an audience large enough for the interest of major advertisers in the mid-'90s who still required large audiences at low costs per thousand. The second approach looked toward an even more competitive future. It aimed to draw the interests of sponsors such as stockbrokers and fishing-rod firms who cared about narrow audience niches.[29] Also, and perhaps just as important, it intended to carefully craft a detailed image for the network and its viewers that would stand out in an environment where hundreds of formats vied for attention. So, for example, the president of E! Entertainment Television said that his broad target was eighteen- to forty-nine-year-old entertainment enthusiasts. By contrast, he described his "super core" as eighteen- to thirty-four-year-old female entertainment enthusiasts who were slighly better educated than most viewers (even more than most cable viewers) and who tended to be urbanites.

Across cable networks, going after these audiences meant trying to get the most bang out of the building blocks of cable programming in order to create compelling brand images. One set of building blocks involved promotional activities. Starting with the logo that most cable networks placed on the right lower corner of the screen, they helped viewers identify the channel in the cacophony of channel switching and quickly grasp its intended audience. A second set of blocks consisted of compatible reruns, programs picked up after they have aired on other stations, usually the broadcast networks. They became a fact of life on many of the cable networks for the simple reason that the networks could not afford to generate enough of their own material for a twenty-four-hour service.

The people who fashioned promotional materials for a cable network and the others who sculpted program flows out of compatible reruns took it as their task to cast up images that could telegraph the personality of their networks and, by implication, of the people who were viewing it. In the feverish competition for core and super-core viewers, that led to promotional styles that were frequent, idiosyncratic, and intended to cause the "right" channel surfers to stop and take a look.[30] Programmers used phrases such as "attitude" and "in your face" when they discussed attracting the right people.[31] By creating an attitude, they meant designing a format to have a spirit that would appeal to the particular target. An in-your-face attitude meant that a format or part of a format called out to its audience noisily.

Cable network executives intended the largest noise in their branding arsenal to come from the third set of their schedule's building blocks, signature shows. From a channel's standpoint, they were a little like an especially forward magazine cover, only with sound and motion. A signature program is a series created expressly for a particular programming network as an explicit on-air statement to audiences and advertisers about the personality of the network. The concept emerged during the 1980s, and by the mid–1990s every video network was struggling to maintain at least one signature show. Cable executives were acutely aware of the programs that stood for themselves and others. In the mid-'90s, *Beavis and Butt-head* and *The Real World* were among the series that stood for MTV; *Ren and Stimpy, Double Dare,* and *Clarissa Explains It All* were the Nickelodeon network's signature shows; *Crossfire* was one of CNN's contributions to building its personality; while *Talk Soup* and *The Howard Stern Show* were E!'s main personality statements.

The advantages seemed obvious. Properly crafted signature shows sparked publicity for the network in other media outlets that reached the target audience. They got people in the target audience talking with one another about the network. The publicity and "word of mouth" encouraged regular tune-ins to the network—a phenomenon TV people called "appointment television"—with the result that viewers stayed around to sample other shows. The hoopla around a successful signature show also encouraged advertisers to pay more attention to its network. Moreover, it created a sense of excitement among advertisers that had already bought time, especially when at least some of their commercial spots were placed around the series itself.

People in the cable business believed that successful signature shows had to carry an attitude that telegraphed for what and for whom their network stood. Sometimes, ideas about the preferred audience was simply part of the program's subject. The Discovery Channel's *Invention* and A&E's *Biography* program were examples of flagship series that by their very existence in the center of prime time signaled that those networks stood for an upscale, highly educated audience. Similarly, by being rooted in suburbia *Clarissa Explains It All* and several other live-action comedies on Nickelodeon telegraphed the upscale nature of its preferred audience. In addition, they, *Ren and Stimpy, Double Dare,* and a few other signature shows continually acted out a generational theme that one Nickelodeon producer said was at the base of its programming: "It's kids against the adult world."

Yet to a number of highly competitive cable network executives during the mid–1990s the subtlety of signature shows such as *Double Dare* and *Biography* was out of touch with the competitive environment. To them, standing out with an attitude meant creating a series with such a fix on separating its audience from the rest of the population that it sparked controversy among people who were clearly removed from the "in" crowd. The resulting publicity across a wide spectrum of media would, they argued, virtually guarantees sampling by the target audience. E!'s marketing director pointed out that executives chose radio star Howard Stern for a network signature program because on radio he reached the age demographics that E! coveted and because his outrageous jokes about politics, race, and celebrity would undoubtedly place the network in the spotlight and draw viewers with lifestyle interests that resonated with E![32]

The classic example of this "in your face" approach was MTV's animated *Beavis and Butt-head.* Centering on two social misfits who spent their time commenting grossly on rock videos and getting into trouble, the series was a nonstop parade of violence and aggressively stupid sexuality—what most parents and other authority figures considered highly objectionable in adolescent behavior. Far from hiding the program, though, MTV showcased it, using it at the beginning and end of its evening schedule. In this role as the network's prime-time bookends, the series tagged its channel with a hard-edged anti-authority personality that MTV's programmers associated with adolescents and young adults who did not watch much TV and whom the network's advertisers were seeking to embrace.[33] Pressure-group anger at the show, far from endangering it and its image, probably served to reinforce it in the eyes of its target audience. In the words of the *Los Angeles Times,* "Say what you will about the moronic duo, they've helped to cement MTV's identity with viewers and advertisers."[34]

Lee Masters, the CEO of E! who had also headed MTV in the past, asserted that he knew of no cable network that intended to antagonize segments of the population when it developed signature programs. The goal, he insisted, was simply to "stand for" the target audience amidst a crowd of channels. He acknowledged, however, that in the process of doing that a series might very well alienate viewers who would not feel part of the network's demographics or lifestyle.

And yet a look at advertisements of cable networks to potential sponsors shows that the idea of pitting one group against another for monetary gain was actually at the forefront of their minds. Those by ESPN International and Comedy Central were particularly direct in heralding their super cores' lifestyles in that way. ESPN's showed a blurred photo of a soccer player overlaid by a design that recalled the crosshairs of a rifle. "A handful of guys cannot be reached through ESPN," the headline stated. "But they're all geeks who wouldn't buy your product anyway." [35]

In Comedy Central's ad, a man in a business suit stood in a court room, back to the camera, with manacles tying his hands. Judging by the hands, the man was white. The headline of the ad read "We're proud to say that when the average Comedy Central viewer is convicted of a crime, it's most likely to be a white collar crime." Below the photograph were lines citing the network as having "the highest prime-time concentration of adults 18 to 49 with an income of over $60,000"; the "best educated 18 to 49 audience in commercial television"; and "the highest concentration of 18 to 49 professional managerial viewers of any network." The copy did not say what the picture and headline strongly suggested: Comedy Central's target audience was white. [36]

The bluntness of Comedy Central and ESPN International was at the far end of a continuum, but other video networks made their messages nearly as direct. One wonders what, if these lines reached the general public, that public would think regarding the portrayals of viewers and (especially) non-viewers. Today, such ads would probably be rejected as too controversial for promotional materials on the channels themselves. But with increased competition leading programmers to constantly push the envelope of acceptability to be noticed, who knows? [37]

In 1995 *Village Voice* writer Leslie Savan saw explicit attempts to divide groups from one another in the advertisements that populate different formats. "The same firm, through different product campaigns, can proselytize for women's rights and run ads on Rush Limbaugh," she wrote. "They are part of a new culture that sponsors rebellion, that provides the conflict that our society . . . would grow bored without. The right mix of love and hate on the knuckles creates just enough tension to enable both sides to make a lot of money."[38]

It is an exaggeration to suggest that the mid–1990s saw a trend to explicitly encourage social conflict in advertisements. Savan is perhaps more correct in suggesting that the heated competition over audiences in the 1990s caused many of the biggest advertisers to have fewer qualms than ever before about placing their ads on media formats that might raise hackles among social activists. The marketers' hope seemed to be that such critics would not learn of their separate, often niche, targeting activities. If controversy did become public (such as when it became well known that Ivory-pure Proctor and Gamble was a major sponsor of tabloid-television talk shows), the gamble was that good public relations and crisis management would help the firm ride the problem out.

Savan was also on target in recognizing that with the growing fractionalization of media, advertisers began to realize that they could imbue a product with multiple images and so send different images to different audiences. Doing that, they often *implicitly* reflected and exploited social divisions through casting of ads, ther tone, and their placement on formats aimed at audiences that could relate to the casting and tone.[39]

If the wrong audiences knew the purposes behind the ads, it might startle them. For example, Saturn automobile's Hispanic American agency conducted research showing that while Mexicans responded favorably to ads featuring Cubans, Cubans rejected Mexicans as opinion leaders. The agency decided to flow with this prejudice. Saturn management agreed that TV commercials for Miami, where many Cubans live, should exclude the Mexicans.[40]

The creation of slightly different ads for different audiences became during the 1990s a trend that warranted its own term: versioning.[41] Advertisers used the technique to achieve different tones when aiming at different slices of the children's market. Typically, they edited the same basic commercials differently depending on the amount of violence and quick-cutting that different broadcast or cable outlets would allow for certain age groups.[42] Somewhat more varied were advertisements designed to reflect race and ethnicity. Executives at black, Hispanic American, and Asian American agencies often argued that their customers would respond best to persuasive messages only if created on their terms. To that end, the agencies created highly targeted ads designed to resonate with the most relevant demographics, psychographics, and lifestyle characteristics of their group. Coordination between the general agency and the minority agency ensured that the basic campaign theme was not totally different. Still, the ads spoke to the groups with images of distinct lifestyles.

Taking versioning even farther, some marketers developed entirely different campaigns for distinct audiences, with editing and casting decisions designed to exploit their understanding of different audiences' different worldviews. That was the idea behind an MCI ad campaign that aimed to speak to Generation X. The long-distance company's executives worried that their broad-based campaign aimed at baby boomers might not be connecting with the cohort that followed them. The company therefore decided to create a relatively inexpensive series of ads that would run on such GenX cable networks such as MTV and VH1.

To carry it out, the copywriter and art director on the project, Gen-Xers themselves, chose three somewhat off-kilter incidents in the lives of young adults into which they expected people of their age cohort could project themselves or their friends: a couple getting married under water, a male Xer in a tattoo parlor, and a young man at a professional baseball game catching a foul ball with his popcorn cup. At the end of each vignette, a voiceover that reflected the age target asked, "So what have *your* friends done since you last spoke to them?"[43]

If the MCI GenXers' departures from the norm sound bland, that was purposeful. According to the copywriter involved on the project, MCI was nervous about associating itself with topics that might spark controversy. Tattooing and marriage underwater were about as iconoclastic as the firm would allow. Consequently, language, quick-cut editing, and music had to carry the job of signaling Generation X sensibilities.[44] A director who could project an MTV feel in the visuals and sound was key to creating the package, the copywriter said. He used the tattoo vignette as an example. "It was everything, from the music to the style, the scenario, what's happening. The way it's shot, the way it unfolds before you. Even though it's a basic guy lying on his stomach getting a tattoo, if you had taken three totally different directors, it would have come off as three totally different messages."[45]

The MCI case is more evidence that marketers varied in how explicitly controversial they dared to be in their ads to attract their audience. Subtly, though, the MCI GenX ads did perpetuate a media-wide announcement that twenty-somethings were virtually a different culture, best left alone in their own media dens. This sort of partitioning by age was being duplicated in countless ways across a wide gamut of age, income, racial, and categories. Market-driven excitement about category slices within categories was encouraging the creation of formats and commercials that pictured a society so split up that it was impossible to know all the parts. In that context, commercials such as MCI's, placed amid compatible formats, might well be saying, "Better stay with with your own kind; it's less confusing and more fun." Said over and over again to different groups visiting different formats and the cumulative message might well be of a society so divided that it is impossible to know, or care about.

In the mid–90s, the social effect of media fragmentation was not an issue that advertising or media executives talked about. To them, the challenge of fragmentation was to get their products noticed by audiences that were increasingly spread thinly across print and electronic media. Their solutions merely deepened the fragmentation and extended its dysfunctional implications.

A growing belief was that target audiences had to be reached in as many places as possible if a company were to truly get the message to them. Marketers began to suspect that using live events in addition to advertising to send the right image for the product to the right audience might prove more effective.[46] Supporting concerts, state fairs, athletic tournaments and other such activities seemed one way to do that. Boosters of this idea believed that as a "three-dimensional, often participatory medium," an event was "capable of delivering an impact that far exceeds either print or broadcast."[47]

As a result, event marketing, as the process was called, grew remarkably. An estimated $350 million business in 1984, it was considered a $4.2 billion industry in 1994. Moreover, the nature of companies involved changed dramatically. Before the 1980s, the support of events was dominated by two types of firms: beer manufacturers, who wanted to encourage consumption by people viewing the events on-site and on TV, and cigarette manufacturers, who had been barred from television commercials in the late 1960s and were trying to plaster the brands as broadly as possible, including sneaking their logos onto the TV screen.[48] By the mid–1990s, the mix of firms had changed. Event marketing was crowded with packaged-goods and service companies.[49]

The industry was in the throes of re-evaluation. Through much of the 1980s, executives eagerly sponsored events they liked personally, giving only the faintest nod to concerns about their effect on sales.[50] As boards of directors became generally more concerned about executive accountability than in the past, as fragmented audiences forced outlays to be spread more carefully, and as event-related promotions took up more and more cash, corporate leaders began to demand that the sponsorship of events be tied to clear sales-related goals. Many of those objectives related directly to the consumer—encouraging a corporate image that would help long-term growth in sales, for example, or even spiking purchases during the time of the event via coupons given out with tickets. Just as often, though, event marketing was ammunition in the battle over retailer shelf space. It aimed to give local retailers the confidence that the sponsor was committed to pushing its products in their market, and confidence would give the retailers an incentive to give the company more shelf space. That, the sponsor hoped, would lead consumers to see the products more than before and so buy more of them.[51]

Event-marketing practitioners agreed on three points. One was that event marketing was by its very nature target marketing. That is, it involved matching particular categories of people with particular lifestyles to particular occasions they would probably enjoy. The second point was that to be most effective events should be promoted through properly targeted traditional media, such as radio, television, newspapers, billboards and cable. And the third was that the sponsorship of events ought to actively promote a sense of relationship with users of the brand. The idea was that by supporting activities close to the hearts of carefully targeted customers, marketers would solidify an image with them that both specialized and general advertising would reinforce.

As event marketing evolved in the 1990s, it was becoming part of what might be called a horizontal display of lifestyles. Trying to locate a fractured and peripatetic American population, marketers had decided that concentrating on advertising in one or another medium was no longer enough. That was especially considered true for eighteen- to twenty-four-year-olds, whose media habits were traditionally difficult to track anyway. They now thought it crucial to adopt what many dubbed an integrated marketing approach. It involved using events, publicity, public relations and traditional advertising to follow targets—often more than one set of targets—across a variety of both nonmedia and media locations.

In event marketing, the trick to gathering the right people efficiently was to make sure that advertisements for the event functioned like a magazine cover: they had to signal who was invited and why. Sometimes, the signaling didn't work efficiently enough. According to event-marketing consultant Lesa Ukman, Kool cigarettes founded the Kool Jazz Festival in a number of places around the U.S. with the express goal of reinforcing African Americans' interest in the brand. Kool executives were chagrined to find, however, that whites typically outnumbered blacks at the concerts. That lessened the festival's utility from a target-marketing standpoint, and the company ultimately abandoned it.[52]

To event marketers, though, such failures simply meant that firms had to be more careful about the fit between the activity they chose and the lifestyles of their intended audiences. The first half of the 1990s saw a torrent of sponsored events; in 1994 there were more than eight thousand.[53] They staked out more lifestyle territories than ever before. New aspirants kept appearing with their sights at bringing together people with lifestyles that national marketers wanted to reach—from the National Cyberfootball League Tournament to the Chicago Centennial Challenge classic car race to the National College Music Video Contest.[54] Most national advertisers found it useful simply to affiliate with a preplanned event that mirrored the consumer group they were tracking. Professional sports was an especially popular vehicle. Although a few mega-events such as the Super Bowl made it appear that athletic sponsorships always went after the largest number of people possible, marketers made clear distinctions between the few events that seemed geared to "everybody" and the many that were, in the words of one sports marketer, "geared or rifle shot" to particular kinds of people who buy particular kinds of products.[55] These happenings ran the gamut from intramural college sports to Black rodeo to women's golf.

Relying on research, matchmaking firms claimed that they could often signal as specific an audience as the marketer needed, both through the event and via televised coverage, advertising promotion and publicity surrounding the event. Careful distinctions by gender, income, buying habits, ethnicity and race were quite common. In the words of the president of such a company, "The client says, 'Yes, we know that 60% of our product are purchased by females and those females are part of a family unit that has a medium income of $75,000 or $100,000 plus a year, and etc.' So what we do is take the [audience] demographics of a sport [from the various associations representing the sport] and match it up with that."[56]

A growing area of event marketing consisted of companies whose sponsorships aimed to create a sense that certain people were part of a special group with special interests, even if they didn't know previously that the group existed. The athletic shoe business was particularly adept at that. It did a major job through the 1980s and 1990s of getting people of different ages, genders, abilities and avocations to feel that their lifestyles needed to be marked by different types of footwear.

In the mid–1990s, for example, Reebok, Adidas, Avia and other firms believed that a new niche existed for "trail runners." These were shoes for people who liked to navigate terrain far rockier than the gravel paths typical runners used. Whether a substantial number of individuals existed who fit that profile was open for debate. Adidas' Response Trail shoe for that purpose (with more traction, snugger toe boxes, and snugger toe bumpers than standard running shoes) was a big seller in Boulder, Colorado. Some store owners and industry watchers, though, said it was bought as a fashion statement rather than for its function. Others added they did not see a need for a new shoe when a regular running shoe would do best. "Just because a runner is running off road doesn't mean his biomechanics need change," said one shoe executive.[57]

Nevertheless, in an industry hot with feverish competition over niches that spoke to different lifestyles and high profits, the possibility of what *Footwear News* called a new "small pot of gold" attracted attention.[58] The targets were "a growing number of runners who are opting for the back-to-nature experience of rustic trails over hard pavement and noisy city streets."[59] Vendors such Avia, Brooks, Saucony, Asics, and Reebok produced their own trail runners; Nike was even contemplating a new niche, trail *walkers*. More important, to cultivate greater awareness of the product and the lifestyle trail running implied, they sponsored well-publicized regional happenings designed to celebrate the difference of trail running from other sorts of running, to suggest that the people who do it are special, and to hype the shoes that help them.

So, for example, Rockport lent its name to the Leadville 100, a run through the highest region in Colorado. Others sponsored the Pike's Peak Ascent. Avia's event was a "scrambled race through the wild" that targeted "outdoorsy people" aged 20 to 35 with a desire to be different.[60] Promotions for the meet, staged in the wilds of Santa Barbara, California, Stratton,Vermont, and New York City, emphasized links between the personalities of contestants and the trail runner shoe as much as the race itself. Participants in what was called "the Avia Scramble" were told via GenX radio and print to show up for a race having no idea about the course or the distance. To deepen the mystique, an entry blank warned all comers to anticipate sagebrush, wild boar, boulders, cows, gullies and snakes.[61]

By the mid–1990s, these sorts of target-driven happenings were becoming so entrenched in marketers' strategies that expenditures on them were taking the place of some traditional advertising purchases.[62] Magazine, radio, cable, and other media executives who pursued select audiences realized they had better help advertisers pursue target audiences across many places if they wanted to avoid losing a great deal of ad money. Their rallying cry was that in a fractured, frazzled, and mobile society the time had come for media to think of promotions and events—and media in general—in new ways.

The "old way" was still alive and well. It was to use concerts, sweepstakes, bumper stickers, and the like as ways to remind people what the media outlet stood for so that the relevant audience would go to the outlet, advertisers would meet them there, and the outlet would make money. *Black Enterprise* magazine, for example, reinforced its identity as a company that could bring together affluent blacks by sponsoring golf and tennis tournaments, among other events, for that audience.[63] MTV, Nickelodeon, and a few other cable networks found they could license some of their "signature" programs—*Beavis and Butt-head,* for example—for clothing, toys, and books that fans could buy. Burger King started a "Kid's Club" to lure children to its fast-food outlets and then keep them coming back with magazine-like ads mailed to their homes.

But some media executives began to question the very idea that a media brand should remain in one place—a radio station, a cable network, a magazine. They began to distill their media formats—their logo, values, interests, and sponsors—across as many technologies as possible. The aim was to provide them and their sponsors with platforms to signal their connections with the values and lifestyles of their target audiences wherever possible. Media executives told potential advertisers that they were not merely buying space or time at a competitive cost per thousand. Rather, they were associating themselves with a media brand that many consumers saw as a badge signifying important relationships in their lives.

Carrying out that horizontal display of lifestyles effectively, media executives knew, presupposed two things. First, it meant that their ad vehicles required strong brand identities. Second, it required huge resources. Not surprisingly, then, the first half of the 1990s saw giants such as Time Warner, Bertelsmann, News Corporation, Sony, Disney, Capital Cities/ABC, Hearst, Conde Nast, Meredith, and Hachette test the cross-media waters. They planted their brands, alone or through alliances, in a variety of new and old media. One goal was to help ad-driven subsidiaries corner media markets for their preferred demographics and their lifestyles. Their desire to stake out claims where they thought their audience might go led them into some regions, such as the Internet, which were only beginning to be hospitable to ad-supported materials. Awareness that much about such new media was hype mixed with conviction that they could not be left behind. When the president of Conde Nast's magazine division announced spending "a serious seven-figure investment," to launch an "upscale"-looking ad-supported Internet site for several of his periodicals, he admitted that project projections were uncertain. Still, he insisted, "I think this will be an enormous business for us someday."[64]

The conglomerates' magazine divisions, well known for their ability to selectively deliver upscale audiences, were taking the lead in cross-media work. Meredith's *House & Garden* lent its name and editorial bent to a cable network. Hachette and Conde Nast began creating events and custom magazines that aimed to apply their expertise in reaching upscale readers to the special needs of individual advertisers.[65] Hearst, powerful in a variety of magazine subject areas, attempted to transfer those strengths. The company started a new-media division that, among other projects, announced plans to create CD-ROMs aimed at "women and men passionate about the home."[66]

Time Warner's Sports Illustrated subsidiary became a model for tar-

geted cross-media activities. The company defined itself as standing for
relatively well-off males of various ages who cared deeply about sports.
Its traditional business, *Sports Illustrated* magazine, reached more than
3.2 million readers (subscription and single-copy sales) weekly in 1995.
That was large by magazine standards, yet Sports Illustrated's president
estimated that year that only 75 percent of his division's business actually
derived from this "core" magazine. The remaining amount—and the
most rapid growth—came from other activities.[67]

A good part of the 25 percent extended *SI*'s name in traditional directions: the licensing of sports clothing and the creation of events
to reinforce advertisers' association with *Sports Illustrated*. *SI*'s famous
swimsuit issue was as much a promotional event as a magazine issue. The
photos of women modeling skimpy clothes became an expression of the
brand's male sensibility in broadcast TV programs and on home video
as well as in the magazine.

More innovative from the standpoint of target marketing was Sports
Illustrated's decision in the early 1990s to create vehicles that would
publicly signal the existence of subsets of its audience and encourage
sponsors to associate themselves with the subsets. *Sports Illustrated* itself
encouraged subscribers to declare if they were avid golf and/or football
fans. Those who nominated themselves received a special sponsored section with their magazine, written for *SI*'s subpopulation of golf or football enthusiasts, up to forty times a year.

Another way to break up readership with the potential of extending
it was to emphasize different ages of sports lovers. *Sports Illustrated for
Kids* focused on gathering preteens and early teens around sports. The
SI College Tour was a traveling mini-amusement park backed by companies such as Gillette and Gatorade. *NBA Hot Shots* was a one-time magazine from *SI*'s custom-publishing division. Supported solely by Gatorade, it aimed to bring the sports drink's message to "young men" who
were basketball enthusiasts.[68]

Yet another place for the Sports Illustrated brand in the mid–1990s,
with articles and advertisers, was Pathfinder, the Time Warner site on the
Internet's World Wide Web. The implied purpose for Sports Illustrated's
site was to display the brand's affinity with computer-oriented sports enthusiasts. Just as likely, the company's executives simply did not want
to miss getting in on the ground floor of what many in advertising and

media were promoting as the next great place for reaching likely prospects.

Those who enthused about the online population in the mid–1990s couched their comments in the caveat that very little was really known about the few million plugged into the commercial online services (mainly Prodigy, America Online, and Compuserve), the supposedly thirty million linked to the Internet, and the estimated two million users of the World Wide Web, the multimedia part of the Internet.[69] Yet the profile that marketing magazines and speeches presented was of a universe that stopped marketers in their tracks: mostly young white men, mostly well educated, computer proficient, and so-called early adopters of technology.

While these people as a group formed an alluring target, the way they arrayed themselves online made them even more attractive. Online services encouraged their members to choose from among an enormous variety of chat groups or bulletin boards dedicated to particular subjects. An integral part of the Internet, for example, was Usenet, a conferencing system composed of individual "newsgroups" with topics from Bosnia to bestiality. From a marketing standpoint, that meant the people were segmentable by a broad gamut of lifestyle interests. As one consultant noted, "[Online] customers coalesce into 'newsgroups' and information services that are specifically targeted toward their interests."[70] For marketers, the challenge was to find ways to signal their relationship to those groups—or to create new groups—in persuasive ways.

The first half of the 1990s was a tentative, exploratory period in marketers' approaches to online audiences. Ironically, media firms and marketers, long tethered together in traditional media, found they had to establish new ways to work together. Many marketers felt that they could go it alone when it came to showing their stuff over online services. Yet media executives argued that in cyberspace as elsewhere, associating with a strong media brand would play a key role in bringing the right consumers to the right advertisers.

Advertisers using the Internet had the technology to bombard the online population selectively or completely with ads in the form of electronic mail. Yet that kind of direct targeting was a Trojan Horse they felt they could not use. Ad executives were quite aware of "flaming" or "spamming" incidents in which the online population reacted angrily en masse to receiving unsolicited commercial messages. Executives also believed that online users detested commercial messages that simply reminded them of what they already knew. By the mid–1990s, they accepted the notion that in the new-media world "advertising has to be news, not noise" to the audience receiving it, in the words of computer futurist Nicholas Negroponte.[71]

One sneaky way to create advertising that targets would not scorn fell under the rubric "public relations." It involved sending a message to one or more bulletin board or Usenet groups with topics that matched the product or a profile of its consumers. Another way to entice online populations to read ads was to label them clearly as advertisements but offer discounts to people who acted on them.[72]

But while targeted publicity and promotional tactics sometimes bore impressive results, they did not bring with them the kind of long-term building of an image and relationship with consumers that national marketers craved. It was around this desire that the interests of media and marketers began to converge. Marketers wanted to create online sites that would reflect a brand image customized for that part of their target audience that existed online. They wanted people to come to their online sites, and they wanted data about the ones who did. Media firms, too, wanted to reach certain people with a brand identity; they wanted data about their audience; and they wanted two streams of revenue— one from consumers and one from advertisers.

Their ability to work together online began in earnest with the appearance in 1993 of multimedia capabilities on the Internet's World Wide Web as well as on commercial online services. Ambitious to be associated with the cutting edge, many marketers from AT&T to Dial a Mattress to a small greeting card company called Greet Street established sites in cyber "malls" or "home pages" on the Web. Many advertisers saw these sites as interactive magazine ads that signaled their personalities and those of their preferred consumers. Some programmers, annoyed by the static metaphor they felt magazines implied, emphasized that online marketing sites had to be interactive to attract users and keep them coming back.[73] Online browsers were invited to explore the company's message by clicking on "buttons" that would give them details about products, see pictures, hear music, and let them send messages to the advertiser. Sometimes, the consumer could purchase products, though the lack of online credit card security as late as 1995 meant that payment often had to be made over the phone.

When the home page's purpose was not to directly sell things, advertising agencies had still not settled on methods through which to judge the number and nature of people using particular online sites. They accepted as a truism, however, that the key to success lay in "finding ways to get people to come back again and again," as one ad agency's new-media executive put it.[74] To entice target consumers to their home pages, companies began to develop online equivalents to in-your-face programming. Their aim was to signal quite clearly that the site represented one location where a distinctive community that identified with the product could gather.

Creators of online "home pages" for marketers and media firms also argued that attracting customers in cyberspace ought to go beyond simply laying out lifestyle signals, as magazine covers and cable networks tended to do. They felt that, more in the style of many radio formats and promotional events, an online site should foster a sense of camaraderie among the people its creators wanted to draw to it. This intention to emphasize a sense of belonging may well have been spurred by marketers' awareness that some of the most popular aspects of the Internet involved interactions through bulletin boards. Real-time conversations in "relay groups" and "multi-user domains" provided even more possibilities for role-playing and acting out values. Enthusiasts quickly found areas they liked, or started their own, and they became involved in intellectual, emotional, and even sexual relationships with people they had never seen.[75]

Marketing and media executives tried to adapt this idea to their needs. Some, taking aim at upscale young computer-savvy males, tried to ingratiate themselves with this market by making a virtue out of virtual vandalism. The trend began when teenage and college-age computer hackers broke into marketers' World Wide Web home pages to change illustrations, alter games, or leave graffiti-like messages. Instead of prosecuting the intruders, or making it harder to get in, some firms promoted the activity gleefully as an example of how popular their home pages had become. Each hoped the publicity about the escapade and the firm's generous reaction would encourage more young adults to visit its home page, in the process receiving a favorable image of the company and its products. In one case, Metro-Goldwyn-Mayer/United Artists, the marketer of the flick *Hackers*, was so successful at turning the story of virtual vandalism to its home page into positive PR for the film that some suspected the studio of engineering the prank itself.[76]

Beyond these incidents, the home pages of marketers and media increasingly exuded a sense of having lifestyle affinities with the brand and those who used it. They provided displays about the company's products and its image, and they gave those who entered the ability to send messages to the company as well as to interact with other people who cared about the firm and its products. As one consultant put it, "The heart of the Internet is people talking to people in an open and sharing environment." For marketers, he said, "tools are just now becoming available that make it far easier to create not just repositories of multimedia information, but true communities of common interests, where people congregate to share communities and insights, as well as to learn and to shop."[77]

The Zima clear-malt alcoholic beverage provides an example. For the Adolf Coors Company, Zima's owner, encouraging computer users to get involved in the electronic Zima site was a way to link up with people who were good prospects for what the firm positioned as a Generation X drink. According to Zima's brand manager, using the Internet was "the perfect matchup with the type of people we were going after, people who are open to new things and who are leading their peer groups in using new technology."[78]

The brewery printed Zima's Internet address (zima.com) on the labels of Zima bottles. Visitors to its World Wide Web home page did not get a traditional pitch for the beverage. Instead, they got to follow the continually updated adventures of a techno-savvy twenty-something named Duncan who had asked his fellow office worker Alexandra on a drinking date. Users also got to pick slang words and vote for the color of an electronic refrigerator on Zima's home page built around an interactive freezer and come back to see it being built.

To solidify the connection with the Zima site among people who found it fun, users were asked to fill out a Tribe Z registration request for names and e-mail address in order to become an "official member of the Tribe." A subsequent electronic letter sent to all "members" was titled "Welcome to the Tribe!" Combining stereotypical GenX irreverence with a desire to be taken seriously, it read in part:

You may have been wondering . . . where your life was leading in this new relationship with Zima; what kind of free stuff
you might be getting. . . . Anyway, here's what you can expect
as a member of Tribe Z:

- free transferable Zima logo patch.

- entrance to the Freezer.

- [e-mail] directory of other members.

- notification of Zima events in your area.

- the opportunity to win free t-shirts and merchandise.

In other words, the online note promised to bring to Zima's Internet
audience event marketing, public relations, consumer promotion, and
even product placement (in the interactive Zima Fridge exploration).
These activities echoed Zima's signals to its customers outside the Internet. The uniquely online twist, the e-mail directory, furthered the
notion that Zima enthusiasts had activities, interests, and values in common. Other companies were pursuing their Internet lifestyle targets with
similar signaling ammunition on their home pages.

The challenge, of course, was for marketers to get users who fit target profiles to find their ad sites in a world where hundreds of businesses
were setting up their tents and trying to get people into them. Print
magazines such as *Wired* did alert readers to sites that their writers considered particularly interesting. In addition, online reviewers such as
Point Communications and search indexes such as Yahoo, created by
students at Stanford University, sent users to thousands of places. Nevertheless, even though some firms encouraged their listing in indexes, they
had little power over placement in such listings, and it was quite possible
for them to get lost in the shuffle. The long-term problem of matching
people with the appropriate lifestyle interests and demographics to the
right home pages remained.[79]

That is where branded media formats that were setting up shop on
the Internet, America Online, and other services entered the picture. In
the late 1980s and early 1990s, one could legitimately ask how media
firms intended to profit when many of their traditional advertisers were
establishing major electronic homes without them. America Online and
the other commercial services did pay an online outlet every time a user

accessed it, but the amount was minimal. On the Internet, media firms made nothing at all from access. Some companies did not carry ads, preferring first to experiment on their own. Even most of the media sites that involved ads made little direct profit from them. Instead, they carried advertisers who bought time or space from their media firm's core outlets—its magazine, television network, or radio station.

Media firms, in other words, treated online advertising as a "value added" promotional activity that cemented relationships with sponsors. It was a "come-on" part of a larger ad package, not an independent moneymaker. CBS Television, for example, spoke to two very different targets in the service of different advertisers. On the Web, it signaled GenXers with a *Late Night with David Letterman* theme. On Prodigy, which supposedly had more women and somewhat older users than other online services, the TV network hyped prime time programming such as *Murder She Wrote* and *Dr. Quinn: Medicine Woman* that its online executives felt would appeal to that audience.[80]

By the mid–1990s, this attitude was beginning to change. A growing number of companies were seeing online magazines as places where they could eventually make new money from advertising and maybe even from subscribers. The word was out, however, that the way to do that was not simply to recycle an online version of the printed matter. Consultants insisted that computer users expected new information. Consultants also urged that media firms offer chat and bulletin board functions. In line with this idea, Newsweek's multimedia magazine on Prodigy included onscreen buttons that encouraged readers to access its "archives," to "talk to us," and to even get a recorded "welcome" message.[81]

Interactive ads from Honda, Chrysler, and Fidelity Investments were also part of the Newsweek package. They had accepted the idea that an association with Newsweek's home page was an efficient way to get recognition from the right kind of internet audience. Media firms, however, had discovered that cyberspace was allowing them to cater to advertisers with the best of both worlds. Marketers could have their own home pages. But they could signal the existence of those home pages, and get people to them, by purchasing space on media home pages.

Internet marketing consultants such as Modem Media and Onramp were encouraging advertisers to see that a media format could be a terrific way to lead consumers to an advertiser's online site. Links that marketers purchased on media sites were leading users to the marketers' stand-alone home pages or to other home pages that would reflect a marketer's self-image. Companies were also making deals to attach their own media sites via links with online media firms that had compatible audiences and advertisers. So, for example, Zima in 1995 had 125 connections to its site from other sites. According to the company's agency for online work, most of the 125 were simple connections to other home pages on the Internet. Ten, though, were paid media buys that ensured the firm large banners to signal compatible customers.[82] For example, the company paid to place its home-page button on Hotwired, the Internet site for *Wired,* a popular print magazine aimed at twenty-somethings with interests in the online world. It also bought a compatible location on the Point Web's site for Internet reviews.[83]

More ambitiously, the creators of the Yahoo Internet index formed an alliance with Netscape Communications, creators of the most popular software used to "browse" the World Wide Web. The agreement was that Yahoo's home page would carry the Netscape logo and Netscape would route users of its browser to Yahoo, which was beginning to sell advertising links. The general idea in all deals such as these was to connect media and advertisers searching for the same kinds of audiences in as many ways as possible.[84]

The plan—to link more and more compatible sites via onscreen buttons and banners—was an elegant way to extend to cyberspace the horizontal parade of lifestyles that marketing and media brands had been establishing across media and through events outside cyberspace. In fact, in their marketing and non-marketing areas, the Internet and other online services emphasized a greater array of lifestyle interests than any other medium. The online audience was continually receiving signals that even its relatively small stratum of American society—young, up-scale, and educated—should best be thought of as a melange of often unrelated lifestyles and values. Moreover, a growing number of marketers were rewarding them with a sense of community—or of Tribe—for thinking that way. Particularly when placed against the signaling of social divisions in print, radio, and cable TV, it was hard to miss the message that society was so divided that it was becoming impossible to know, or care about, more than your tribe or set of tribes.

Anyone could see, too, that the online parade of lifestyles was only beginning. The hype regarding online enterprises was enormous, and few, if any, companies were actually making money yet. Debates raged among executives about whether such interactive access to media and marketing sites would ultimately be more widespread through computers or through the more omnipresent television sets, via cable or phone lines. Still, most media and marketing executives saw interactivity, with the targeted signaling it represented, as integral to the future of marketing. To them, the real question was not whether it would work but how to integrate media-based signaling with other marketing activities to establish the most effective relationships with potential customers. Many believed that the key to such integration lay not just in signaling but in tailoring messages to individually targeted customers based on information that marketers could find about them. This "direct-response" approach provided yet another engine for cultivating a sense of America as a hodgepodge of separate, disconnected worlds. It is the subject of the next chapter.

TAILORING DIFFERENCES

As chapter 5 showed, executives in the 1980s and early 1990s believed that they could divide, attract, and keep customers they cared about most through signaling. Signaling involved trying to beckon certain types of people via traditional advertisements, publicity, public relations, and events in ways that would encourage those consumers to link their identities with those of the advertisers. Yet many marketing executives came to believe that signaling was not enough in their complex, competitive environment when it came to their most desirable consumers. They decided that it was crucial to find ways to achieve stronger, more individualized bonds with them. "Not all customers are equal," said a consultant in 1994. "You have to put golden handcuffs on your very best customers."[1]

To do that, executives turned to new information technologies to help them home in on the individuals within those target populations and cultivate them for their products. Conferences and trade papers in the first half of the 1990s were filled with enthusiastic declarations of benefits from direct-response marketing, database marketing, interactive marketing, and especially relationship marketing. Consultants and marketing executives insisted that to maximize power in the new-media environment a marketer had to link the signaling of populations to individual relationships with consumers. Media executives began to take action when they realized that they might lose advertising monies to interactive ad projects excluding them. They tried to design news, information, and entertainment services that were tailored to individual subscribers and that advertisers could sponsor along with their signaling activities.

The hype about direct and relationship marketing was often greater than the activity, especially on the part of manufacturers of food, soap, and other package goods. Moreover, companies often made the specifics of their data-gathering and tailoring activities proprietary, so it was hard to gauge exactly what they were doing. It was clear, though, that customized activities were not as widespread or developed as the signaling of distinction through targeted advertising and media that was discussed in chapter 5. Moreover, in tailoring to individuals entertainment and news media were far behind direct marketers, who used mail and telephones to accomplish many of their tasks. Still, a growing number of U.S. executives were placing bets on the idea that deep associations with particular customers represented their best chance for success in a segmented and ferociously competitive world. By the mid–1990s, national marketers of all sorts were rushing to develop expertise with direct-response advertising and particularly its database, interactive, and relationship offshoots.

One consultant, noting that the growth rate of "direct" was greater than that of mainstream media advertising, predicted that the total monies spent on customizing relationships with individuals would one day surpass non-tailored forms of selling.[2] The editor-in-chief of *Advertising Age* also saw it as a major transition that was changing the ad and media businesses. "[Mainstream] advertising used to be the marketing tool of choice," he wrote. "Now it's down on the list, and when interactive media arrive in a big way, traditional media will be a relic. Does anyone doubt that direct marketing works?"[3]

It was a popular issue throughout the media system. Getting much less play, however, were the implications that these activities had for the views that Americans were, and increasingly would be, receiving of themselves and their world. What relationship marketers were trying to do was to create different virtual neighborhoods. Using sophisticated databases, they were searching out people with similar demographics, interests, values, and activities; starting similar conversations with those people; and then tailoring ensuing conversations to their responses. Here was neighborhood redlining joined to a contemporary version of the door-to-door salesman.

By surrounding individuals with mirrors of themselves, their values, and their activities, relationship marketers emphasized to their targets a world that began and ended with their personal needs. Along with signaling, relationship marketing furthered a vision of a fractionated society where it was unnecessary and sometimes even too difficult for people to move in circles unrelated to the interests of their primary communities. Where relationship marketing went beyond signaling was in the parade of distinction. Creating relationships often meant highlighting entitlement tailored to lifestyles, as when airlines encouraged business travelers to anticipate certain rewards based on their mileage frequencies.

Marketers were aware that the public policy of privileging people based on lifestyles could spark social antagonisms. As long as these antagonisms did not hurt their business, though, they insisted that they had to continue partitioning consumers and speaking to them differently. The pursuit of their best customers—what some called "the golden 20%"[4]—required bold steps that might well alienate some people who were deemed less important.

As late as as the mid–1970s, the elite of the ad world looked down on "direct" work.[5] They associated it with the selling of shoddy or quirky mail-order products—breast enlargers and Ginsu knives—by preying bluntly on the audience's fear, guilt, greed, and desire to be exclusive. Mainstream ad people mined these same psychological tactics, or Great Motivators, as one direct practitioner called them.[6] Yet they saw themselves doing it much more subtly than direct marketers, via campaigns that enhanced the long-term reputations of brands.

The cultures of the two ad businesses were quite different. A common example of direct marketing was an ad in a magazine that encouraged a reader to write for a free catalog. Another was a set of coupons mailed to the home. In both cases, sales could be tracked by the company giving the discounts. Direct marketers saw their ability to get clear feedback from their work as the heart of what they did. A 1982 article in *Advertising Age* described the business as "an interactive system of marketing which uses one or more advertising media to effect a measureable response and/or transaction at any location."[7]

Mainstream agency people stressed image-making over that kind of feedback. They typically revered ads that encouraged their competitors and their audiences to wonder at the imagination that made them. They gave prizes to each other for "creativity" in advertising. *Advertising Age* even published a magazine called *Creativity,* which explored the processes behind the beauty of contemporary ad work.

Direct marketers snickered at that meaning of creativity and scorned prizes for it. They argued that kudos should be awarded only for campaigns that demonstrably increased sales. That, they contended, was something mainstream advertising had a hard time doing because it was often impossible to draw a causal link between a commercial message and a consumer's purchase response. To prove that certain appeals directly caused sales to jump required unusual circumstances such as a cable system that sent different commercials to separate, but demographically similar, parts of a city. Often lacking that, ad people measured bumps in sales that took place around the time of an ad campaign. Long-time direct practitioners were not persuaded by these indirect methods or by research into whether people recalled seeing or hearing an ad, another indicator of an ad's success used by mainstream advertisers.[8]

Despite these marked philosophical differences, by 1982 fifteen of the top twenty advertising agencies had bought or started a direct-marketing capability.[9] It was primarily their clients' growing interest in computer-guided targeting of niche markets that brought them to look at direct practitioners with grudging respect. Large direct-marketing firms had been keeping lists of people on computers since the 1960s. Beginning in the late 1970s, their new techniques for dividing and tracking consumers according to an enormous number of demographic, psychographic, and geographic categories led target-minded executives to look at the business anew. At the same time, developments such as the 800 number (for quick responses to TV and catalog offers), ink-jet printing techniques (which allowed mailers to personalize messages to individuals), and the personal computer (which allowed easy data storage and access of sales results) generated a conviction among direct-marketing practitioners that the advertising world was moving their way.

A Dun and Bradstreet executive saw the changes as paralleling the multiplication of U.S. media channels and the distribution of audiences across more outlets than ever. The traditional hallmarks of direct marketing—precise audience identification, individualized media communication, and speedy full-satisfaction order fulfillment—meshed constructively, he said, with the new technologies.[10] Futurist John Naisbitt was even more blunt. "Direct marketers are at the forefront of where everybody is going to be," he predicted in 1983. "We can all learn from them."[11]

The range of direct work grew wider in the 1980s than ever before.

The number of commercials that invited viewers to use 800 numbers and credit cards to buy products by mail increased drastically. Their creators often placed direct-response spots on cable channels and non-network ("independent") broadcast stations that sold time cheaply in low-rating time periods. Cable and independent outlets were also vehicles for infomercials—audiovisual ads that displayed the attributes of a product in a program ranging in duration from several minutes to a half hour. Taking the infomercial one step further were shopping channels that invited immediate purchases by phone twenty-four hours a day.

But while TV-based platforms for consumer responses were especially visible in the 1980s, it was via the mail and the telephone that most targeted advertising took place. Catalog mailing and other solicitations also increased dramatically through the decade. In the second half of the 1970s, advertisers doubled their direct-mail expenditures, reaching $10.5 billion in 1981.[12] During the 1980s, according to *Direct Marketing* magazine, mail expenditures soared from $12.7 billion in 1983 to $17.2 billion in 1986. By 1989 direct-mail spending had climbed to $23.4 billion and in 1993 the number reached $27.3 billion.[13]

Use of the telephone for marketing, often to order from the mailed catalogs, grew even more dramatically. According to *Direct Marketing*, companies spent $34 billion in 1984 on marketing transactions via the telephone. By 1990 that number had risen to $60.5 billion and in 1993 it was $73 billion.[14]

Direct response shared a number of characteristics with mainstream advertising, publicity, and promotions. Direct marketers' penchant for dividing consumers fit with the movement toward increased specificity about audiences in those other activities. Nielsen TV audience data; MRI and Simmons syndicated data on demographics, psychographics, and purchasing patterns; geodemographic extrapolations from PRIZM and Conquest—these and other storehouses of information were scavenged by direct tacticians as well as by standard ad, promotion, and publicity people. Too, in direct-response work, as in standard advertising, public relations, and event marketing, the focus was on reaching out—signaling—to a particular population with certain categories.

Where the direct-response business diverged from the mainstream, and where marketers saw its greatest possibilities, was in the connections that its practitioners could make with their targets. The 800 number and the personal computer made it much easier than in the past to link up with potential customers quickly. The technologies also made it easier than before to track the "pull" of an ad.[15] On a cost-per-thousand basis, this approach was clearly more expensive than using magazines or network television. Direct practitioners insisted that what they lost in efficiency of reach would be more than made up in the careful selection of people likely to act on the sales pitch. The trick was to get good lists of likely prospects.

That in itself was not a new challenge. Companies were purchasing names for marketing purposes in the nineteenth century.[16] The computer's ability to store and sort the names of millions of people and their characteristics, however, moved the list business—now called the database business—into overdrive. By the 1990s the buying and selling of names and information about them had become a major industry. Broadly speaking, direct marketers used two resources for name gathering: universal databases and transactional databases.

Universal databases are compilations of information on every individual and household in an area, even an entire nation. Companies that sell this intelligence often glean it from public records. In the 1990s, R. L. Polk took advantage of the availability of auto registrations in thirty-eight states to anyone who cared to look. It matched each car with the name and address listed on ownership records. From other sources, the name and address were then connected to a raft of information about each person: age, home ownership, occupation, family size, income, leisure interests, credit card ownership—even their past response to mailings. The organized material was then placed on sale.[17]

But Polk's work was just the tip of an iceberg of companies rummaging through public information about individuals. Records of births, deaths, marriages, divorces, property sales, building certificates, and mortgages were freely available for almost everybody in the United States. At least one outfit, Jefferson Mailing Lists, even sold lists of recently backrupt consumers, adding thirty-five thousand names per month from court records. Because bankruptcy was declarable only once every seven years, such consumers might be seen as relatively good short-term credit risks.[18] As two direct-marketing consultants noted in 1993, "Almost anything that is in the public record has already been collected and compiled into a database by some enterprising mailing list company somewhere."[19]

Building on top of these public records were firms such as TRW,

Equifax, Donnelley Marketing, and Claritas. They gathered and sold storehouses of bytes on individual creditworthiness and other data available privately rather than publicly. Donnelley's Conquest/Direct system, for example, offered marketers the profiles of potential customers by demographics, lifestyles, and retail sales expenditures. The company claimed that its database covered 90 percent of all U.S. households. Its software allowed clients to generate customized color maps of target market areas. Mailing-list services included the ability to select names based on responsiveness to mail appeals, creditworthiness, vehicle information, psychographics, lifestyle details, financial investments, hobbies, occupations, census demographics, and more.[20]

There were many other firms offering a variety of services to help marketers winnow their prospects. For example:

• National Decisions Systems, a subsidiary of Equifax, claimed to have classified every household in the United States by price sensitivity, coupon use, brand loyalty, television use, and other characteristics of interest to consumer product marketers. NDS also sold access to a list of about one hundred million employed individuals. Clients could dial into the database and analyze it via a personal computer.

• Telesphere Communications, using caller-identification technology, offered telemarketers a way to retrieve names and addresses, calling frequency, and broad lifestyle classification. That information could be made available to telemarketing operators before they answered the phones.

• Epsilon Data Management promised to help not-for-profit organizations learn more about their donors and expand their numbers. "Who are your best customers?" an Epsilon brochure asked potential clients. "Where do they live? What charitable 'products' are they buying . . . and why?" The company added that it "analyzes more than 3,000 lists and 65 million prospect names every year—giving us firsthand knowledge of which lists are the best lists to help you acquire the most new donors."[21]

As the Epsilon example suggests, a large amount of the energy that direct-marketing firms expended was on trying to locate people who would fit their profiles of likely, even ideal, customers. Inferring buying interest from a range of demographic, psychographic, and broad lifestyle information was often helpful as a starting point. Yet many direct practitioners of the 1980s and 1990s followed the long-held dictum of their business that led in a different direction: the best predictor of future behavior is actual past behavior.

This proposition underscored the importance of transactional databases. A transactional database is a list of people who explicitly responded to a particular marketing or fund-raising appeal. Marketers would often purchase names from other marketers with products that reflected compatible lifestyles. So, for example, names of men who paid for season tickets to sporting events might attract a company trying to sell sports memorabilia. Similarly, a frequent-flier list would likely draw a hotel chain with an eye on the business traveler.

The basic assumption driving the lists was summarized in an equation that Warshawsky/Whitney, a list firm, promulgated to its clients: "Segmentation + Selection = Success." In an ad in *Direct Marketing* magazine, Warshawsky/Whitney focused on its ability to split up auto owners into a variety of categories. It had information on four million mail-order buyers and requesters and one million credit card holders. It knew their age, income, education, current employment, marital status, children, and addresses. The Warshawsky/Whitney ad noted that an overwhelming number of its listed people (80 percent) were married, an indication to ensure clients that they could reach the solidly middle class and higher. Moreover, clients could infer lifestyle interests from the kind of vehicle each person on its roster owned.[22]

Prices of people lists varied depending on the list owners' perceptions of their attractiveness to marketers. Consider the Best Mailing Lists company. In the early 1990s, it offered hundreds of segmented mailing lists with prices ranging from $45 to $85 per thousand individuals. Space scientists were at the low end, sociology department heads were going for $60 per thousand, and teachers of high school mathematics were priced at $65 per thousand. Lists that identified a person's political contributions by party or provided the home addresses of prominent men were unpriced in brochures, suggesting perhaps that they were quite a bit more expensive and, at the same time, negotiable. One analysis of lists suggested that the most valuable people were white, middle-aged, high-income male consumers, especially when they had purchased high-cost consumer items such as computers or automobiles.[23]

Donnelley Marketing's "Carol Wright" program in the mid–1990s contained some elements of universal and some of transactional databases. Every few weeks the company distributed millions of six-page questionnaires with the picture of fictional Carol Wright via Sunday newspapers and into mailboxes around the US. Donnelley promised to send "samples, cents-off coupons and money-saving offers all year long" to persons who filled out the questionnaire and mailed it in. Donnelley used the returns to flesh out its general store of information about Americans and their buying habits.

The Carol Wright portion of Donnelley's database included over thirty million households. For each of the individual households, a Donnelley client could find out about dress size, pets owned, military veteran status, type of antacid preferred, and other information. Moreover, the fact that Carol Wright recipients took the trouble to fill out and return the questionnaire was in itself important information. It meant that they were to some extent responsive to direct-marketing appeals.

That lent to its database a transactional flavor. So did the presence of questions about specific products purchased. Besides reviewing them, a Donnelley client could buy its own proprietary queries on a special survey sent to Carol Wright homes. Heinz's Weight Watchers unit could ask if a household used a diet center. Pepsi could look for Diet Coke drinkers.[24]

The expense of buying millions of names for prospecting led catalog firms, banks, credit card companies, and food marketers such as Heinz and Pepsi to be as specific as possible in the characteristics they wanted.[25] Increasingly, a marketer's goal in list culling was to maximize the chances of yielding individuals who mirrored the marketer's most desirable current clientele. This mandate encouraged them to examine carefully what they knew about their own customers before going prospecting.

One way to continually update information about customers was to use interactions with them by phone to request demographic and product-use information. A marketer that knew names and addresses of its customers could also use a company such as Database America to learn more. DBA took a list and matched it against data on more than eighty-four million households. The resulting merged file could supply the marketer with a wealth of new information about each customer's purchasing behavior, estimated income, credit extended by mail-order firms, credit cards, investments, and charitable and political contributions.[26]

To learn more about their own ("house") files, direct marketers often broke their lists into ten segments, or deciles. The top decile indicated the most desirable customer in terms of how often they bought and what they spent. The bottom deciles were infrequent purchasers of inexpensive items.

Data analysts examined the customer deciles by age, income, gender, race, and other demographic factors as well as lifestyle factors that were known and geographic categories such as zip codes or even smaller geographic units. Having created a model of their best customers (the ones in the top deciles), they matched it against geodemographic databases such as PRIZM. That helped them determine the demographic and lifestyle features of the best customers' zip codes. Knowing those features might allow them to prospect directly in the customers' zip codes or in zip codes that mirrored the features of those areas.

Direct marketers called the process cloning. "The best targeting that most companies can use these days," said a direct-marketing consultant, "is [to say] 'let's find people who are just like the people we have.'"[27] It meant that individuals with similar attributes in databases were increasingly sharing the same direct-mail pieces; often demographics and lifestyle were more important than precisely where they lived.

As important as cloning was, though, continuous learning about one's own customers and dividing them into groups from most to least desirable had an even more important purpose. Increasingly, beginning in the mid–1980s, direct marketers focused on paying more attention to the customers they already had. Doing that, executives contended, required going beyond signaling to potential customers. It required, instead, "managing" the customer roster—"rewarding some, getting rid of others, improving the value of each of them."[28] That meant, in turn, establishing "dialogues" with the firm's loyal consumers that reinforced their fidelity with marks of distinction: signs that the company was tailoring its activities to their needs and those of the people like them.

"Knowing your old customers is not just good business sense," wrote one direct marketer. "It's less expensive and more profitable than acquiring new ones."[29] The head of a direct firm stated that "ninety percent of a manufacturer's profit comes from the repeat purchasers" and only 10 percent "from trial or sporadic purchasers."[30] Moreover, "it costs six to ten times as much to get a new customer as it does to retain a loyal one."[31]

A loyal consumer over many years could bring in lots of money, marketers pointed out. A General Motors vice president for consumer development estimated that a devoted GM buyer would spend $400,000 with the company and its dealerships over a lifetime. Similarly, two marketing consultants concluded that a business traveler who flew between coasts once every other month would, during the course of a business career, easily generate more than $100,000 in revenues.[32]

Repeat customers were especially important when a brand's customer base was relatively small. To a growing extent, this was also the case for even the largest marketers. Efficiencies in manufacturing technology encouraged small production runs that had previously been uneconomical. Moreover, the new computer-based techniques for dissecting America into very specific demographic, psychographic, and lifestyle categories had helped to identify niche markets. In the face of rabid competition, these tendencies led to an explosion of products and services that aimed at particular demographic and lifestyle slices—golfers, for example, or even "senior citizen golfers who drive luxury sedans and are in the market for new ones."[33]

Ironically, recognition of the crucial value of repeat customers came at a time when executives said they faced an escalating difficulty winning and keeping them. In many industries of the 1980s and 1990s there was a sense that customer loyalty in the U.S. was generally plummeting. Reasons abounded for the alleged breakdown. Some excoriated producers for using discounts, giveaways, and other promotional gimmicks to spike short-term profits instead of working to maintain brand identities that would withstand price competition. Still others emphasized retailers' tendency to use lower prices on generics and store brands to exploit customers' lessening fidelity to manufacturer's brands.

Critics of the marketing status quo maintained that growing clutter in mainstream advertising, promotion, and publicity made it harder to convey brand images to people. They contended that the number of ad messages reaching out to people had become so great—by one count five thousand a day—that the odds of their remembering any particular ones were less than in previous generations.[34] Making the chances of recall even smaller, marketers believed, was the rushed nature of American life in the final quarter of the twentieth century. People, they felt, often didn't have time to sort through the welter of ads trying to flag them down.

Direct marketers used corporate concerns about brand loyalty and growing disenchantment with mainstream advertising as an entry point to plug their business and extend it. Direct work, they noted, was regularly tracking individuals and trying to keep them as customers. "Brand loyalty is a kind of continuity program, and we should treat it as such," exhorted Lester Wunderman, the influential founder of a major direct-marketing agency. He repeated the proposition, increasingly recognized in his business, that the high road to profits for any company or brand is the number of loyal repeat customers it could acquire and keep.

Signaling potentially good customers through standard advertising or by giving prospects samples or coupons was simply inefficient, Wunderman insisted.

> Most advertisers and their agencies who seek to expand their share of market believe that their major leverage is to multiply the number of consumers at large who try their product. . . . In search of . . . tactical but temporary advantage [over competitors], they waste hundreds of millions or even billions of dollars in advertising, sales promotion and marketing costs in an attempt to promote consumer trial—and too often they stop there. Because they rarely get names and phone numbers, they do not know how or whom they should try to build ongoing relationships. They practice the tactics of acquisition without the corollary strategy of customer retention.
>
> The grim fact is that a one-time sale or "product trial" doesn't cover its cost. . . . Ninety percent of a brand's profit comes from repeat purchases. . . . Of the 84,933 products launched between 1980 and 1990 only 14 percent have survived. What a waste and what a disaster for the companies, their employees and their shareholders.[35]

The ability to help a firm not only target and signal the right kind of customers but keep them was, Wunderman continued, direct marketing's great asset. "Our task is to collect and safeguard the 'Crown Jewels' who create almost all of the profit. Mass advertising and mass marketing cannot do that job efficiently. We know how to help build a 'share of loyal customers' strategy because in our business we have learned that relationships are everything."[36]

As perspectives such as Wunderman's caught on, "building loyalty" through "relationship marketing" became the primary catchphrases in direct work of the 1990s. The notions proposed that a customer's value lay in purchasing not one product but a variety of products from the company over many years. Relying on signaling was no longer enough to ensure loyalty to the company and its output, practitioners generally agreed. What was needed was an ongoing conversation with every desirable customer.

This approach to selling therefore implied two other efforts that were then getting much play in the advertising world: database marketing and interactive marketing. The first was the art of using computer files to segment customers by demographics, psychographics, and lifestyles, and to pursue the most valuable ones. The second referred to the customer's ability to provide immediate feedback regarding a firm's products and services.

Relationship marketing took these activities one step further, however. The idea was to go beyond interacting with all carefully selected customers in the same way. Instead, the aim was to tailor all contacts with individual customers to each customer's particular activities, interests, and values, as known through a database. That, many believed, was the only way to have a chance of connecting in the right way with the right customers in an increasingly frenetic, fractured society. "Today's customer is a moving target," a writer in a 1992 issue of *Direct Marketing* magazine admonished his readers. "And the customer database allows you to reach this target."[37]

To keep the conversation—and the purchasing—going, practitioners were to build connections with individuals by linking the door-to-door salesperson's ability to relate to individual customers with the computer's ability to come up with more information about the customer than ever before. That information was to be updated continually through customer purchase patterns and other contacts. The reason the seller would not be overwhelmed by the number of people was because most of the interactions were taking place by machine. A computer would sort the most appropriate appeals and turn out customized messages by mail, by phone, or online. Every now and then, live representatives of the firm would get involved.

Writers dubbed the process mass customization. Done properly, wrote two consultants, it meant that "[e]very dialogue with any customer is an opportunity to build the scope of your relationship with that customer. Every shred of information about an *individual* customer's needs, perspectives, whims—every item of learning gained from a dialogue—can be used to ensure a tighter, more productive, and long-lasting relationship." [38]

In practice, the idea translated into using databases and "dialogue" to overlay the buying experience with qualities that reflected the special customer's characteristics and lifestyles and linked them to the product or service. In the 1980s and 1990s, this idea was put into practice mostly through so-called loyalty programs. These activities aimed to tie targeted consumers to a company by long-term incentives, with benefits and privileges tailored to individual characteristics.

The approach gained special prominence as a result of airline "frequent flier" programs. In 1981, American Airlines started a club that rewarded its members with free air trips, car rentals, special check-in lines and nominally priced upgrades from coach to business or first class depending on the number of miles they traveled with the carrier. American kept in special touch with those customers and tried to track, and cater to, the needs of the very best ones.

Competitors copied the practice. The carriers were sure that the goal, to give individuals a reason to stick with an airline, worked. Research revealed that in 1980 the average business traveler had a half-hour tolerance for delay before changing airlines. That is, the person would walk to another airline if a scheduled plane was more than thirty minutes late. By the late 1980s, this tolerance had increased to three and a half hours. [39]

The frequent-flier program set the standard for the many loyalty programs that followed in the next decade. The key to successful loyalty programs, direct marketers told each other, was to go beyond simple gifts. Gifts and simple discounts, they said over and over, were not primarily what customers wanted; nor would they automatically instill loyalty. "Our best customers [already] get all the discounts," said a marketing executive. "Offering them more . . . wouldn't be much of a retention program at all." He distinguished his firm's loyalty plan from a promotion which gave 1 percent back on all store purchases. "That has nothing to do with loyalty. It's like Pavlov's law: Buy something, get something back."[40]

Knowing what privileges to offer required what one executive called a "quiet conversation" between the company and each individual that combined database and mass-customization technology with periodic interventions by salespeople.[41] For example:

• The Waldenbooks chain created the Preferred Reader program, with a membership charge of $5, later raised to $10. The goal was to inform a reader when a title was available that matched the reader's interests, as evidenced by previous purchases. When such a book was identified, a card with that information would be sent to the Preferred Reader; the card also served as a coupon offering a small discount.[42]

• General Motors instituted a credit card with no annual fee and the accumulation of credit toward discounts on the purchase of GM cars. From GM's standpoint, the benefit of the program was the opportunity to track the habits of five million people who had chosen to get a GM credit card. It also, according to an executive, allowed the company "to have a very rational, and very logical, reason to mail our five million people each month something regarding automotive. And more important, it's something they expect because they have raised their hand and said, 'I want to be a GM card customer.'"[43]

• The Ritz-Carlton Hotel chain constructed a database of its more frequent customers that tracked their preferences. By the mid–1990s, the firm had recorded 400,000 expressed preferences in their reservation system. Their tack was not to ask a person to fill out a survey. Rather, any time they asked for something unusual—a firm pillow, a high floor, a minibar without liquor—it was duly noted in the computer. The result, said one writer: "If I stay at the Ritz-Carlton Hotel [chain] and I order white wine from my room service tonight in L. A., and I say, "Oh, put an ice cube in my white wine," two months from now or two weeks from now or two years from now, when I stay at the Ritz-Carlton in Atlanta and I order white wine from room service, they'll almost certainly ask me if I'd like an ice cube in it."[44]

These sorts of programs proliferated during the early 1990s. A company that tracked them in different industries found that clubs and loyalty programs rose from 130 in 1992 to 153 the following year to 167 in 1994, an increase of 28 percent in two years.[45] By mid–1995, the number had climbed to 250.[46] Industries as diverse as fast-food chains, financial services, retail stores, and telecommunications hoped to garner the same sort of success as the airlines. "Frequency marketing is moving out of the industry where it has grown up and moving into industries where there are new applications," said one consultant.[47]

What was particularly changing in the 1990s was the attitude of manufacturers of inexpensive "package goods"—diapers, cereals, soups, inexpensive cosmetics, over-the-counter pharmaceuticals—toward tracking and wooing individuals. A few package-goods loyalty programs—such as Huggies New Mothers—had existed since at least the mid–1980s. Traditionally, though, executives argued that the low-involvement, low-cost products made any sort of direct marketing irrelevant because costs per individual target were high when compared to mass media. During the 1990s, package-goods marketers began to acknowledge that they could very much benefit from one-on-one interactions with consumers.

• In 1995, Coca-Cola was involved in a number of database efforts aimed at improving customer retention. The company was selectively distributing a Coke catalog, featuring four hundred licensed products with the Coca-Cola logo. It was using a 350,000-name mailing list to reach collectors of Coke memorabilia. It was considering a brand loyalty program aimed at the lucrative teen market. And it was sending coupons to existing customers to boost their brand loyalty. The coupons had codes on them that allowed the firm to track which households redeemed them and which didn't, and which should be further encouraged by mail. "We're segmenting our consumer database for a variety of promotions, from tactical coupon mailings to loyalty programs directed at heavy consumers," said the beverage giant's public relations manager.[48]

• Zima, the clear malt beverage, was one of many marketers pursuing data about, and the loyalty of, college students and GenX techies on the Internet. In addition to signaling a sense of community through the home page as described in chapter 5, Zima used mass-customization techniques to portray an individual relationship with the Tribemaster who represented the company. The Tribemaster asked Net users to fill out a survey to join the Tribe. The Tribemaster sent e-mail messages to members and exhorted them to inform Zima when they changed their e-mail address. Each Tribe member received a unique password that would allow the user into the Zima refrigerator, an interactive graphic that the user could explore and "paint" in a unique way. Further emphasizing the importance of the individual to Zima was a promise to hold online marketing focus groups and reimburse participants for their time.

• The Weight Watchers Food Company, owned by Heinz, started a relationship-marketing program in 1993 that used as a core database the people who joined the Weight Watchers reduction regimen run by an unrelated company. "It was designed to build a relationship while people were in Weight Watchers groups. Members got bonus points for attending classes and going to meetings. They also received bonus points for every dollar spent on Weight Watchers foods. Members could use their points to buy merchandise, including "top-line apparel" from a members-only catalog. The approach illustrated an emerging trend: More package-goods marketers such as Heinz were beginning to follow the airlines' lead and use customer data to develop loyalty programs that rewarded continued use with more than just coupons. "Couponing is usually the first resort of most package-goods marketers because that's the traditional method that's been used," said one executive. "But as database marketing evolves, we'll have to test additional devices."[49]

The key to believing that all this was worth the effort lay in recognizing a repeat customer's lifetime value. Enormous competition for shelf space in supermarkets and department stores forced executives from even the largest manufacturers to find ways to explore the hypothesis that repeat customers, properly handled, could help keep brand prices up and niche brands on the shelves. If a company saw a person's purchase of a box of corn flakes as a single incident, then direct marketing of any sort made no sense. Shooting a message at millions of people on network TV made for a much lower cost per thousand people, even if the great percentage viewing the commercial did not end up buying the cereal. If, by contrast, the marketer could see that a known corn flakes purchaser would be making one of thousands of decisions to purchase the corn flakes over a lifetime, then the consumer's value would take on a totally different perspective. Taken further, if the marketer would identify the loyal consumer of corn flakes as someone who would likely buy a range of the firm's products over a large number of years, related to the particulars of the consumer's habits, the lifetime value of that person would be even greater.

The proposition presupposed getting information about those heavy users, and marketers were increasingly adopting a variety of methods to gather data about their best customers. They were asking for information from consumers on sweepstakes forms, mail-in rebates, product-registration cards, and in-box coupons, as well as through 800 numbers and at events aimed at their target audiences. According to a study commissioned by the Direct Marketing Association, by 1994 two thirds of the leading retailers in the U.S. were using databases to build customer relations and store traffic by collecting and linking customer data with transactions. Among those retailers who did not have database marketing programs, 40 percent claimed they were planning to start one in the near future.[50] Among package-goods firms, the ten most highly committed consumer database builders in 1995 were marketing giants: Ralston Purina, R. J. Reynolds, Quaker Oats, Gerber, Philip Morris, Dowbrands, American Tobacco, Kraft Foods, Sara Lee, and Kimberly Clark.[51]

"What we're seeing are major attempts by package-goods companies to find a way to make this kind of relationship marketing work," admitted a direct practitioner in 1993. "Efficiency is the challenge—can we make it work so that it's profitable?" He also said: "Package-goods marketers . . . are enthused about the possibilities of database marketing, but no one has yet cracked the code."[52]

"Cracking the code" became the Holy Grail not just for package-goods manufacturers but for their retailers as well. All kinds of retailers joined the fray, from upscale department stores to discount chains.[53] Among retailers, supermarkets had the most to gain from relationship marketing. With low profit margins, supermarket executives recognized the utility of loyalty programs. Any setup that would turn occasional customers into loyal customers, and loyal customers into even bigger spenders than in the past, would be of great benefit.

The activity did have precedent. Retailers around the country in the 1950s and 1960s used green stamps as a major loyalty vehicle. They dispensed stamps based on the amount the customer purchased. A customer could collect the stamps in many places and redeem them for gifts. But green stamps as carried out at the time did not mesh with '90s marketing philosophy. The program was indiscriminate; it gave incentives to everyone to buy green stamps almost anywhere. Nineties thinking, by emphasizing social differences and brand loyalties, ruled out such across-the-board approaches. Nineties thinking also emphasized the value of data that helped marketers to ferret out social differences.

One company that traded elegantly on this interest in separating people efficiently was Catalina Marketing. Its system, found in about 8,500 stores in early 1995, printed electronic coupons at the checkout lane based on the products that the checkout person had scanned.[54] The coupon could be created for the product being purchased, a complementary product, or a competing product. The maker of charcoal briquettes, for example, might pay Catalina to print a coupon each time a customer bought mustard. Or the maker of one brand of mustard might pay for customers to receive coupons for that company's sauce when they bought a competitor's mustard. A drawback, however, was that the Catalina system did not use data from the past to determine how the buyer should be reinforced for present purchases.

Supermarket executives realized that with a number of adjustments to their cash-register system they had the capability to collect those data, and more. Handled properly, that would allow them to tailor promotional coupons and other incentives based on an individual customer's demographic information and buying pattern. The idea was to increase customer loyalty through frequent-shopper programs with valuable and attainable gifts; to promote higher-margin goods in the store, such as flowers, meats, and prepacked salads; and to find out who the best customers were and what their buying patterns and background said about how they might be rewarded.

In the 1990s, many supermarkets were shaping relationship programs to do just that. Smitty's, of Phoenix, Arizona, was particularly successful, boasting over 800,000 members at the beginning of 1995.[55] Those kinds of numbers, and the stored information they implied, intrigued package-goods suppliers. Supermarkets were already inundated by manufacturer-sponsored ads that associated lifestyles and products via in-store media such as signs, radio announcements, and electronic shelf markers. Supermarket databases pointed to ways that package-goods firms could move beyond broad-based signaling to interacting with individual consumers at the point of purchase.

Supermarket executives indicated a willingness to share some of these data with their suppliers—for a substantial price. Because the supermarket companies were typically confined to particular regions of the U.S., package-goods firms typically had to make their deals on an area-by-area as well as company-by-company basis. Trying to become the exception was a company called Advanced Promotion Technologies. It aimed to use its Vision Value Network to knit the databases of various supermarket chains into a nationwide system supported by package-goods firms. The system would provide those firms and the retailer with a frequent-shopper program, targeted promotions, and financial services (such as the use of bank cards) tailored to the personal background and buying history of the individual customer. The high cost of a nationwide rollout led some to suspect that Advanced Promotion Technologies would have a hard time remaining solvent.[56] Nevertheless, marketers in the mid–1990s were convinced that deep and ongoing relationship-marketing programs would play a key part in the future of all sorts of retailers and manufacturers.[57]

What they tended not to discuss very deeply, though, were the social implications of those growing activities. Judging by the direct-marketing trade press and most business books on the subject, robust discourse about relationship marketing's role in American society tended to begin and end with comments on how the industry could prevent public concerns about the violation of consumer privacy from inhibiting business. Certainly, that was a volatile issue. Traditionally, direct marketers had been relatively free to collect and resell information about Americans.[58]

Nevertheless, the direct-marketing trade press was dotted with concerns that consumers were annoyed because they believed that too much information about their lives and personal preferences was being exchanged without their knowledge. It also seemed clear to practitioners that people believed they were receiving too much "junk" mail and too many telemarketing solicitations. Moreover, pollsters and academics were predicting that the growth of online services would increase worries about privacy, as more ways of collecting personal information would be created.[59] The thought that an upsurge in anger might result in legislation made the industry skittish.

The industry's main lobbying group, the Direct Marketing Association, issued suggestions for gathering data that it felt would take the heat off its constituents. It revised them periodically as new public pressures built. The DMA also used as a defense the ingenious argument that the invasion of privacy had its positive side: the more specific the information that marketers knew about people, the more relevant individuals would find the messages sent to them, and the less likely they would be to complain about receiving junk mail.

Since not all direct marketers thought the Association was proactive enough to stop public ire from eventually spilling over into legislation, self-regulation proposals routinely floated through the industry. Supporters of relationship marketing did not disagree with these ideas. They asserted, however, that the collaborative logic of their work drastically reduced the chance that privacy would become a regulatory issue. "If you and your customer are collaborating, you are *friends,*" wrote influential consultants Don Peppers and Martha Rogers. "And the essential ingredients for any friendship are dependability and trust. They can count on you, and they can trust you with their secrets. It is possible, in fact, to make money, more efficiently, by increasing the level of trust enjoyed with every customer relationship, *protecting* your customer's individual privacy rather than intruding upon it."[60]

Notwithstanding their stress on building two-way relationships, Peppers and Rogers were quite clear that the power guiding the collaboration should remain with the marketer, not the customer. They accepted the idea that relationship marketers could sell their lists to other organizations as long as the seller handled the name sorting and mailing for the buyer. They recognized that the precise ways that a marketer used consumer data should best be kept from consumers, despite the collaboration. And, Peppers admitted to the readers of *Forbes* business magazine, sometimes the need for facts had to give way to a pragmatic bargain: "You pay customers if necessary. [You say,] 'We'll give you this benefit, if you will share some information about yourself.' [Or,] 'If you will tell us your purchase intent, we'll give you this coupon.'"[61]

The idea that relationship marketing was a collaborative act that benefited consumers so much that they did not mind having their privacy invaded seemed to calm executives in the growing number of service companies, retailers, and manufacturers that had committed themselves to building databases about their customers. The federal antiregulatory tone of the mid–1990s may have further stilled fears. In 1994 a study commissioned by the Direct Marketing Association found that the overwhelming majority of "major retailers" indicated that they "no longer saw privacy concerns of customers" as an obstacle to capturing customer data.[62]

When relationship marketers discussed guidelines to chart their future in a business where customer privacy was a settled issue, they agreed on two propositions that underscored the importance of extending divisions in American society. The first was that relationship marketers should sell to their customers with menus and prices tailored to the differences between them. "Today we are moving rapidly into marketing on the differences [between people]," a well-known consultant told *Progressive Grocer.* "With databases, you can learn those differences and adjust promotion and advertising accordingly."[63]

Building on this proposition, an executive at Spiegel Catalogs suggested that the nation was already pretty well divided in half between people who were on direct marketers' lists and those who were outside the direct-marketing loop.[64] He also noted that those targeted were continually divided further. Companies analyzed information on their best customers and used databases to clone virtual neighborhoods of people similar to them. They sold those names to other firms, who sent the same people other materials in common.

These people might or might not know they were part of those groups. They might or might not know that they were being surrounded by a growing proportion of mail and telecommunications messages that was customized for them, often based on how they had responded to other offers. They also might or might not know that only they, or people that marketers considered just like them, were getting certain ad pitches, certain kinds of coupons with certain discounts, certain options for joining clubs and acting loyally to certain brands. Either way, said an *Advertising Age* writer, "loyalty-marketing experts argue that companies must discriminate among customers." The writer quoted an expert who put the issue bluntly: "We argue strenuously, strenuously against naive sentimentalism on the part of companies who insist 'We love all our customers and we love all our customers the same.'"[65]

This emphasis on individual differences led to a second proposition about the way relationship marketing should be applied differently to different consumers. The proposition was that to maximize their profits, marketers should not only reward their very best customers, they should push away, even alienate, those who were less valuable. In these situations, people *would* know when marketers considered them part of attractive lifestyle groups.

Loyalty programs pointed the way. "Frequent flyer programs are nothing more than a means for differentiating an airline's most valuable customers from its less valuable customers," wrote two consultants.[66] As noted earlier, these programs aimed to make dedicated customers more dedicated, increasing what marketers called an airline's "share of customer." The customers that an airline wanted most to cultivate were naturally the ones that had the most business to offer the carrier. As a result, they shaped frequent-flier programs to reward them the most, offering premium levels of service to what many in the industry called "road warriors."[67]

American Airlines offered some customers the standard Red-White-Blue AAdvantage Card, others a Gold card, and still others a Platinum one, depending on the miles flown per year. In other airlines names, not colors, indicated status. Northwest, for example, had a WorldPerks Preferred card, while Continental called its top-of-the-line loyalty marker the OnePass Elite. People who did not qualify for such badges were clearly treated differently than the ones who did.[68]

For the highest tiers of customers, the rewards of continued business came not just in the form of mileage prizes. Airline computers marked them for special treatment by all employees who dealt with them. Platinum-level individuals were pampered with special privileges, convenience, and all-around solicitude. They were given low-cost upgrades to First Class or Business Class, special reservations phone lines, special check-in counters, priority baggage handling, and private airport lounge privileges.

It was a lesson not lost on hotel, telephone, car-rental, banking, and other types of companies with loyalty programs. "To maximize the value of a relationship," wrote one consultant, ". . . reward . . . long and high-purchasing customers with a VIP customer program that offers exclusive benefits and services. Make them feel like 'insiders' or 'family.' Encourage other customers to reach VIP status. Emphasize that continued high-level purchasing will maintain benefits, *while decreasing purchases will risk losing that status.*"[69]

The head of the Retail Strategy Center offered similar comments when suggesting how loyalty could be inculcated among supermarket customers. He dismissed the time-honored idea that supermarkets should charge the same prices to every customer. Instead, he championed an activity he called "Customer Specific Pricing" (CSP). Smart stores, he said, were finding ways to examine their customers' buying habits and, based on them, to offer different specials, discounts, and/or unique prices to different individuals, "depending on their past and potential value to the retailer." Some stores using CSP were even sending out personalized thank-you cards to cherished patrons. The cards were often "co-sponsored" by major manufacturers that shared an interest in associating themselves with the lifestyles and purchasing habits of these special customers.[70]

The tension of distinctions was quite evident in the upscale world of frequent fliers. Airline executives were aware that travelers hesitated to drop a frequent-flier program once they started accumulating miles. As a result, the executives felt secure that they would retain members even if they punished them—demoted individuals in card status, for example, if their annual mileage decreased. One road warrior noted that when he cut back flying on American Airlines, he was downgraded from a platinum rank to a gold one. "It was a terrible ego blow," he remembered.[71]

Airlines also distinguished between people within frequent-flier levels when it came to distributing popular perks such as upgrades. "Just for grins," said one loyalty-program expert and United Airlines traveler,

> go to an airport on a busy day at a United Airlines counter. Listen to the business men, and women too, who want to be upgraded. They want to sit in first class. 'And because I'm a 1K cardholder [they say], I should get to sit in first class.' And then it comes down to— [United is] actually able to access how good a 1K customer you are. Have you flown 500,000 or 400,000 miles. And the person with 500,000 gets the seat first.
>
> And you should see them! I have heard some of the most profane language coming out of very well-dressed businessmen because of this. They know they deserve that first class.[72]

The key to managing such anger, relationship marketers understood, was to make the customer see tension-inducing rules as almost an interpersonal issue between the company and the customer. "Failure" to get benefits within the scheme would then be a two-way rather than one-way phenomenon, a private issue resulting out of the rules of collaboration rather than one needing public remedy. The approach still could blow up into public trouble. American Airlines was hit by a class-action suit of travelers who believed that it was illegal for the company to retro-actively change the rules for round-trip awards. Still, direct practitioners believed that properly configured, tailored one-to-one interactions could keep legal discrimination in the interest of marketing a private matter.

From a relationship standpoint, a 1995 announcement to the press by First Chicago Bank can serve as an example of how to discriminate in a strategically improper way. Bank executives said they were setting a $3 per fee visit for some customers each time they used a human teller in-stead of an automated teller machine or telephone banking system. Only customers who would keep either $2,500 in a checking account or $15,000 in a combination of checking and interest-bearing accounts would continue to have free, unlimited access to human tellers.[73] The principle was one that on the whole banking industry executives ap-plauded. Large banks around the U.S. were generally trying to keep their biggest depositors with few transaction fees and a panoply of perks. At the same time, they were loading other customers with lots of costs.

Lower-income customers were often profitable for banks because they often did not meet the minimum balances needed for no-fee check-ing and so wound up paying hefty monthly and per-check fees. Bankers also found that lower-income customers were less demanding than middle-income ones, and when they bounced checks they would not plead for waivers of the charge, as many middle-class customers would do. The worst middle-class customers, according to bankers, were those whose lifestyles led them (for reasons of age, infirmity, or personality) to use live bank tellers frequently instead of bank machines. The cost of maintaining live tellers for them was making their business unprofitable.

It was these "transaction hounds," as they were known in the bank-ing industry, that First Chicago Bank was after when it promulgated its rules publicly. Apart from trying to encourage its wealthiest customers to stay, the bank was also publicly signaling that some customers were not worth the cost. Amid discussions of the economic reasons for such a decision were the inevitable grumblings that certain types of people were being singled out for greater burdens, and some for greater re-wards, than were others. "If nobody changed their behavior, 80 percent of my customers would never see the $3 charge," contended a First Chi-cago executive. "For the other 20 percent, I want one of three things to happen: I need for them to change their behavior, I need for them to be willing to pay more, or I need for them to find another bank."[74]

From a public-relations standpoint, it backfired. As long as a month after bank officials made the policy public, members of Congress were warning of boycotts and competitors were tweaking First Chicago about what it had done. Some observers suggested that bank executives had used poor rhetoric with the press in their original announcement.[75] Other banks, wanting to do the same thing, were holding back and looking for "kinder, gentler" ways to selectively reward and punish their customers, according to the *New York Times*.[76]

To relationship marketers, the solution was a no-brainer. A month before First Chicago's actions, a banking consultant in *Bank Marketing* magazine suggested that by using computers and its private customer list a bank could do what First Chicago did, but without the public fireworks. The trick was to use mass-customization technologies and loyalty programs to reward and alienate individuals on a one-to-one basis. Databases, he noted, had made it easy to determine the top 15 percent of customers. The databases had also made available ways to determine which of the mediocre customers—"the apathetic 75 percent," he called them—could be raised to top status by encouraging them to consolidate their cash, stocks, loan, and other accounts from a number of firms into the bank. The databases had also made it easy to determine which customers were not worth holding. Taken together, he observed, the considerations implied that using a bank's own channels to make its own customers more loyal—and to discourage customers who are unprofitable—should take much greater precedent than marketing outside the bank's channels through the mass media.

> Just as important as protecting and expanding the best customer relationships . . . [i]t is necessary to de-market unprofitable customer relationships. . . . As a matter of pure economics and sound profitability management, you should in fact make it very convenient [through bank procedures] for a certain percentage of your customers to bank elsewhere.
>
> . . . Market share and share of customer are not mutually exclusive but compatible concepts. As the bank's customer base continues to grow, so will the number of customer relationships included in the 15 percent group of most profitable relation-

ships. . . . [C]apturing the share of the customer market of the
bank's existing portfolio—bringing to the bank all of the products and services the existing, less profitable customer relationships maintain with bank and nonbank competition—will
provide the pipeline to expand the bank's best customer relationships. Therefore [economic thinking] requires than banks
allocate 80 percent of their sales and marketing resources to the
existing customer base and 20 percent to the mass market.
Banks are not in the business of selling corn flakes.[77]

Actually, as the previous pages have shown, even the manufacturers and
sellers of low-priced package goods were experimenting with increasing the loyalty of known customers in the 1990s. There were certainly
slipups, the most well known being the demise of Quaker Direct, the
Quaker Oats Company's ambitious 1990 attempt to reach eighteen million households with trackable coupons.[78] Nevertheless, not long after
Quaker Direct was shut, some Quaker brands returned to experimenting
with forms of relationship marketing.[79] Other firms that had also not
found the keys to relationship-marketing heaven kept trying again. Their
executives were convinced that at least some part of their firm's marketing future lay in using databases and customized interactions with consumers to encourage loyalty as well as the purchase of a wide array of the
firm's products.

The growth of direct marketing was among the developments in the
1980s and 1990s that made executives in television, radio, newspapers,
and other media nervous. They saw the mail, telemarketing, and in-store
promotions drawing unprecedented cash. They knew that the idea of
data-based, interactive relationships with individuals was gaining popularity among marketers. But they knew, too, that presenting news, information, and entertainment in individually tailored formats that could
draw tailored ads presented formidable challenges.

Of the traditional print and electronic industries, the magazine business was the quickest to adapt to the interest in customization. In the
vanguard was a venerable agricultural business periodical, *Farm Journal*.
From the 1950s, its management had been searching for sophisticated
ways to send different versions of an issue to subscribers with different
crops or animals. The breakthrough came in 1982, when the invention

of a new computer-driven binding system enabled the company to put together customized contents to match the special farming needs and interests of each of its 825,000 readers as noted in a database gathered in periodic telephone surveys. By the early 1990s, each *Farm Journal* issue was coming out in two to three thousand different versions, though the record was 8,896 concatenations for a single issue. Moreover, advertisers had the option of matching their ads to the individual subscriber profile. So makers of hog-farm equipment and supplies could talk only to hog farmers, with no waste in circulation.[80]

Three consumer magazines, *Games, American Baby,* and *Modern Maturity,* soon followed *Farm Journal's* lead, though not in quite so ambitious a manner. At the turn of the 1990s, *American Baby* was offering its advertisers an ability to divide its 1.1 million readers into new parents and parents-soon-to-be (including expected birth date), based on information provided by new subscribers. As a result, the Gerber baby food company ran different personalized ad messages in the magazines for mothers of two- to three-month-old infants and mothers whose babies had reached three to four months. The ads featured the appropriate product for each age group.[81]

Signs that the industry was really moving in a new direction came when Time Magazines, Inc., subsidiary of Time Warner and the nation's largest magazine publisher, made a decision to enter the business of selective binding and imaging. Initially, *Time, Sports Illustrated, People,* and *Money* magazines used the technology for advertisers alone. The magazine firm reportedly spent two years assembling the equipment and gaining the data-management expertise needed for the job. At a premium price, an advertiser could specify that its ads should go to certain individual subscribers and not to others, depending on the advertiser's needs and the information about the readers in a Time Warner database. Moreover, using ink-jet printing technology, the advertiser could alter on-page copy to reflect the information in the database.[82]

Marketers seized on the idea quickly.

• In 1993, for example, Philip Morris worked to match its cigarette customer list with the magazine subscriber lists of several Time Warner magazines with the goal of sending ads to cigarette smokers only.

• A year later, the targeting got even more specific in an ad campaign for the new Chrysler Cirrus that took aim at Japanese auto competitors.

Time Warner researchers matched car registration from R. L. Polk and Company with subscription lists from *Time, Sports Illustrated, Money,* and *Life*. As a result, owners of four-year-old and newer Honda Accords, Toyota Camrys, and Nissan Altimas received an eight-page insert with detailed Cirrus product information bound into the November issues of those magazines. While auto marketers previously had aimed magazine ads at specific zip codes, the Chrysler-Time Magazines venture marked the first time a campaign had had "this degree of specificity," according to a Time Warner spokesperson.[83]

• In 1995, Time Warner's database was used to create a lifestyle model that would predict car-buying choices. The effort, for Chevrolet's Cavalier, involved *Time, People, Sports Illustrated, Entertainment Weekly,* and *Life*. Again matching Polk car registration data with Time Warner's demographic and lifestyle information, Chevrolet's agency developed a mathematical model for which subscribers were seen to be Cavalier coupe or sedan prospects. Each of the fourteen million subscribers to the five publications received an ad for either a coupe or a sedan, depending on what the model concluded about their buying interests.

While customized printing was primarily the province of ads in consumer magazines during the early 1990s, it began to be used in editorial matter as well. *Sports Illustrated* in January 1994 began selectively inserting a special sixteen-page section, "Golf Plus," at no extra cost into the issues of a portion of its readership. The magazine decided whom to target by first sending questionnaires to all its subscribers. Through the responses, it was able to identify 400,000 hard-core golfers and learn their playing habits, golf equipment, and other information that would attract advertisers. "Golf Plus" showed up in about forty-two of fifty-two issues.

Several months later, in the fall of 1994, the magazine went further with another four-page insert, "NFL-Plus." For this section, about 800,000 subscribers paid an extra $5.20 a year for inserts about their favorite divisions or teams during the football season. A Seattle Seahawks fan living in Philadelphia, for example, was able to request more detailed coverage of the team than was available in the regular magazine.[84]

Going further, *Time* began to regularly tailor its national section to inform subscribers how their particular members of Congress voted on certain issues. The company's executives saw such expensive activities as necessary for preserving their business. "The future of marketing will be more and more characterized by the ability to create a relationship with your [individual] customer," said an executive. "The magazine can become the primary vehicle for making this happen."[85]

By mid-decade, the president of Time Magazines estimated that about 10 to 15 percent of its advertisers were using the company's database for marketing. Other magazine companies were following its lead. Conde Nast, publisher of *Vogue, Vanity Fair,* and the *New Yorker,* among others, was finding that dangling its database in front of advertisers could overcome their reluctance to buy space without bargaining over the price. Selective binding and segmented subscribers were becoming popular across the consumer magazine spectrum. One executive opined that computer customization would be required in an inevitable competition between media over differentiating audiences. "Magazines will have to fight hard against other media," he said.[86]

Hard news and information providers also were beginning to have some success at customizing their products in the mid–1990s. Unlike magazines, the success was in electronic delivery rather than printing. While news companies did deliver papers with sections of articles and ads keyed to different neighborhoods, the papers were not keying their editorial matter and ads to different people. Instead, the cutting edge was in electronic clipping services personalized to match the needs of individuals.

• The Los Angeles Times Syndicate sold *Financial Fax.* For a subscription charge of $12 a month, a customer would receive daily information about up to fifteen stocks the customer wanted tracked along with a small (two-by-three-inch) advertising message.[87]

• The Reuters Money Network, an online computer service, searched daily in a variety of sources for business topics that the subscriber deemed important. Users could specify areas of interest, and Reuters could create what it called a "personalized newspaper" of current articles on the subject.[88]

• Dow Jones offered two services. The less expensive of the two, called *Personal Journal,* allowed subscribers to list ten subjects (companies, topics) that the company would retrieve for them every weekday from the firm's *Wall Street Journal* and the Dow Jones News Service. Subscribers would access these articles by computer through a local number or an 800 number. The more pricey service, called Clip, searched a larger number of topics from a larger number of sources and deposited them into an electronic folder which the subscriber could access by computer.

• An entrepreneurial venture called Individual Incorporated offered three information products customized to individual and corporate requests. *First!*, with a price over $5,000 a year, was aimed at corporations for distribution over their computer networks. *HeadsUp,* which cost about $70 a month, was sold to executives on an individual basis. *iNews,* the least expensive at about $15 a month plus $2 a page, was aimed at occasional users and included fewer news sources than *First!* or *HeadsUp.* In 1995, Individual announced that its *iNews* personalized news service would go on Microsoft's new online network, MSN. "Individual's advanced filtering technologies and broad access to news sources will be of great benefit to MSN members by delivering to them their own personal, daily newspaper," a press release quoted Microsoft's general manager for online services.[89]

These tailored information services made money straddling the fence between business and consumer audiences. Almost all the activities in this realm were experiments. There were lots of those, and it was still unclear which would come out on top.

It *was* clear that whoever came out on top, the project to fractionate society would continue. In the presence of signaling, relationship marketing, and tailored media, upscale individuals were more and more being encouraged into media worlds that rewarded their distinctive lifestyles by reflecting the lifestyles back at them. With just a little effort (habit, actually), they listened to radio stations, read magazines, and watched cable programs that paraded their self-images and clusters of concerns. With no seeming effort at all, they received offers from marketers that complemented their lifestyles. And with just a bit of cash, they paid for technologies that could further tailor information to their interests.

This environment was certainly not total; the people could seek other media interests, and even block direct-marketing blandishments from reaching them, if they chose. Increasingly, though, the easier choice was to go with the familiar flow of media and marketing paraphernalia. Moreover, in the face of the daily tensions of work, family, and immediate community, it might be difficult to turn down marketers' proposal to set an environmental climate control that blocked out what was not directly relevant and reflected only the small world the individuals really cared about.

In the future, it might be possible that individuals at a variety of income levels could enjoy media that marketers would fashion just for them. Still, with so many media and marketers reveling in differentiation, how many would stress similarities among people and urge them to cross the fissures that they saw appearing all around them? Was an image of America being built into the new media world one in which people addled by fractionalization inside and outside the media would simply retire to their own tailored environments and give up caring about people who didn't fit?

Rare were the marketing practitioners who even came close to raising these questions in the mid–1990s. They were more interested in making sure that the elements of the emerging media world would come together in a way that would suit them. What role, if any, should the traditional broadcast TV networks play? How should relationship marketers approach niche cable television channels? Where should interactive technologies fit in? Through their discussions, though, they did express a vision of where they and the media had come from and where they wanted it to go. As the next chapter will show, it was a vision that took signaling, tailoring, and social segmentation even further in the name of efficient marketing.

SEVEN

PLANNING A FRACTURED FUTURE

"**OUR MOST IMPORTANT AD** medium, television, is about to change big time, and we have one whale of a stake in these changes. From where we stand today, we can't be sure that advertising-supported TV programming will have a future in the world being created . . ."[1]

If uttered by any number of futurists during the 1980s and early 1990s, these words would have been either mildly accepted or shrugged off by media and advertising executives, depending on their point of view on the urgency of new-media changes. As delivered by Edwin Artzt to the American Association of Advertising Agencies, though, the speech caused an unprecedented stir. For Artzt was the chairman of Proctor and Gamble, the world's largest advertiser. P&G was pumping more than $3 *billion* annually into advertising—and 90 percent of it into network television advertising—to keep brands such as Tide, Pampers, and Crest in the forefront of American consumers' minds. When top Proctor and Gamble executives spoke, the ad industry listened carefully.

Now, in May 1994, Artzt declared that his firm and others were in danger of losing the ability to get Americans' attention because marketers and their agencies had not ensured that the new-media world would be advertiser-friendly. He worried that the firms generating new-media experiences were moving down a road that would allow Americans to turn away from commercials. He shuddered at a vision of cable-, satellite-, and telephone-delivered television with pay-per-view programming. He trembled at the notion of virtual home shopping malls and interactive CD-ROMs that people would buy and pay for themselves.

"There is," he warned, "a very real possibility that the majority of programs people will be watching will not be advertiser supported."

By all accounts, the speech made a deep impression on the ad-agency owners, creative directors, and CEOs who comprised the 4A audience. One observer wrote that they sat in "uncomfortable silence" as Artzt sketched a scenario "that was nothing less than American Advertising Agency Apocalypse."[2] Afterwards, many disagreed with Artzt that advertisers had to fear that a new media scene could arise without their help. Others pointed out that ad agencies, and even the 4A, had already been quietly doing some of what Artzt was enlisting them to do.

Nevertheless, his concerns did spark a lot of discussion within ad agencies and in the trade press on the strategies that marketers should take toward the evolving media world. The discussions encouraged more visible action than before on the part of agencies and advertisers to work toward an environment that would reflect their interests. Leaders of traditional ad agencies, looking for a key role in that environment, pushed the idea that they could help coordinate the new vision. Focusing their predictions primarily on the short term, they left it up to other groups—new-media executives and direct-marketing consultants, especially—to elaborate the future. These, in turn, forecast a system of entertainment, news, information, and advertising that would profoundly change the way even package-goods companies relate to consumers.

Both the short- and long-term prognostications built their assumptions about the future on notions of America that marketing people had been advancing during the 1980s and 1990s, as described in earlier chapters. The basic proposition was that society was increasingly fractured, frenetic, suspicious, and individually self-indulgent, and that emerging media were reflecting that. Ad people believed that their role was not to challenge this idea or to work against it. Rather, it was to exploit it for their own purposes by making sure they could signal target audiences and customize commercial messages for them in as many media as possible. The visions that resulted pointed marketers in directions of both the targeted signaling that chapter 5 described and the customized approach to advertising elucidated in chapter 6. Inevitably, all advertisers were converging on a direct-marketing view of the world in which the ability to "slice and dice" a population, to quote one consultant,[3] was far more important than the ability to bring it together.

The Artzt speech was perhaps most remarkable because the P&G chairman expressed his certainty that advertisers had passed the point of no return when it came to media fragmentation. P&G was the quintessential mass marketer of package goods, trying to reach "everybody" as often as possible in the most efficient way possible. Artzt admitted that Proctor and Gamble, in a given year, had to sell four hundred million boxes of Tide. To do that, he said, the firm had to reach its consumers over and over throughout the year. The only way to do *that*, he insisted, was with "broad-reach television."[4]

Still, to Artzt there was no naysaying the fact that the opportunities given consumers to get audiovisual images apart from broadcast TV were growing by leaps and bounds. Commercial online services were claiming that by the end of 1994 they would have six million subscribers. Their revenue, $795 million in 1994, was expected by forecasters to jump to $1.7 billion by 1998. Interactive television in 1994 was a $37-million-a-year business and was predicted to grow to $4.2 billion in 1998. Wholesale earnings for the CD-ROM industry was likewise expected to soar from 1994 to 1998, from $2.5 to $3.5 billion.[5]

So while Artzt believed in the importance of broadcast TV, he also believed he had to consider these new options for consumers. In his speech, he suggested that he was willing to consider a variety of methods beyond the major networks to get the "broad reach" the firm needed. Proctor and Gamble had already begun to use customer-segmentation and target-marketing techniques. What worried P&G's chairman primarily was not that new technologies would encourage more targeted or tailored advertising. Rather, it was that emerging media technologies were giving people the opportunity to escape from advertising's grasp altogether.

As Artzt saw it, the issue had been brewing for twenty years. Back in the 1970s, he said, ABC, CBS, and NBC were successful at creating a flow of programs that would discourage viewers from getting up and changing the channel. Of course, advertisers had long been aware that commercials gave viewers the opportunity to go to the kitchen, the bathroom, or simply see what was playing on another channel. Often, though, they stayed in their chairs. Artzt insisted that the strategy helped advertisers as well as the networks.

He quoted Barry Diller, who at the time owned the QVC home-shopping channel, as noting that the power of the lineup to hold audiences to a channel began to diminish in the 1970s. According to Diller, the culprit was the remote channel changer. The "remote" led viewers to emphasize individual shows and pay less attention to channel flow as they surfed their increasing number of channels and sometimes ignored commercials altogether. But, warned Artzt, "remote controls were just the beginning. They'll soon be replaced by program navigational services that will fundamentally change the dynamics of TV viewing."

> These "navigators" will be heavily-marketed subscription services. They'll tell viewers what's on tonight—and more. They'll know the kinds of programs a viewer likes. They'll even remember everything a viewer has watched.
>
> TCI is now working with TV Guide to develop a navigator called "On-Screen TV Guide." Their vision is that subscribers will go immediately to their navigator channel whenever they turn on the TV. And the navigator will have done its homework—it'll recommend a lineup of programming, drawn from this three or five hundred channel universe. It may even recommend two or three alternative lineups. And once viewers have said, "OK," they won't even need their remote. The navigator will turn channels for them.[6]

Artzt saw a gaggle of navigational tools emerging in what was being called interactive television, where the viewer could send back a message and get an immediate response. Viacom was testing Star Sight while Bell Atlantic was developing Stargazer. These services, he predicted, would "rapidly erode the whole idea of channel identity." Network lineups would be replaced by navigator lineups. The idea of a spot on the dial would no longer be important, or even relevant. Signaling to viewers and tailoring to them would be done only around individual programs.

That, said Artzt, could drastically affect the ability of advertisers to get their messages across. Without network lineups to keep people tuned to a particular channel, ad spots between programs could easily disappear. ("Right now," he noted, "these spots represent 15% of TV advertising.") He added that "another chilling thought" was the "very real possibility that the majority of programs people watch will not be advertiser supported. Pay-per-view movies are a good example. People will flock to these because they offer all the functionality of home video plus the convenience of never leaving home."[7]

Tom Murphy, the chairman of Capital Cities/ABC, presented one solution to the P&Gs of the world: Resist the new media and help the broadcast networks preserve their power. "If we got down [with television] to the point [of fractionalized audiences] where . . . radio is today," Murphy claimed, "then the cost of delivering advertising messages . . . would be very, very high." That, he continued, would make it difficult to introduce new products, since reaching huge numbers of people would become an expensive chore. Murphy implied that P&G should not support the kind of channel fragmentation that would severely undermine the major broadcast networks and their still-huge audiences.

Artzt sounded somewhat sympathic to that argument. But he clearly believed that P&G's role was not to fight a rear-guard holding action against developments he felt were inevitable as consumers began using these new services. "What we've learned," he said, "is that what people want is choice, convenience, and control. And they're willing to pay a fair premium to the programmers and media suppliers that meet these needs."[8]

Artzt, like most marketers, had little doubt that the multiplicity of choices that new-media enthusiasts were predicting would materialize. The growing number of electronic options, these enthusiasts argued, would come from a wide spectrum of news, sports, shopping, and information sources, not from what people traditionally called entertainment. Moreover, they suggested, the notion of entertainment would broaden in the new media environment beyond traditional TV series and feature films to include games. Observers who doubted the feasibility of so many choices tended to argue that costs of creating "network quality" programming would be too high to be supported by relatively small target audiences. Yet those people ignored the rapidly growing trend to consider the worldwide market in the revenue streams of media materials in the 1990s. U.S. producers such as Disney were cranking up production to create huge libraries in anticipation of worldwide payoff. Similarly, companies in Europe and Asia were poised to contribute to a flood of audiovisual options targeted to different population niches in America and elsewhere.[9]

"The question is," Artzt emphasized, "if [consumers] get what they want—and I have no doubt that they will—how will they use television? And what will it mean for advertising?" He exhorted his audience to work toward answers. He paid homage to the personal computer "as a formidable future vehicle for advertising and even programming," and he said CD-ROMs and online services were "bound to produce major changes in marketing goods and services to the public." He reminded his audience that the advertising industry had worked in the past to shape the media to their needs. He urged both the 4A and the Association of National Advertisers to move urgently to consider how the new world would impact advertising and how they could shape it to the ad world's benefit. "We may not get another opportunity like this in our lifetime," he said. "Let's grab all this new technology in our teeth once again and turn it into a bonanza for advertising."[10]

On the record, individuals who were in Artzt's audience voiced their approval of his talk. That was understandable. It would have been dangerous for any major ad-agency executive to publicly pick a fight with the world's largest advertiser. Moreover, P&G had a track record for changing media and advertising. Many who listened to the speech might have remembered that during the early 1980s P&G had been a powerful force in establishing the legitimacy of cable television and home video as advertising vehicles.[11] The company had also been instrumental in forging new units of TV commercial time and new rules for the way merging agencies should think about potentially conflicting clients.[12] While not bringing that up, Artzt did remind his audience that P&G had been in the forefront of setting the agenda of the advertising-media relationship going back to the company's creation of the soap opera for radio. His message was clear: When P&G decided to act, many other major advertisers acted. And ad agencies had to follow.

But a number of agency executives said privately that Artzt's fears were unwarranted. They insisted that the new media would not be able to survive without ads and that their creators could be brought to understand that. The executives added that they and their colleagues were troubled by the broad sweep of Artzt's assertion that agencies were doing little to bring their clients into the new-media environment. They were particularly stung by his claims to the *New York Times* that ad agencies were "a bit reactionary about the rapid onset of all this change." The P&G chairman had said after his speech that agency executives were reluctant to explore the utility of new technologies out of a fear that by helping to bring down the traditional media they would be helping to erode their traditional sources of revenue.[13]

"We were all frankly quite annoyed," one executive who was interviewed for this study said, reflecting on discussions that people from several agencies had about the speech. She added that some of her counterparts had said "well, maybe we're not getting enough publicity. Maybe people don't realize what we're [already] doing."

Another executive, co-director of interactive development at the Bozell agency, noted that the 4A already had a committee to study new-media issues before the P&G chairman's exhortation that such a committee should exist. She added that many agencies had been exploring advertising via emerging technologies through various committees in small "pockets" of their firms. They were doing it secretly so that they could stay ahead of their competitors in understanding new media and impressing clients. It was too bad, she said, that the P&G chairman had not recognized their efforts.[14]

Suzanne Kaufman, executive vice president and director of new technologies at N. W. Ayer and Partners' Media Edge unit, agreed that much was being done behind the scenes. What some took as conservative, even reactionary thinking was to her the complex process of separating futuristic wheat from chaff. Kaufman said that ad agencies had a responsibility to their clients to disentangle the hype about new media from the actual benefit they brought to advertisers. Much of the criticism that the major ad agencies were neglecting future technology was coming, she suggested, from members of small new-media startup firms who were angry that the agencies were not supporting them with advertisers' money.

She said that in the early 1990s she was frequently visited by technology wizards from those companies. They had proposals—for example, an interactive travel guide—that they were hoping her client, AT&T, would sponsor. The problem, Kaufman noted, was that her visitors typically had no idea about the needs of major advertisers from the standpoint of audience verification. Moreover, they demanded as much as half a million dollars for an advertising spot carried by an unknown media product that had not even gotten off the ground. She was sure that the money request was based not on any real consideration of the value of their activity to AT&T but on the idea that AT&T was rich and could support startups. Sent away empty-handed, those technology wizards "come back to the press and say advertising agencies have no imagination. They really don't want to use new media." So, she concluded, "I think you need to look at where that criticism is coming from."[15]

Criticism of the large ad agencies was also coming from direct competitors: so-called "interactive specialists" that offered their services to help marketers plan and create materials for online services, CD-ROM, and interactive television. Modem Media and Onramp were among the most prominent of these small firms. They were in the business of setting up home pages on the Web and designing them to attract target audiences. They also helped their clients buy space on other home pages that could reach compatible audiences and lead them to the client's own home page.

That kind of expertise available outside a traditional agency threatened to diminish the value of agency planners in the new-media environment. It also threatened ad agencies in another key area: creative work. In fact, a variety of developments of the late 1980s and early 1990s challenged the accepted notion that ad agencies were the font of aesthetics in the service of marketing. Infomercial companies, direct marketing firms, event marketing firms, and even Hollywood talent agencies were nibbling at the ad agencies' role in creating commercial messages. The sky was not falling, but some industry leaders clearly felt that the potential for disaster did exist.

In 1995, Martin Sorrell, the head of the powerful British ad conglomerate WPP, offered the opinion that advertising agencies could be put out of business by the coming of interactive media.[16] Allen Rosenshine, the chairman of the BBDO Worldwide agency, felt compelled to give a speech to the International Association of Advertising Agencies in which he disputed Sorrell's claim.[17] *Advertising Age* owner and columnist Rance Crain suggested the same year that as marketers took increasing responsibility for their interactions with the public they were finding agencies more and more irrelevant.[18] The ad-agency world seemed to be in the throes of an identity crisis.

Suzanne Kaufman and others noted that part of the way for a large agency to present an image of being secure with its role in the 1990s was to show expertise in the new media. Agency executives realized that in many cases clients' determination to explore experimental media was part of their own agenda for prestige. "You've got marketing execs who want to do this because it's going to look good for their marketing department or their résumé," said one agency executive. Agency people felt they had to join them even though the work brought few concrete rewards. "If they don't participate," noted *Advertising Age*, "they leave the door open for interactive specialists [such as Modem Media] to steal the business. It's also a tacit admission the agency is not up to snuff in new media."[19]

As a result, raiding other agencies' clients to be their "agencies of record" for interactive media became a status symbol in 1994 and 1995. Far from trying to stultify new-media growth, a growing number of ad-agency leaders began to see the Internet, CD-ROM, and other high-tech platforms as avenues that could lead them to new credibility and long-term profits. With the Artzt talk as catalyst, their public and private discussions about harnessing these areas grew.

They tried to increase their legitimacy by arguing that, unlike the specialty organizations that might be aiming to edge them out, they were uniquely able to carry out two interconnected activities. One was the development of strategies that allowed for the best possible coordination of new and old media to meet clients' audience-targeting needs. The second was the encouragment of ratings systems that would give credibility to the use of interactive media for marketing. Both tacks took for granted the proposition that, used properly, these tools would help clients keep on top of a fragmenting America by learning where the consumers they wanted were and acting to target them with the right message at the right time.

Ed Artzt was certainly not the only executive fixated on controlling America's transition from an era of mass-market television to an era of target-market, interactive video. Interest among advertisers in new media was reaching what *USA Today* called a "fever pitch" as more consumers were purchasing high-tech equipment for their homes.[20] Philip Guarascio, vice president and general manager of marketing and advertising for General Motors' North American operations, was one of those laying out millions of dollars to experiment with what they hoped would be cutting-edge ways to forge relationships with their customers. He argued that the primary job of agencies ought to be helping clients to make sense of the new-media forest "as idea makers and strategic partners."[21]

Comments such as these were echoed by other marketing leaders. Not so gently, they gave ad-agency executives the word that their ability to remain major players in the decades that followed would depend on an ability to come up with planning advice and creative work for a much larger part of the media than was traditionally the case. To do that properly, agency people would have to dramatically change their idea of what advertising was and could be.

It wasn't a wholly new notion. Now and again during the previous two decades, writers in trade magazines and speakers at conferences had urged ad people to realize that the proliferation of new media and the changing nature of American society were making standard ways of describing their work outdated. The most common target was the practice of thinking of advertising as the distribution of discrete commercial messages to target audiences through paid media. Critics pointed out that the approach separated "advertising" from other important ways to communicate with intended groups—for example, public relations, sponsored events, the telephone and the mail, even gossip ("word-of-mouth" in the marketing business).[22]

As chapters 5 and 6 have shown, by the 1990s many marketers were involved in a range of communication activities that could be brought together in an integrated package. A buzz word for this activity which was increasingly popular beginning in the late 1980s was integrated marketing. Several colleges, including Northwestern University's journalism school, even offered a degree in the subject. It was still unclear to many executives, though, whether an ad agency or some other company would be the best organization to take the lead in bringing these diverse efforts into a coherent shape. A number of ad-agency leaders argued that this ought to be their role. They were struggling to make sense of their position in an emerging environment where discrete ads in paid media were increasingly giving way to event-marketing and other promotional efforts.[23] Consequently, they argued that their firms' expertise in media planning and creative thinking positioned them as the logical parties to work hand in hand with their clients on integrated-marketing efforts in the new media world.

Arnie Semsky, executive vice president and worldwide media director at the BBDO Worldwide agency, put the case in a way that emphasized an agency's ability to bring together what he called a variety of "communications options"—traditional and nontraditional ad routes to the public—in the client's interest. Ad-agency practitioners, he noted, were beginning to make sure that the selection of these options preceded decisions about what the message should be like.

> In the past, agencies set marketing objectives, developed copy strategies and creative executions and, finally, moved to planning and buying media. Today, a new way of thinking is emerging. Agencies are being asked to develop broad communications strategies.
>
> First, we address key media questions, such as who the target audience is; then we identify communications options that best reach that audience. Only then do we move on to what we will say and how we'll say it.[24]

Semsky and others suggested that to survive the ad agency had to become an operations center that guided marketers toward targeted consumers in an enormously fractured, changing environment. The integrated-marketing perspective directly addressed Artzt's fear that some media would not carry traditional ads. An ad agency's territory was now every kind of message that could sell a product, paid for or not. Magazine ads, newspaper ads, radio commercials, in-store marketing, direct mail, telephone selling, sponsored events, and public relations activities—these and other approaches would have to be used in a coordinated manner to make sure that quick-moving target consumers would come into contact with the sales messages that would be relevant to them in as many places as possible. Coordination of all communication options meant using any medium that helped in the strategy—from buying commercial time on a cable channel, to placing a product in a movie aimed at a certain audience, to arranging for stories about the product to appear in targeted magazines, to arranging for coupons on Catalina supermarket checkout systems.

From a self-promotion standpoint, adopting this integrated perspective allowed major ad agencies to argue they had become legitimate platforms for helping to organize their clients' "communication options" whenever new options arose. It would allow agencies and clients "competitive leverage," Semsky said, in a media environment that would continue to fragment. The growing marketing possibilities implied in interactive media were an example. "[F]or the foreseeable future," he told *Advertising Age,* "the media environment will be governed by one word—more. Around the world, we'll see more media, primarily electronic, more direct selling to consumers, more interrelated communications and more customer interactivity." [25]

Ad-agency leaders moved quickly after the Artzt speech to show that they were shaping the burgeoning interactive environment and tying it to their integrated model. One major way they did that was through an organization they formed in response to the speech. The organization was called CASIE—the Coalition for Advertising Supported Information and Entertainment. Its members came from the interactive divisions of major ad agencies and pointedly excluded their upstart cyberspace competitors. A primary Coalition goal, according to Bozell agency executive and CASIE member Judy Black, was to make sure firms shepherding interactive television, online services, and other technologies understand "that the consumer is not going to support this new world of media. And that advertising is going to be needed to make this environment happen." [26]

It didn't take much jawboning. Even telephone companies, which historically could count only Yellow Pages in their advertising experience, were building advertising revenues into their future plans. BellSouth, for example, formed an advertiser advisory board to help design an experimental interactive television system in the Atlanta area. [27] As for the computer domain, many of the most ambitious content providers for online services and CD-ROM were giant media firms that had been making money off advertising for decades in magazines, newspapers, broadcast television, cable TV, direct mail, and other media. They saw their movement to the new technologies of the '90s as no different from their movement to cable TV and database marketing when these were new. Their actions were based on the conviction that competition would cause advertising in one form or another to spread inevitably beyond their traditional bases and that they had to follow it or lose revenues.

A number of months after the formation of CASIE, several media giants even saw a common interest in creating a trade association that would nudge agencies and their advertisers to move more rapidly to support their online activities. Called the Cyberspace Content Coalition (CCC), its founding members were the interactive divisions of Time Warner, Hearst, the Tribune Company, the *Washington Post,* Reuters, and Newhouse Newspapers. Also a member was *Wired* magazine, which had shown strong interest in garnering advertising for its HotWired site on the World Wide Web.[28]

An immediate need that the CCC identified was to standardize advertising formating rules on Web sites to make it easier for ad agencies to place the same ads or hyperlinks on different sites. "Advertisers and content providers are anxious for ways to play in the new media that gives them some efficiency," said the general manager of Hearst's HomeArts Web site, which drew for content on the firm's upscale magazines about the home. "There aren't many standards in the marketplace. Everyone is trying something new and we'd like to all share that information so we can learn from each other."[29]

That was very much the attitude that CASIE members wanted to hear. In the course of their first year, they had laid the groundwork for a full-scale surge of advertisers into the fabric of emerging technologies by working on three areas: creating a legislative/regulatory game plan that would ensure advertisers' ability to reach whomever they wanted, understanding the spread of new media among consumers, and finding ways to measure consumer activities with new media.

The first area spoke to Artzt's concerns that government rulemaking or funding of new media might somehow make it harder for advertisers to control them. The Coalition's position was that business competition and advertising, not government taxes and subsidies, were the best ways to ensure that Americans could afford access to the information superhighway. Education and social service groups, CASIE said, wanted to be on the dole, "saying they would like to be put on this information superhighway and would need government support to get there."[30] CASIE urged the cash-strapped Clinton administration to think of advertisers as a refreshing contrast.

At one hearing of the U.S. Commerce Department's Telecommunications Information Administration, a P&G executive in charge of advertising and information services represented CASIE in making a blunt pitch for the full inclusion of advertising on the information superhighway. If the Administration were to succeed in its aim of guaranteeing universal access to that highway, he said, then ad-supported programming was the only way to go. Without ad subsidies, the cost of participation would be so great that only a select few would be able to afford it, while the less moneyed would be stranded at the side of the road.

He dramatized the industry's affordability argument, saying the average monthly household TV bill would be $350 without the $30 billion that advertisers currently spend every year to support programming. "Where entertainment or information is offered viewers at a price, advertising will enable them to be provided at the lowest practical cost," he added. "Additionally, we anticipate there will be consumer interest in advertising support for many other services that may become available to consumers over the highway." [31]

CASIE was interested in monitoring that interest as well as the general interest of consumers in media without ads. One report that the Coalition commissioned pointed out that in 1995 86 percent of U.S. households had VCRs and that more than a quarter of those households rented movies very often—six a month, on average. A third of American households had video games. Nearly a third had home computers; 7 percent were subscribing to online services. The average household with a computer spent almost nine hours a week on it for non-business purposes. The head of the firm that wrote the report concluded that "all of this [use of other media] means less time for television" with traditional ads. [32] Here were areas that advertisers had to penetrate.

But penetration was only the tip of an iceberg of business issues regarding new-media audiences that ad-agency executives believed they had to address. They saw measurement of interactive media as a way to help their clients and themselves. They knew that ad-agency executives had historically enhanced their reputations with clients by insisting that third parties, not media firms, should be the ones monitoring audiences for marketers. They undoubtedly also realized that in the past the start of credible ratings marked a watershed for a developing medium. It was, for example, only after agencies along with their advertisers pressured cable networks to agree to accepting Nielsen's People Meter as a measure of viewership that cable advertising really took off in the mid–1980s. [33]

Consequently, CASIE members and advertisers that supported them made it clear that serious money could come to the interactive media only if a ratings system was put in place that satisfied the researchers and planners at major agencies. If network TV had its Nielsens, if magazines had their Audit Bureau of Circulation and Simmons figures, if radio had its Arbitrons, then it stood to reason to agency people that interactive programming coming through cable TV sets, computer online services, and CD-ROM vehicles should have their routine audits, too.

In February 1995, CASIE suggested that a universal standard be developed for measuring the use of computers and interactive TV. While executives from large ad agencies saw the recommendation as a triumphant step, the cyber-agencies that were making their fame crafting Web pages and online plans seemed to see CASIE's measurement proposal as part of a broad-ranging attempt to co-opt their world. A Modem Media executive claimed that marketers already had all the relevant data about users of their Web pages, since the computer devices (called servers) that kept their material on the Web also tracked usage. Several firms, including Modem Media, were analyzing these data for their clients with proprietary software.

"There's no need to go anywhere else," the Modem Media executive argued. "Employing a third party to authenticate usage is a print- or TV-based model, which has only limited use in this medium." Bringing the struggle between the new and old world into the open, he added that traditional agencies "don't know the first thing what this stuff is all about." He also opined that "[i]t's in the interest of the Arbitrons and Nielsens of the world to control the data because that's how they make money."[34]

CASIE members naturally had a different viewpoint. The overall aim, they emphasized, was not just to monitor the way people use individual "screens" of entertainment, information, news, or marketing content on computers and interactive TV. Just as important, the goal was to understand the patterns whereby different types of users moved from one screen of content to another. They announced two major guidelines for such a system. One was that it should track the ways that individual remote-control and mouse users interact with their television or computer screens. The other was that this auditing system should accommodate second-by-second measurements of online or interactive television usage, as opposed to the fifteen-second increments that were standard for conventional TV.

CASIE moved quickly to show what it wanted. In March 1995, the Coalition rolled out a measuring service that it said conformed to its guidelines. Called the Interactive Information Index, it was created by a firm ad-agency executives trusted—Arbitron—in conjection with two smaller firms. General Motors announced it would support trials of the Index, and BellSouth followed quickly. Not to be outdone, Nielsen, another firm traditional agencies felt they could depend on, weighed in with its own system and said that it had support from phone companies trying to track consumer activities during their experimental tests of interactive video.[35] Both the Arbitron and Nielsen tools derived their power from tracking the content associated with clicks of the TV remote controls and computer mouse.

This "clickstream" auditing technique built into the evaluation of new media an approach to media audiences that had become the norm among agencies and their clients in the 1980s and early 1990s. Traditional advertising categories such as "general household TV viewing" and "magazine subscriber profile" had given way during that time to emphasis on every individual "user" of a medium within the household, including guests. Ad people broke up the household into gender, age, and income (including kids' spending) categories; they related each of these categories to lifestyle activities; and they compared their findings across racial, ethnic, regional, and other lines.

The clickstream method also reflected that advertisers' conceptions of Americans as rabidly mobile had reached a new level. Gone was the notion of the 1980s that the American family's growing freneticism manifested itself primarily *outside* the home. Agency researchers were convinced that in the mid–1990s individuals were becoming fast-moving targets even in the house, with zappers and clickers shifting quickly from screen to screen on the TV set and computer. The realization convinced them that the People Meter's ability for tracking viewing changes every fifteen seconds was anachronistic and that second-by-second measurement was needed.[36]

CASIE members believed that when integrated with audits of those other media by firms such as Nielsen and Arbitron, the new measurements would allow a level of signaling previously unheard of by marketers. Media outlets and marketers saw themselves applying the tactics discussed in chapter 5 to computer home pages and highly fragmented TV programming. With more accuracy and specificity than before, they could urge populations and even individuals in an increasingly fragmented society to consider that particular media and product images spoke most clearly to people like them.

Leaders of the direct-marketing world, including those from direct-marketing subsidiaries of traditional agencies, boasted that they could go even further in targeting than that. Stressing the interactive aspect of the new TV and computer technologies, they said they could now fulfill a direct marketer's dream: to bring the complex tracking and relationship-building activities used in direct-mail and telephone work to the heart of electronic media. Using even more sophisticated databases than before, they would be able to go beyond signaling to start actual conversations with individuals of specific demographics, interests, values, and activities; to tailor responses that matched the individuals' concerns; and even to get similar customers to interact with one another.

As chapter 6 showed, three key words in direct practitioners' lexicon of the 1990s were *relationship, difference,* and *customization*. It was not that direct marketers held that the mainstream advertising industry was always wrong to signal to targeted groups of consumers through an integrated-marketing plan of events, public relations, and promotions. To them, such activities might be used to find new customers. They believed that ultimately, though, the best way to complete a sale and inspire customer loyalty was to contact each person in those targeted groups directly through mass-customization techniques. Their aim would be to exploit an ongoing dialogue with consumers about the product and the company to learn how each one could be impelled to continue buying, and to buy more than in the past.

"Our consumer targets must be differentiated and specific," said direct-marketing guru Lester Wunderman in 1993. He noted that many media corporations were building new media around direct-marketing principles. He quoted Marshall McLuhan's prediction that "instead of peddling mass-produced commodities, advertising is going to become a personal service to each individual." And he predicted that the direct practitioners would rise above an underappreciated past and guide marketing in the new media system.

> Who first understood that media had to be segmented? Who first discovered that segmented, information-based advertising was more effective than mass irrelevance? Who discovered that information had to become the main component of messages and media? . . . Who first began to use information and dialogues to strenghthen consumer loyalty? . . . And who has the most to gain from the success of interactive, information-based media?

The answer to all of the above: direct marketing. Until now, we alone have been the architects of the connective link between manufacturers, consumers and the media. For the near future, we will have to remain so. But before the end of the century and the beginning of the next millennium, we shall become the partners of manufacturers, retailers and consumers who will use our skills to express and transact their needs and services with each other.[37]

A 1994 "white paper" published in the fall of 1994 by Redgate Communications carried this vision further. Redgate was deeply involved in interactive marketing. "Ten years from now," its manifesto read, "more real-time conduits [than ever] will link all of us directly to the information, products and services we are interested in."

Imagine a personal newspaper or information service in every home or office that displays headlines, summaries and topics capable of being printed out selectively. This scenario is already underway through growing special interest on-line services companies. In less than twenty years, some observers predict, electronic newspapers will outnumber printed ones.

Such services won't be confined merely to the young and computer literate but will be available to anyone who can use a touch-screen display. The programs will learn our interests by remembering our choices. Advertising will appear between messages and the service will record our responses. Ads will trigger our immediate responses by delivering rebates or coupons via a printer connected to our TV or PC, either of which will be able to serve as the source of both our information and entertainment.

Advertising effectiveness will be measured by our behavior and response, not by the number of possible "exposures," as it is today. Cost per thousand (CPM) will cease to be a term used by ad space representatives to convince prospects of the effectiveness of their media. And advertising agencies will be paid according to the number of sales transactions generated by their creative application of new media tools, not merely for production or as a percentage of the media buy.[38]

A theme of direct marketers was that the description of '90s consumers as fractured, frazzled, self-concerned, and hard to convince applied to their counterparts in the coming decades as well. As Redgate put it, the consumers of the future would "want what they want when they want it." Comfortable with high tech, they would not just expect interactivity in their dealings with marketers, they would demand it—"at the click of a button, a key, a remote pad, or even via voice recognition by the information appliance." Consumers wouldn't be willing to sit through a commercial "unless they are getting something in return for their time." They would also be willing to pay more for services and information "tailored to their preferences."[39]

The challenge, ultimately, was no different than earlier years: to reach people who would be likely to purchase the marketer's product or service. People in the "direct" tradition still needed to create or buy lists of likely customers. They argued that the new interactive arsenal would accommodate new ways to separate people into different lists according to lifestyles they expressed in viewing and computer use. One consultant exhorted marketers that "hundreds of thousands of names and addresses are floating on the Internet, waiting to be listed, organized, sliced, and diced." After all, he pointed out, "the Internet is essentially one giant agglomeration of special interests."

He suggested that an entrepreneur roam the Internet searching for names, mailing addresses, or phone numbers that individuals displayed in "chat rooms" and computer bulletin boards devoted to particular subjects. The entrepreneur would lift the names or addresses and transfer them to a relational database where they would be linked to attributes inferred from the topic of the individual's message. "Suddenly, an [Internet user] is silently captured in a database and will soon receive information through the mail tailored to specific interests. What was learned cruising the Internet has been vacuumed and converted to a targeted selling proposition."[40]

In the case of interactive TV, one benefit for marketers of gathering individual names was the ability to use an "insertion" technology that allowed an advertiser to send a commercial to specific homes at specific times no matter what people were viewing. Homes could be divided in a multitude of ways—by income, parents' age, buying patterns, race, ethnicity, vacation habits—and commercials signaling the different categories would cut into viewing during commercial time. "Say I like your home," said an interactive-advertising executive at a major agency, "and whatever you're doing at nine o'clock I want my commercials to run. I don't care whether you're playing a game, I don't care whether you're doing your banking, I don't care whether you are watching a movie, and I certainly don't care what movie you are watching."[41]

Many direct marketers and new-media executives would add that this home-targeting strategy was only a prelude to the insertion of person-specific commercials. They believed that the TV navigation that worried Edwin Artzt could actually be a boon to marketers. In the future, when turning on the set a viewer would activate a personal navigator. In turn, the navigator would signal the release of commercials intended specifically for that person, based on advertisers' categorization of him or her. Watching those commercials would become part of the commerce of subscription TV, lowering the cost for consumers who would be valuable to certain advertisers and be willing to watch their commercials.

"In a sense," predicted two direct marketers, "this means commercial messages, in and of themselves, will be bought and sold like entertainment programming. If I want to watch a live football game, Miller [Beer] might offer to sponsor my viewing, but I might have to 'pay' for this subsidy by interacting during the company's commercials."[42] Sometimes, payback for that subsidy might be filling out a questionnaire. Marketers understood that with interactive television, as well as with online services, users could often be encouraged to provide information that would help ad people divide them more carefully, and keep even more careful track of them than before.

Many new-media proponents described ways in which interactivity could take even more sophisticated forms. Say Ford Motor Company wants to ingratiate itself with an upscale thirty-six-year-old lawyer who, the company's computers have learned, is shopping for a mid-priced automobile. To encourage her in Ford's direction, the company might offer to pay for two nights' viewing. (For people likely to buy a particularly expensive car, the automaker might spring for a week's viewing.) If the programs chosen support time for commercials, Ford might insert spots likely to interest her. If some of the programs carry no commercials, Ford might propose that in return for the gift the woman watch a short documentary about a car that Ford expects might be of interest to her. Ford might even inform her of events in her area that it is sponsoring and that relate to her interests. Based on her phone response, the company might follow that up with direct-mail packets and computer disks with comparative car information.

But Ford might push even further. Unknown to viewers, the company might have placed several of its cars in movies or TV programs that its research suggested would match the interests of upscale professional women between the ages of eighteen and thirty-four. To encourage women who fit that profile to watch those shows, Ford might pay the company that coordinates the navigator to highlight the programs on a list of recommended shows in professional women's personal suggestions. In fact, Ford might well analyze the types of print and electronic materials used by individual women likely to buy a car. In that way, the automaker will be able to ensure that cars will show up in those clusters of media. Everywhere the women turn they will see the same Ford cars with tailored messages.

Futuristic scenes such as this that were painted at advertising conferences increasingly presented a picture of an ad business that would be able to use mass-customization technologies in its coordinated approach to selling. The idea was that to be most effective, marketers should tailor commercial messages to individual consumers so that the commercials would mirror the customers' backgrounds. In more targeted ways than ever, messages for products would become crafted appeals to an individual's own personal needs, values, and activities, as translated through databases shared by noncompetitive marketers who traded or sold names to one another.[43] The ultimate in effective appeals, marketers believed, would be to surround individuals with mirrors of a world created for them or, at least, people like them. In the coming world, perspectives reflective of other people's habits and marketing needs would be deemed inefficient.

A direct-marketing practitioner at a unit of the Young and Rubicam ad agency conglomerate took the next logical step. He predicted in 1994 that in years to come a brand "will be like a chameleon, looking and acting differently to different people while satisfying, servicing and shaping individuals more intensively." For example, he said, computers would use lists to decide what discount coupons, free gifts, or other promotions different types of people should get. In the case of the target audiences for a family movie such as *The Lion King*, computer "agents" would decide what "individual combinations of *Lion King* product endorsements, educational applications, and home shopping opportunities to [offer to] customers depending on what they own, consume, prefer and signal." In fact, even the movie might be edited differently to reflect the ads for different audiences. "In this hyper-customized world, the inter-relationship of advertising and programming increases because customer tastes and preferences are known in advance."[44]

Direct-marketer Lester Wunderman went still further. He argued that in the new-media environment marketers should see each individual person as the brand, with all products pitched to that personality. "The new definition of a brand will be that it represents a cluster of a consumer's needs," Wunderman told a Direct Marketing Association audience. "It is each consumer who is becoming a brand. I am a brand—and each of you are brands. Brands defined by the needs and priorities which are unique to us. There are, in fact, some 260 million brands in the United States [matching the number of people]."[45]

This emphasis on individual differences to the point of redefining brands as distinct people surrounded by commercial mirrors of themselves was played out in an early form through the loyalty programs discussed in chapter 6. With their eye on new interactive technologies, direct marketers saw additional ways to tailor brand images to individuals based on their demographic and lifestyle characteristics.

It would not be difficult to suggest how the signaling activities of particular newspapers, radio stations, cable systems, and magazines on CD-ROM could be coordinated with the customized activities of direct mailers, online information providers, and interactive television services to target different segments of the U.S. population. As chapter 5 noted, the trend among advertisers and media firms in the 1980s and 1990s was to emphasize divisions rather than overlap in preferences that population segments have for entertainment, news, and information. Looking to the future, ad people and media people saw this emphasis growing. They believed that clickstream audits and other research would give them a greater ability than in past years to describe the media habits of narrower and narrower segments of the population. They also saw a growing ability to influence those media habits by making sure that the right publicity and discounts got to the right audiences.

The technology to do this and even more tailored marketing already existed in the mid–1990s. Its feasibility in small-scale studies was being shown in a variety of tests conducted by various alliances of telephone, media, and computer giants.[46] Among the fifteen or so U.S. experiments on interactive television alone were the following:

• The Knight-Ridder media firm and Bell Atlantic telecommunications company were developing news, entertainment, and advertising for delivery into the home via Bell Atlantic's planned Stargazer network;

• General Telephone and Electronics intended to provide video programming over a phone network capable of giving users selections from more than five hundred choices;

• AT&T and Viacom were going forward on an interactive TV test in Castro Valley, California, that aimed to sell merchandise from the Comp-U-Card International direct marketing firm;

• Time Warner was committing $5 billion to the development of its Full Service Network starting in Orlando, Florida. It was promising on-demand access to Warner Brothers movies, interactive shopping, and other aspects of participatory television.[47]

There were hindrances to rolling out these and other high-tech projects on a large scale. One problem was that some of the technology, while feasible with small populations, could not yet to sustain large numbers of participants. Another was that it was unclear to media firms if the cost of implementing certain innovations would outstrip the amount that marketers and the public would want to pay for them. Still another issue was that media firms were unsure as to the final form that consumers would prefer their electronic services to the home. Predictions of the ascendancy of one or another technology were running in cyclical fads. In the early 1990s, for example, interactive television seemed to be the horse to bet on, while by 1995 online services had taken the better position in ad executives' minds. Time Warner, which had hands in both, was among the firms predicting that both would succeed through the ultimate merging of computers and television in the home.[48]

Making these issues even more difficult were reports in the mid–1990s that might lead an observer to question whether existing media firms had to do anything at all regarding the so-called interactive future. Revenue results suggested in 1995 that the broadcast television networks and the leading cable services were bringing in ad money in record amounts. The printed version of *TV Guide* in 1994 became the first periodical to surpass $1 billion in ad revenues. And Blockbuster Video, a movie-rental company that pundits were forecasting would be crippled by cable-based alternatives, was spilling off profits at a rate that surpassed all the other subsidiaries of its owner, Viacom.[49] The mass-market media's hot streak seemed to belie the claim that the broadcast networks were on a downward slide, that electronic navigators would replace printed video guides, and that interactive television and computers would take revenues from traditional electronic and printed sources of entertainment, information, and news.

But even the leaders of the firms that were raking in the cash contended they knew the handwriting was on the wall. They realized that in late 1995 Wall Street was placing a higher monetary value on some cable networks such as ESPN than on broadcast networks because of what investors saw as the wired world's enormous growth potential.[50] They were convinced that technological change and the loosening of federal laws that restrained competition between telephone and cable companies would cause the expected interactive television universe to take off in the next few years. That, they believed, would fundamentally change the tools of advertising.[51] The general sense was that change was inevitable and that they had to get out in front of the curve or be left behind. "While nothing's going to replace network television fast," explained the president of an NBC division that was developing targeted extensions of, and alternatives to, the broadcast networks, "five years from now we don't want to say, 'Gee, where were we?'"[52]

Most new-media observers agreed that navigation equipment would be consumers' primary entry into the new video world after the turn of the century.[53] In a navigation-driven environment, channels would be replaced by choices that could be "dialed" up from a central "bank" of programming that would be receiving some shows in real time and would hold others in its memory. In this scheme, ABC, CBS, NBC, and Fox would therefore merely be selections among a multitude of other options. They might present more than a single selection at a time.

A Thursday-night viewer, for example, might be able to choose, for free, the real-time flow of NBC's comedy block; local-affiliate programming might follow after 11 P.M. Or the viewer might decide to watch—perhaps free, perhaps for a charge or an advertiser-promoted discount—

a network drama episode from the previous Sunday evening. Of course, a viewer cruising with the remote control might watch parts of all of these and more.

This consensus on the network future after the turn of the century led to a vigorous discussion of networks' role, and the role of other broad-reach media such as billboards and in-store signs, in a world where huge numbers of targeted and interactive choices would hold sway. The traditional view of the importance of the broadcast networks and other mass-market media was that they were crucial for building widely shared brand images. Allen Rosenshine, head of the BBDO agency, made this point when he asserted that "mass media will not go away because brands are not built one-to-one; they are most effectively transmitted through broad-based media."[54] Making a related point, Robert Herbold, P&G's head of advertising and information services, argued in 1995 that the low-cost, frequent-purchase products that were his firm's focus did not cry out for targeted interactive programming to connect with their customers. "If you're selling Crest toothpaste, you probably don't need an interactive ad," he said. "What you do need are tons of [TV] messages on a regular basis to constantly reinforce what that brand represents because the purchase decision is so frequent."[55]

Yet a P&G competitor, SmithKline Beecham, tried marketing its Aquafresh toothpaste on the Internet not long after Herbold's comments.[56] Moreover, even Herbold wanted to hedge his bets. Despite his comments about toothpaste and mass-market TV, he quickly followed up on his chairman's pledge that P&G would be a major participant in tests of interactive media and of programming activities that could get around limitations on traditional TV commercials. Herbold himself noted two reasons for experimenting with interactive media. The more important one for P&G, he said, was to learn how to reach huge numbers of consumers with P&G's message as the broadcast networks' ability to deliver them continued to decline. The other was to take advantage of interactive technology's ability to target consumers precisely and provide marketers with better research and database information.[57]

Relationship marketers were convinced that it would be possible for even package-good marketers to gradually move away from using mass-market media to sell products aimed at even the largest number of people. They believed that mass-customization technology would make it possible for print and electronic media to tailor ads to individuals on a broad scale. People with different backgrounds, personalities, and patterns of activity could automatically receive different versions of the ads, even different brand images, with the media materials they would choose. Mass-market media, then, would not need to be used simply to try to persuade huge numbers of people quickly.

Instead, many direct marketers postulated, traditional mass-market messages would continue for two reasons. One would be to reach consumers who would actually never be expected to buy the product. The reason, consultants Don Peppers and Martha Rogers noted, was that "many products and services will continue to be sold for their badge value," the value that it has because others aspire to it or cannot get it.[58]

This approach to widely shared media already existed in the mid–1990s with luxury items. The Lamborghini automobile company decided to advertise its vehicle in large U.S. circulation magazines, even though the vast number of readers couldn't afford it; in fact, the firm expected to sell only 100 cars in America during all of 1995. The reason for advertising rather broadly was not to reach the small number of expected buyers, whose characteristics the company knew and who would best be reached in person, or by mail. It was, rather, to inform broad numbers of Americans of the exclusivity of the car, that it was beyond their reach. That, the marketers felt, would make the vehicle more valuable to the people who *could* afford it.[59]

The second, and major, use that direct marketers expected for broadly viewed media would be to signal as many people as possible that a product or service has wide appeal. McDonald's, Coca-Cola, Pepsi, Chevy, Reebok, and other major brands would undoubtedly still want "everyone" to appreciate their national visibility. At the same time, relationship marketers predicted that the creators of a company's national ad campaign would increasingly have to take care not to contradict the different integrated marketing programs crafted for highly targeted segments of the population. Because of the priority of target-marketing strategies, a "national" campaign might sometimes be little more than an eye-catching audiovisual logo designed not to interfere with the different messages that different audiences were getting about the company.

The more specialized images would show up in the clusters of primary media that even fairly heavy viewers of broad-based TV, billboards, and in-store ads would call their own and turn to for identity as well as personal credibility. Traditional network programs might even feed this appetite for separation. A CBS program might tout Reebok's sponsorship of a show and display its logo to every viewer at the program's start. During the show, though, CBS might route different ads for the athletic shoe company to different types of people. Reebok could decide, for example, that it wanted CBS to send commercials with one perspective on the company's products to people categorized as "African American teen viewers" and those with another perspective to "healthy upscale retirees of any racial background."

Viewers might not be aware that various customized versions, reflecting the lifestyles and values of other groups, existed. In fact, in all likelihood even the logos of Reebok and other firms would invoke different "scripts" of associations among many different groups when they were seeing them together on billboards, in-store signs, and broadly shared TV programming. The reason is that companies such as Reebok would be spending so much energy on separating Americans through integrated target marketing—through the distinct clusters of magazines, events, CD-ROMs, and other media that would surround distinct audiences. Unknowingly, people might be reacting to very different histories of association. So even when people would be watching together, they would be encouraged to think of different things, to consider different market-driven worlds.

EIGHT

IMAGE TRIBES

AT ITS HEART, this book has been about the way advertisers and the media worked to construct America from the 1970s through the mid– 1990s. During the period, both industries showed a greater interest than ever before in detecting and exploiting social divisions. What consequences will their activities have for the way Americans see themselves and others in the coming decades? The findings here suggest answers that are disturbing.

Before exploring them, though, it may be useful to step back and consider what this study has to say about the general process through which advertisers develop images of people and their lives. Here are four propositions about the industrial construction of society. They might be tested against the advertising-media relationships of other eras, even of other countries.

• *The industrial construction of society is a purposeful activity, though not a conspiratorial one.* Throughout this investigation, it has been quite clear that the corporate imaging of society is not an accidental by-product of marketing activities. Understanding society is, instead, a major and explicit goal for advertisers, their clients, and the media firms with whom they deal. They spend lots of money supporting research organizations inside and outside their own firms that can advise them. They believe that expertise in this area affects their ability to reach consumers.

While a good deal of the data and interpretations to this end are proprietary, a substantial amount does get into the trade press and industry meetings. An examination of the sources reveals that the discussions of society by media and marketing practitioners are pragmatic, speak to the needs of their clients, and rarely reflect on the social or moral meaning of their work. The free flow of contentions over one or another point of view is evidence that no central committee of the media system guides the discussions. When consensus appears it is because an idea makes sense to the people involved or because one or another organization pushing it has clout. But no one organization has all the clout, as the next proposition notes.

• *The industrial construction of society is an integral part of a company's struggle for position.* Within marketing and media firms, the need to understand America is linked closely to the need for efficiency and effectiveness. Useful ideas about society are therefore coins of exchange among research firms that maneuver for clients, ad agencies that plot to get advertisers, and media firms that jockey for sponsors. Both large and small firms are intensely involved in this competition. Small firms often use debates about trends as a way to tell the industry that they are at the cutting edge of strategic thinking. Large firms want to prove to current and potential clients that they haven't lost their edge.

The upshot is an unending stream of public and private rhetoric by companies that aim to show that they are able to analyze and package those portions of the population that their constituencies want to reach. Where they get their ideas about society and how they make them useful are questions addressed in the next proposition.

• *Companies look both outside and inside their industries to decide about how society is changing and what to do about it.* When it comes to looking outside, marketing and media practitioners find some areas more relevant than others. They tend to ignore religion, the fine arts, and literature. Instead, they look to government, academic, and private reports for trends on the economy, the family, and the population as a whole.

Chapters 3 and 4 show, for example, that during the late 1970s and early 1980s ad people found broad significance in the political victories of Ronald Reagan; the increasing gap between rich and poor; the changing dynamics of the American family; and the huge growth of Latino, African American, and Asian American populations. These developments became lenses through which executives thought they could understand and predict Americans' consumption patterns. They tested and expanded their ideas through focus groups and surveys.

While these notions about society came from outside the advertising and media system, the way marketers implemented them was very much driven by internal business concerns. The result was a portrait of America that, while borrowed from other institutions, was shaped to fit the demands for efficiency and effectiveness in advertising. Marketers and media firms channeled the insights they gleaned from outside sources in ways that might have even run counter to the aims of the people who generated the original data.

It is doubtful, for instance, that the academic and governmental groups that released reports about widening divisions of income in America would have expected that their information would be exploited to sell products. That, however, is what happened, as ad practitioners merged income details with other data in order to separate groups worth pursuing from those that weren't. When it came to blacks and Hispanic Americans, the separation involved drawing stark lines between winners and losers. As chapter 4 notes, ad people ignored members of those groups that could not meet expectations. At the same time, they reveled in data about high-consumption middle- and upper-middle-class blacks and Hispanic Americans that they divided even further by gender and lifestyle.

Marketers searched for gold in many social slices. Media firms were quick to develop formats that would create demographic and lifestyle labels that the advertisers equated with gold. Nickelodeon's executives talked of programming that would draw upscale suburban kids; executives for online companies exulted in the high-achieving early adopters that their services were chasing; the publishers of women's magazines fell over each other trying to prove to media buyers that the tone and topics of their articles reached out to the "best type" of working woman; and catalog companies touted their ability to create "books" tailored to a panoply of different wealthy lifestyles.

This point about formats can be generalized:

• *The ideas about society that companies develop are embodied in the structure of the media as well as in their content.* More than a few writers have observed that the commercials, songs, articles, and programs which appear throughout the media system mirror their creators' perspectives on society. This look at the ad world shows that the struggle of marketers and media firms over the nature of U.S. society goes even further. It affects the distribution and nature of formats—the very structure of the media system.

Media executives decide whether the layouts and "tones"—the formats—of their outlets are acceptable to the audiences that they think marketers will find attractive. Drawing on their business priorities and visions of consumers, they continually assess the existing mix of formats in magazines, newspapers, radio stations, online services, and other ad vehicles. Marketing executives, for their part, decide whether the number and nature of outlets are acceptable from the standpoint of audiences they want to reach efficiently.

This format-building process sets the ground rules for selecting content. Doing so ensures that marketers' assumptions about audiences are reflected in the different formats that they support. When high-visibility formats in magazines, cable, and the Internet emphasize upscale twenty-somethings, for example, it seems logical that there wll be much hunting for entertainment, news, and information with these consumers in mind. By contrast, the relative lack of advertiser interest in men and women older than fifty—and especially over seventy—will mean a smaller and less visible part of the media mix aimed at them, fewer formats targeted to them, and therefore less content with them as central, active characters.

Inertia is an important feature of the media system. It takes much effort to make major alterations in the media mix and the formats that populate it. When significant changes do take place, they signal that executives are going through a major rethinking of either society, advertising, or media. The decades covered in this book are remarkable because they show the beginnings of a paradigm shift in all three areas at the same time.

Beginning in the late 1970s, national advertisers and their agencies advanced the notion that Americans were becoming more fractured, frazzled, self-indulgent, and suspicious than ever before. They said that U.S. consumers were getting harder to reach, and were sharing fewer common views of the world, than in previous years. They noted that the growing social divisions paralleled an increasing fractionalization of U.S. media, as seen in the growing number of radio stations, magazines, cable networks, VCRs, video games, and computers.

Advertisers believed that the social divisions and media fractionalization presented opportunities to create and sell new products. But this would work only if they understood the new social realities and if the media targeted the groups that marketers wanted. As a result, both marketing and media executives worked to develop a shared understanding of how America was splitting up and to make sure that changes in media would take place in ways that would help advertisers persuade their chosen segments as efficiently as possible. As chapters 2 through 4 show, the discussions reflected a broad range of demographic and lifestyle labels. Advertising and marketing practitioners jockeyed to present their versions of the way men, women, blacks, Hispanic Americans, suburbanites, seniors, and a wide spectrum of other groups were changing.

Chapters 5, 6, and 7 note that with these activities came an appreciation of media that could help marketers meet their targeting needs. Proponents of these media argued strongly, and increasingly successfully, that while people might use mass-market vehicles such as network television in their everyday activities, they identified more strongly with the worlds portrayed in formats aimed at them. Reaching the right groups with "rifle shot" efficiency became an important part of marketing plans. Media formats that signaled an interest in people with specific backgrounds and lifestyles grew in popularity.

Momentum toward creating targeted spaces for increasingly narrow niches of consumers accelerated despite the consolidation of giant media firms during the 1980s and 1990s. The deals that linked Time to Warner, Viacom to Paramount, and Disney to ABC were not consummated with the aim of turning back the clock on media fractionalization or audience segmentation. If anything, the conglomerates' global reach could speed the segmentation process along, since it gave them the ability to amortize the costs of targeted ventures not just across audience segments in the U.S. but across their counterparts around the world. In addition, the conglomerates' multimedia ownership meant they could make additional money by spinning different versions of the format or content to the target audiences in a panoply of media locations. Viacom's MTV could stand for upscale young adults on U.S. cable, on international satellites, on clothes, CDs, and on a variety of printed paraphernalia.

All this meant that the cutting-edge competition was no longer over the creation of mass-circulation media with huge audiences, as it had been in the first three quarters of the twentieth century. Rather, it was over the creation of primary media communities that covered a variety of places. The aim for the media firms as well as for the marketers was to make the target audience feel part of a tight-knit extended family, attached to the program hosts, other viewers, and sponsors, wherever they went.

In tandem with these developments, a sea change was taking place in the forms of advertising that marketers used. The business of "advertising" was broadening far beyond its traditional meaning of discrete messages that were clearly meant to persuade. During the 1980s and 1990s the money spent on time and space for ads in traditional media typically remained level or rose slowly compared to previous decades. By contrast, the cash channeled into other ways of getting persuasive messages in front of targeted consumers—ways such as product placement, in-store promotion, discount coupons, sponsored events—took off.

So did direct marketing. A previously disdained area of the business, it began to look good as direct practitioners' ability to use databases to pinpoint and customize persuasive messages to individuals and groups grew in sophistication. Advertisers' interest in direct work suggested that they would naturally grab onto an interest in interactive television and the "mass customization" of news, information, and entertainment.

Some interactive technologists groused that advertisers were slow to appreciate the potential of their business. Advertisers responded that the practical implementation of their futuristic ideas was not yet clear and that realistic targeting could take place elsewhere. As chapter 7 notes, by the mid–1990s the largest marketers and their ad agencies were proclaiming that they would move decisively to influence the new interactive world as it developed. Interactive TV proponents expected that the amount of subscription and pay-per-view programming would rise in the future (implying that advertising would decline). Yet more and more advertisers declared that they were ready to associate themselves with these domains even if no commercial spots would be allowed. They would do it by subsidizing the use of interactive TV for consumers whose attention and loyalty they cared to cultivate.

In general, all signs indicated that marketers' support of the media in return for hyping their products to audiences would remain a cornerstone of the media world. Whether the activity was product placement in movies and computer games, subsidization of cable and VCR programming in return for publicity, or payment for links on Internet home pages, marketers viewed the new ad tactics as helping them reach the consumers they wanted in environments conducive to selling.

The heads of major technology firms, media corporations, and marketers clearly feel that there is no turning back from the growth of print and electronic choices aimed at narrower and narrower groups of people. The feverish growth of the Internet is ample proof. Certainly, the high cost of introducing interactive television in the mid–1990s derailed the plans of some companies and caused skeptics to argue that high-tech scenarios wouldn't ever come to pass. But suggestions about the future based on disappointments of the moment are as misguided as blue-sky futuristic pronouncements. The competition to develop interactive technologies has not faded, despite the changing strategies of particular firms.

The momentum toward segmentation is both national and global. As the previous chapters have noted, media practitioners are already being rewarded for delivering homogeneous audiences to marketers in clusters of primary media communities. All signs indicate that this will continue to be the case in print and electronic media and that new technologies will speed the process along, especially after the start of the twenty-first century. The capabilities of print and electronic media will allow virtually all media to adopt two major characteristics of direct marketing that have traditionally made mainstream advertisers jealous. One is selectability—an ability to reach an individual with entertainment, news, information, and advertising based on knowledge of the individual's background, interests, and habits. The other is accountability to advertisers—an ability to trace the individual's response to a particular ad.

Such "rifle-shot" power will be hard to turn down in favor of mass-market tactics, which will appear as inefficient scattershot in comparison. Certainly, as discussed in chapter 7, there will be companies that want to get their brands out to the broad population as quickly as possible and so will find mass-market media useful. They will support the presence of billboards, supermarket signs, and TV shows such as the Super Bowl, the World Series, and the Miss America Pageant that are designed to grab millions of viewers in a short period. That kind of programming will help create immediate national awareness, and maybe word-of-mouth, for a new car model, a new athletic shoe, or a new computer to as many people as possible.

An impulse toward mass-market media will probably also exist in the interest of media firms' efficiency. To make back the high production costs for a TV movie about the Chernobyl nuclear disaster, Warner Brothers Television might try to reach as many people as possible by targeting their personal navigators with plot descriptions that are tailored to their backgrounds. Descriptions might be written for people old enough to remember the incident, others for people interested in science, others for people who have a habit of viewing films with the lead actor, and so on. As another example, NBC might set up its election coverage so that it can be tailored to viewers with different interests. People who care especially about foreign affairs, people specializing in agricultural issues, people who want to know about environmental issues on a state-by-state basis—they and others may be given the option of choosing versions of the network feed that add experts in their areas in addition to generic NBC coverage.

But this desire to combine production efficiencies of mass marketing with the audience draw of tailored materials may well end up pushing separation over collectivity. Over and over, the different versions of news will act out different social distinctions for different people. And even when the content is the same for the various segments (as in the Chernobyl movie), producers will promote the firm differently to different types of viewers or households. In addition, commercials clearly tailored to certain types of people, or to certain media communities, will encourage the perception that the viewing experience in America is an enormously splintered one.

It is likely that producers of news and information will be able to customize content to a greater range of demographic, psychographic, and lifestyle catgories than will those who create expensive movies. The reason is simply that, at present at least, it is less expensive to customize news and information programs than top-of-the-line entertainment. From an economic standpoint, shopping, video games, light entertainment, and many sports are closer to news and information than to high-cost films. It seems likely they will become major platforms for tailored television and online materials in the years to come. That will drastically splinter audiovisual audiences.

The major consideration driving these audience-slicing activities is the notion of identity. Marketing and media executives are sure that people gravitate to materials that most closely zero in on their likes and dislikes, their sense of themselves. But marketers also believe the converse: that people prefer not to confront materials that cause them discomfort. Advertisers already avoid associating with controversy if they can help it, since they believe that the displeasure people feel rubs off on them and their products. It stands to reason that when targeting becomes an efficient alternative to sending the same materials to everyone, even more sponsors will hesitate to support touchy topics and perspectives if they go to certain viewers. Research will explore who is angered by what, and media will adjust their formats accordingly. In both print and electronic domains, customized magazines will try to ingratiate themselves to readers and sponsors by trying to mirror the readers' ideological viewpoints.

This picture of the emerging media system is closer to the prediction of "image tribes" that chapter 1 ascribed to Don Peppers and Martha Rogers than to the more optimistic balancing of the *Daily Me* with the *Daily Us* that Nicholas Negroponte augured. The reason, this book has shown, has to do with an aspect of the media world that neither Peppers and Rogers nor Negroponte consider: Marketers and media firms hold vested interests in constructing certain versions of the world and not others.

Negroponte argues that individuals will always be able to search out materials that move them beyond narrow concerns and link them to the larger society. His examples of social outreach—Sunday crossword puzzles, bargain hunting in the general classifieds, Art Buchwald's column—may fuel conversations around the office water cooler between people who typically belong to different primary media communities. Yet the assertion that people will pay serious attention to *The Daily Us* rather than *The Daily Me* has first to be weighed against the question of whether individuals, if they can help it, truly want to relate to issues faced by people unlike them.

Negroponte himself admits that he would spend far more time with *The Daily Me* than *The Daily Us* and would naturally consider *The Daily*

Me closer to his needs. Marketing firms see this preference on a wide-spread basis, and they try to exploit it. With their ever more sophisticated databases, they hold a growing ability to learn what aspects of entertainment, news, information, and advertising specific types of people, or even particular individuals, would be in the mood to buy. It may be difficult for audiences to turn away from attractive materials that are associated with a feeling of narrow, close-knit identity, particularly in view of the discounts and loyalty programs advertisers may offer. Advertisers are convinced, and will act to ensure, that in the new media world the "Us" will lose out to the "Me" and the image tribe.

There is much reason to believe that marketers will continue to find reinforcement for their views of a divided America in a range of places. Popular and expert opinion in the mid–1990s seems permeated with the belief that America is moving through an incredibly centrifugal phase. Books with titles such as *The Disuniting of America, American Apartheid, The Next American Nation,* and *Alien Nation* have trumpeted the appearance of increased divisions in U.S. society.[1] Newsmagazines have amplified the books' influence.

The consensus seems to be that at every level of society Americans are separated by their own problems, allegiances, and interests. Many suggest that the nation's White Anglo-Saxon Protestant power elite has given way somewhat to a professional and managerial class containing a broader mix of races and ethnic backgrounds at the top. Yet the same analysts note that competition within this multifaceted "overclass" has itself become intense. This is because of a belief that the U.S. economy will no longer lift everyone up with it. The sense is that turf battles have become the norm for individuals within and across income, gender, age, race, ethnicity, and lifestyles.[2]

Accurate or not, this widespread talk about social schisms is quite likely to continue shaping the way that advertisers, their agencies, and media firms approach Americans in the last years of the twentieth century. In view of the discussions of social conflict and alienation swirling around marketing and media, executives in that business might protest that it would be foolish to act differently. After all, they might say, their mandate is to channel developments of U.S. society into tools for selling. Ad people, in particular, might note that their campaigns are more subtle and less inflammatory than those provided by many radio talk-show hosts, cable television programs, and magazine columns.

In the face of such protestations, three key points of this book are worth repeating. One is that the advertising industry depends heavily on ideas from other areas of society. The second is that advertisers are not passive regarding these ideas. They take action to incorporate them into their business activities, which often means trying to find ways to exploit social problems rather than to ameliorate them. The third is that the ad industry affects not just the content of its own campaigns but the very structure and content of the rest of the media system. The advertising industry's cash and philosophy provide the principal supports for those explicitly divisive talk shows, cable programs, and magazine columns. Whether ad people like it or not, they are centrally responsible for images of social division.

A parallel example of the way that perceptions of social division are being built into structures that guide people's lives can be seen in the design of communities during the 1980s and 1990s. In areas throughout the United States, home builders have been attracting buyers by creating communities that have gates and guards around them. The architecture critic of the *Dallas Morning News* estimated that in 1994 an estimated four million Americans were already living in gated communities. The number was growing quickly. That year, between one-third and two-thirds of all new housing construction in southern California were gated.[3] The percentage was said to be about one-third in Phoenix, Arizona, the suburbs of Washington, D.C., and in many parts of Florida. Typical features of upscale gated communities were tight security (walls, electronic tag access), exclusivity (homes in the $450,000 to $1.2 million range), and income and lifestyle segregation (what the *Morning News* called "social homogeneity").[4]

Observers agreed that the force driving these communities was fear of crime and its erosion of property values. Tied to that was a skepticism of government's ability to do much about either. In fact, gates and guardhouses were popping up in urban neighborhoods as well as suburban ones, and they were cutting across traditional racial and economic lines. The *Morning News* reported that Dearborn Park, a popular middle-class neighborhood near downtown Chicago's Loop, installed gates and cul-de-sacs. In Los Angeles, several public housing projects erected gates and walls.

One planning expert asserted that the gating of communities indicated a fundamental shift in American life that was related to "a dramatic lack of trust in public order."[5] It wasn't that there was necessarily more crime, added a sociologist, "but that it has become so random. . . . It used to be that if you stayed out of bad neighborhoods you'd be OK. That no longer works." The effects of the fear had even spread to suburban mall shopping. "In the past . . . most malls didn't want visible security," a security consultant told a *Washington Post* reporter. "Now more and more of them want it, because the public wants it. They want to see armed guards."[6]

In that environment, the builders of such communities saw reason to market their developments as "safer, friendlier and more economically stable than traditional urban or suburban neighborhoods." One called its development "a perfect place to live . . . outside the pandemonium of the city," where there can be "a return to simpler times, when you know you were secure within the boundaries of your own neighborhood . . . [and] where children could play unattended and be safe after dark."[7]

Critics of gating didn't quarrel with the desire to protect home and family. They did, however, point out that while gating might be useful for the individual, it was actually divisive for society. That was because communities with gates separated not just the violent and the nonviolent, they put walls between people of different incomes, races, ethnicities, and even ages. Once gates and guardhouses were built, they tended to reinforce the values that created them. Such structures, literally built into the society, would be very difficult to change.

"[Wanting to be safe and hold good property values] are perfectly good motives, right and honorable," said Rice University sociologist Stephen Kleinberg. "[But] [t]he problem with enclaving is that it leads to the deterioration of any sense of connectiveness to the larger community. 'If I'm making it, it's not my responsibility to look after others.' That's the direction American society seems to be going, and it's ominous."[8] University of Pennsylvania sociologist Douglas Massey added a pragmatic warning about the effects of this separation: "A nation so subdivided at home, so miseducated, can't compete in the global economy. . . . If you build up a wall you inevitably pay other prices."[9]

The same conclusion could be drawn about the emerging media world. The wide diversity of media channels, the fascination of the Internet, the excitement of interactivity through cable systems, phone systems, or even satellites are hard to deny, or to want to relinquish. Many people who have moaned over the small number of choices on TV, aimed at the lowest common denominator, may delight at the prospect of a television system that is like the magazine industry. One person can get the *New Yorker* or *Vanity Fair* or the *National Inquirer* or *Field and Stream*—or all of these.

But what cheers the individual may hold problems for the collectivity. Many of the key players shaping the wonders of the new media world have a vested interest in emphasizing differences between people. The social price may be alienation, reduced social mobility, anger, and fear of others.

As it often has been with gating, income is a central issue in contemporary media trends. Ad practitioners construct income in terms of winners and losers. People with relatively low incomes are typically the big losers, since marketers and media executives show little interest in attracting them to specialized areas. By contrast, upscale individuals and families have marketers falling over each other to reach them. They differentiate income further by lifestyle. The more a company can connect someone to a set of high-consumption lifestyles, the more chance that the person will be tracked and wooed across a variety of targeted and personalized media. Wealth follows wealth.

Measured against the problems of getting food and a roof over one's head, marketers' separation of people into income classes may not seem like a problem. Yet the cultural experiences of different income groups are likely to become increasingly divergent. That will happen because people of different income groups will be segregated by different news, entertainment, and information options, sorted by disposable income. People will be attracted to different options in these three areas, according to financial wherewithal. And it will happen because in the name of efficient targeting, marketers and media firms encourage people of different incomes toward certain formats and not others. Mutually reinforcing, these activities taken together will lead some groups more than others to have better and larger windows on the culture of success.

As noted in chapter 7, marketers, ad agencies, and media firms have supported a minimum universal standard so that it will allow them to reach "everyone" through advertising, should they want to do that. But their support is supremely self-serving. Marketing and media folk recognize that hooking up huge numbers of people also allows them to find out as much as they can about them. Then they can selectively target the ones they want, ignoring the ones they don't.

With income differences growing in the U.S. between those designated "upscale" and everyone else, with poor immigrants streaming into many parts of the country, and competition for good jobs enhancing existing social tension between races and sexes, it will only compound the problem to encourage media separation on top of physical separation. Douglas Massey and Nancy Denton in their book *American Apartheid* argue that people's life chances are inextricably linked to where they live.[10] It does not seem too much of a stretch to suggest that the same idea applies to the media worlds in which people live. Because of targeting and tailoring, income and age labels will route people toward certain cultural experiences, certain types of commercials, or certain discounts. As a result, people increasingly will live in different media spheres. Marketers and media will guide the relatively well-off into cultural tracks pointedly designed for their income brackets while they will let everyone else find their own ways on the shoals of "universal service."

But income is only the tip of a broad gamut of prejudices that marketers and media act out. They link income to notions about such categories as age, education, gender, race, and ethnicity. Personality and lifestyle labels are also put into play with the aim of uncovering individuals who are both predictable media users and useful customers. As previous chapters have shown, the "audience talk" that swirled through the ad industry and the media during the 1980s and early 1990s amounted to an eager dissection of U.S. lifestyles. The overall aim was to find many different segments that would please marketers because of their substantial disposable income and thus their ability to buy.

Some advertisers' actions in the name of selling actually opened doors for previously marginalized groups. Consultants, advertisers, and agency executives used the idea of "disposable income" to justify pursuing certain emerging identities in society. Along with rethinking their understanding of the wealthy, the upscale, women, suburbanites, and other clearly desirable groups, ad people rewrote their books on homosexuals; African, Hispanic, and Asian Americans; and seniors. Marketers established that many members of these groups ought to be targeted for their buying abilities.

The down side of this labeling process, though, was that some people who may have considered themselves part of those groups—of gays or blacks or seniors—did not make it into the market-driven cate-gorizations. Those people were labeled as less useful or simply different than other members of their group because they didn't meet the same income or consumption criteria. The resulting targeting and tailoring might well distance upscale blacks from downscale ones, lesbians (espe-cially those with children) from male homosexuals, executive women from others, seniors over seventy years old from younger ones.

The many other demographic and lifestyle labels that marketers acted out during the 1980s and 1990s extended the portrait of Amer-ica as splintered by distinctions. Doing that, they signaled that people should find their own kind in media communities designed for them. They also signaled the irrelevance of many geographic relationships. In an era of satellites, physical distance is becoming less and less a concern for media companies. Huge media firms interested in target marketing increasingly find it far more useful to distribute materials for far-flung consumers with similar tastes than to produce entertainment, news, or information for audiences of relatively narrow geographical areas who have little in common.

These far-flung groups of people may be more like one another in their backgrounds and lifestyles than the people who live in neighbor-hoods two miles away. People may increasingly feel that links to indivi-duals in their immediate space and time—people they work with, see in stores or on the streets—are not nearly as important as their far-flung virtual communities. News about their own neighborhoods will prob-ably draw people who care about schools and property values. Beyond those tangibly important concerns, though, they may care to learn little about people who live close to them—in the same or nearby neighbor-hoods—but whom they consider substantially different. Links between suburbs and cities, already tenuous, will likely become even thinner.

Given the chance to separate themselves electronically from types of people they believe are threatening their well-being, media users are likely to do so. Keeping "different" people out of mind when they don't have to deal with them may become as important as keeping them out with gates. Those who can afford it will deal with the fear of going out by dialing into malls set up for individuals like them. Media firms will customize e-mail, interactive games, and online chat rooms to create vir-tual communities of people from around the world who hold similar interests, and attract similar advertisers.

It will take time, perhaps decades, for the full effects of the emerging media world to take shape. Eventually, it is likely that children growing up in the hyper-segmented environment will see the pictures of division as reflecting the real thing. Compared even to today, the media of the future will be far more fragmented, with hundreds of market-driven options targeted and tailored to carefully calibrated types. While that may engender a tight sense of community among people who share similar backgrounds, it could also reinforce suspicion, lack of empathy, and alienation between people of different backgrounds, income classes, and lifestyles. Primary media communities—image tribes—will guide consumers' sense of social separation by helping them understand whom to label as *not like them.*

In that kind of environment, it is easy to imagine critics worrying that the absence of strong collective media poses a threat to democracy. Society-wide argumentation will be harder and harder to sustain. People who fundamentally disagree may simply not argue with one another; key political and social issues may not be thrashed out as well as they should. With people so accustomed to their own image tribes, they may be unwilling to connect in debates with people outside their circles. And advertisers, traditionally wary of controversy, certainly won't encourage it.

The proper response to this hyper-segmentation of America is not to urge a return to the mass-market world of the 1960s and 1970s. Even if it were possible, it would not be desirable. The explosion of media during the past few decades has led marketers to address many parts of the U.S. population that previously lacked audiovisual identities. Ethnic groups, racial groups, gender groups, and groups arrayed around political positions have seen versions of entertainment and news aimed at them. This sort of cultural diversity ought to be celebrated as the font of a strong, idea-rich society.

But to do that it ought to be shared among the population as a whole. The major problem with the emerging media world is its impulse to keep diversity hidden. Signaling, tailoring, and other targeting activities encourage people to join their own image tribes apart from other image tribes. As a result, marketers' concerns with diversity act to push groups away from one another rather than to encourage them to learn about the strengths of coming together to share experiences and discuss issues from different viewpoints.

Another problem with this approach to diversity is that advertisers have by and large been the ones defining it. In fact, one of the enduring problems of the U.S. media system is that advertisers have had a monopoly on descriptions of America. Terms such as "cost per thousand," "pass-along rate," and "upscale eighteen- to forty-nine-year-old men" have become ground-level labels that determine whether a public medium will survive.

However, there are—or should be—many other ways to characterize populations. One can do it from political, sociological, historical, religious, and literary standpoints. A television program can be geared toward "those who went to Catholic schools" or "those whose parents migrated to the U.S. from Eastern Europe" or "those who somehow feel part of the Old South." These labels describe a lot of people. They are undoubtedly connected to a gamut of "lifestyles" and actions in one way or another. But they are not categories that advertisers use because it isn't clear that they relate in any predictable way to the purchase of products. Should the ability to share the consumer experience be the one characteristic linking us together?

Individuals who are intent that the answer should be no may be able to push against the tide by going out of their way to use media not intended for them and by making it difficult for advertisers to label them. Unfortunately, though, the strength of trends charted in this book do not make one optimistic that growing momentum toward a divided media world will be reversed. Advertisers have been major forces guiding the formats of this new world, and they will resist derailing it. One reason is that companies believe that the American population is in tune with their sense of division. Another is that they suspect that once selling takes off on the Internet, interactive TV, and other futuristic channels, it will be quite profitable.

Once the emerging system is solidified, it will not be easy to change. Media technologies and formats that have been shaped by the values of social division will reinforce those values even when leaders in their rhetoric are trying to bring people together. Like heavy gates separating one community from another, the very structure of the American media world will drive people apart for a long time to come.

NOTES

CHAPTER ONE

1. Quoted in R. C. Morse, "The cable (inter) connections," *Advertising Age,* November 16, 1981, p. S14.

2. Donna Fenn, "Intricate story of a turnaround," *Advertising Age,* October 17, 1983, p. M20.

3. Alvin Achenbaum, "Dominant tv has dominant underbelly," *Advertising Age,* September 25, 1978, p. 1.

4. For discussions of this subject, see, for example, Morris Janowitz, *Community Affairs and the Press* (Chicago: University of Chicago Press, 1967); and David Morley and Kevin Robbins, *Spaces of Identity: Global Media, Electronic Landscapes and Cultural Boundaries* (London and New York: Routledge, 1995).

5. A large and growing literature covers this topic. Of particular interest here is the scholarly discussion of audience construction. See J. Ettema and D. C. Whitney, "The money arrow: An introduction to audiencemaking," in J. Ettema and D. C. Whitney, *Audience Making* (Newbury Park: Sage, 1994), pp. 1–18; Ien Ang, *Desperately Seeking the Audience* (Routledge, 1991), part 1; and Joseph Turow, "The role of 'the audience' in publishing children's books," *Journal of Popular Culture* 16:2 (Fall 1982), 90–100.

6. See Joseph Turow, *Playing Doctor: Television, Storytelling and Medical Power* (New York: Oxford University Press, 1989), pp. xi–xx; and Joseph Turow, *Media Systems in Society: Understanding Industries, Strategies and Power* (New York: Longman, 1992), pp. 1–18.

7. Benedict Anderson, *Imagined Communities,* 2nd edition (London and New York: Verso, 1991).

8. Nicholas Negroponte, *Being Digital* (New York: Knopf, 1995), p. 153

9. Don Peppers and Martha Rogers, *The One to One Future* (New York: Doubleday, 1993), pp. 383–87.

10. Ibid.

11. Joe Mandese, "Five year outlook shows healthy growth overall," *Advertising Age,* July 25, 1994, p. 30.

12. Ibid.

13. While the Veronis, Suhler figures include advertising by both local and national merchants, the national advertisers are of greatest interest here, because they are the major driving forces behind U.S. media trends. Local merchants make most of their impact in neighborhood media—local newspapers, local radio, and regional magazines. Across the country, the impact of these decisions by thousands of merchants is nowhere as coherent as that of national advertisers who drop tens and hundreds of millions of dollars on media plans aimed at making an impact across the country. The amounts that national advertising clients spend individually can affect the health of individual media firms, even that of a media industry.

14. R. Craig Endicott, "US income growth outduels foreign side," *Advertising Age,* April 13, 1994, p. 1.

15. Ibid., p. 54.

16. *Standard Directory of Advertising Agencies (The Red Book),* July 1994.

CHAPTER TWO

1. Quoted in Julie Liesse, "Inside Burnett's vaunted buying machine," *Advertising Age,* July 25, 1994, p. S6.

2. Ibid.

3. Edwin Emery and Michael Emery, *The Press in America,* 5th ed. (Englewood Cliffs, N.J.: Prentice Hall, 1984), p. 198.

4. Ibid., pp. 199–200.

5. Ibid., p. 201.

6. Ibid., p. 233.

7. Frank Rowsome, Jr., *They Laughed When I Sat Down: An Informal History of Advertising in Words and Pictures* (New York: McGraw-Hill, 1959), p. 43.

8. Daniel Pope, *The Making of Modern Advertising* (New York: Basic Books, 1983), p. 139.

9. Ibid., p. 141.

10. Ibid., p. 258.

11. Ibid., p. 258.

12. Erik Barnouw, *The Sponsor* (New York: Oxford University Press, 1978), p. 71.

13. See, for example, James Forkan, "Nets cheered by '78 outlook," *Advertising Age,* January 1, 1978, p. 8; and Colby Coates, "Ratings loss not as bad as first thought," *Advertising Age,* January 19, 1981, p. 104.

14. See, for example, Irwin Gottlieb, "Turning investment management into an art form," *Advertising Age*, September 11, 1995, p. S2.

15. Daniel Boorstin, *The Americans: The Democratic Experience* (New York: Random House, 1973), frontispiece.

16. Ibid., p. 148.

17. See, for example, David Potter, *People of Plenty: Economic Abundance and the American Character* (Chicago: University of Chicago Press, 1954); John Kenneth Galbraith, *The Affluent Society* (Boston: Houghton Mifflin, 1958); Samm Sinclair Baker, *The Permissible Lie* (Cleveland: World Publishing, 1968); and Vance Packard, *The Hidden Persuaders* (New York: D. McKay, 1957).

18. As examples, see Stuart Ewen, *Captains of Consciousness: Advertising and the Social Roots of Consumer Culture* (New York: McGraw-Hill, 1976; Herbert Schiller, *Mass Communications and American Empire* (New York: A. M. Kelley, 1969); and Sut Jhally, *The Codes of Advertising* (New York: St. Martin's Press, 1987).

19. The debate on advertising's role in mass society was joined by intellectuals from a variety of political perspectives. See Bernard Rosenberg and David Manning White, *Mass Culture: The Popular Arts in America* (Glencoe, Ill.: Free Press of Glencoe, 1957), especially the chapters by Paul Lazarsfeld and Robert Merton, T. W. Adorno, Clement Greenberg, Gilbert Seldes, and Dwight MacDonald. See also Neil Postman, *Amusing Ourselves to Death* (New York: Penguin Books, 1986); Richard Wightman Fox and T. J. Jackson Lears (eds.), *The Culture of Consumption* (New York: Pantheon, 1983); and T. J. Jackson Lears, *Fables of Abundance* (New York: Basic Books, 1994).

20. A particularly interesting example is Roland Marchand, *Advertising the American Dream: Making Way for Modernity, 1920–1940* (Berkeley: University of California Press, 1985).

21. Michael Schudson, *Advertising: The Uneasy Persuasion* (New York: Basic Books, 1984), pp. 209–33.

22. Studies for the landmark Payne Fund project on motion pictures and youth along with research at Columbia University's sociology department helped to set the social-psychological and sociological models for understanding media effects. See W. W. Charters, *Motion Pictures and Youth: A Summary* (New York: Macmillan, 1933); Paul Cressey, "The Motion Picture as Modified by Social Background and Personality," *American Sociological Review* 3 (August 1938), pp. 516–25; P. Lazarsfeld and Frank Stanton, *Radio Research, 1941* (New York: Duell, Sloan, and Pierce, 1942); Charles R. Wright, *Mass Communication: A Sociological Perspective*, 1st ed. (New York: Random House, 1959); and Elliot Friedson, "Mass Communication and the Concept of Mass," in Wilbur Schramm and Donald Roberts (eds.), The Process and Effects of Mass Com-

munication (Champaign, Ill.: University of Illinois Press, 1962). An important exception was the work during the 1920s by University of Chicago sociologist Robert Park on the immigrant press. See Robert Park, *The Immigrant Press in America* (New York: Harper and Brothers, 1922). For a useful overview of these streams of thought, see Daniel Czitrom, *Media and the American Mind* (Chapel Hill: University of North Carolina Press, 1982).

23. Earnest Elmo Calkins, *The Business of Advertising* (New York: D. Appleton and Company, 1915), pp. 19–51.

24. Ibid., p. 22.

25. Ibid., p. 185.

26. Ibid., pp. 151–52.

27. Ibid., p. 154.

28. Ibid., pp. 3–57.

29. Susan Strasser, *Satisfaction Guaranteed* (New York: Pantheon, 1989), p. 14.

30. Erik Barnouw, *A History of Broadcasting in the United States, Volume 1: A Tower in Babel* (New York: Oxford University Press), 1966.

31. Quoted in John Tebbel, *The American Magazine* (New York: Hawthorne Books, 1969), p. 234.

32. Ibid., p. 239.

33. Ibid., p. 264.

34. Pope, *The Making of Modern Advertising*, p. 259.

35. Ibid.

36. Interview with James Ramsey, senior vice president-executive creative director, McCann-Erickson, Detroit, October 1994. He was creative director on the Buick account in the mid–1980s.

37. Jesse Snyder, "Buick tv targets yuppie varieties," *Advertising Age,* January 28, 1985, p. 47.

38. Julie Liesse, "Inside Burnett's vaunted buying machine," *Advertising Age,* July 25, 1994, p. S6.

39. Christopher Sterling, *Stay Tuned: A Concise History of American Broadcasting,* 2nd ed. (Belmont, Calif.: Wadsworth, 1990), p. 661.

40. *Broadcasting,* March 6, 1976, p. 45.

CHAPTER THREE

1. Quoted in Jacques Neher, "Turner seeks more ads for his 'super station,'" *Advertising Age,* October 28, 1978, p. 3.

2. Ibid.

3. Ibid.

4. Quoted in John Revett, "Turner tells 4As nets to be eclipsed," *Advertising Age,* October 29, 1979, p. 2.

5. Ibid.

6. Ibid.

7. Herbert Maneloveg, "Marketing—and all society—affected by media changes,"*Advertising Age,* November 13, 1980, p. 56.

8. Ibid.

9. Spencer L. Hapoienu, "Media commentary: How we've evolved," *Advertising Age,* July 27, 1981, p. 36.

10. B. G. Yovovich, "Polishing new research tools for the future," *Advertising Age,* November 18, 1982, p, M26.

11. [No author], "Smith outlines eight trends to watch," *Advertising Age,* August 24, 1981, p. 22.

12. Jeffrey J. Hallet, "Getting ready for the new economy," *Advertising Age,* June 21, 1984, p. 12.

13. Richard Gordon, "Groups cheer coming Reagan era," *Advertising Age,* November 10, 1980, p. 3. See also Leo Shapiro and Dwight Bohmbach, "Consumer watch: Hopeful signs point to jump in buying," *Advertising Age,* April 20, 1981, p. 28; Stanley Cohen, "Consumer issues hard to find," September 21, 1981, p. 42; Sid Bernstein, "Should Kellogg do your voting?" *Advertising Age,* October 5, 1981; B. G. Yovovich, "Now it's the baby boomer's turn," *Advertising Age,* April 4, 1983; and Van Wallach, "New magazines take root in social climate," *Advertising Age,* November 10, 1986, p. S2.

14. Rance Crain, "Reagan to keep ship on same course," *Advertising Age,* November 15, 1984, p. 30.

15. B. G. Yovovich, "Tracking the trends in public opinion: Research companies respond to a growing need," *Advertising Age,* May 23, 1983, p. M30; and Stanley Cohen, "Dog days for consumerists," *Advertising Age,* April 20, 1981, p. 36; [No author], "New AAF, BBB Plan: Local ad review units try again," *Advertising Age,* April 27, 1981, p. 1; Stanley Cohen, "The sights of rebellion still linger," *Advertising Age,* April 18, 1983, p. 24; and Jennifer Lawrence, "States sue U.S. over air-fare ads," *Advertising Age,* May 9, 1988, p. 2.

16. Stanley Cohen, "The more that things change . . .," *Advertising Age,* November 17, 1980, p. 20.

17. Hallet, "Getting ready for the new economy," p. 12.

18. Maneloveg, "Marketing—and all society—affected by media changes," p. 56.

19. Jim Auchmutey, "Graphic changes charted in the middle class," *Advertising Age,* September 12, 1985, p. 16.

20. Ibid.

21. Ibid., p. 15.

22. Jennifer Alter, "Public is still wary of ads: Study," *Advertising Age,* June 23, 1980, p. 3.

23. [No author], "Smith outlines eight trends to watch," *Advertising Age,* August 24, 1981, p. 22.

24. [No author], "Smith outlines eight trends to watch," p. 22; also B. G. Yovovich, "The new localism," *Advertising Age,* April 5, 1982, p. M9; and B. G. Yovovich, "His crystal ball: the daily newspaper; John 'Megatrends' Naisbitt swears by the press," *Advertising Age,* November 11, 1982, p. M4.

25. Judith Graham, "New VALS 2 takes psychological route," *Advertising Age,* February 13, 1989, p. 24; see also Jeff Smith, "A '90s taste for private label: Brands must now 'aspire' to more cost-conscious," *Advertising Age,* April 11, 1994, p. 29.

26. Alter, "Public is still wary of ads," p. 3.

27. Tom Bayer, "Four A's readies new credibility credo," *Advertising Age,* March 21, 1983, p. 3; Jeff Jensen, "Athlete bad? Marketer glad! Sports antiheroes find they're welcome in '90s gritty advertising," *Advertising Age,* September 27, 1993; Theodore Gage, "PR ripes role in marketing," January 5, 1981, p. S10; and Fred Danzig, *Advertising Age,* November 9, 1988, p. S1.

28. See Leo Bogart, "Media and a changing America: A shifting society means new rules and roles," *Advertising Age,* March 29, 1982, p. M52.

29. Ibid.

30. Patrick Riley, "Consumers prove elusive," *Advertising Age,* October 24, 1988, p. S1.

31. Ibid.

32. Maureen Christopher, "Cable viewers a restless lot, study finds," *Advertising Age,* May 9, 1983, p. 62.

33. Jim Benson, "Trouble corralling the grazers: Studies hint at depth of problem, but nets just begin to shake their apathy," *Advertising Age,* November 28, 1988, p. S4.

34. See Yovovich, "Polishing new research tools for the future," p. M26.

35. Ibid.

36. Ibid.

37. Jack Honomichl, "Market research companies," May 17, 1984, sect. 2.

38. Michael J. Weiss, *The Clustering of America* (New York: Harper & Row, 1988), p. 2.

39. Ibid., p. xii.

40. Ibid., p. 340.

41. B. G. Yovovich, "It's 1982—do you know what your values are?" *Advertising Age,* October 18, 1982, p. M31. See also Udayan Gupta, "Mix 'n' match data: Cross-pollinating research provides some useful new hybrids," *Advertising Age,* October 31, 1983, p. 48.

42. Arnold Mitchell, *The Nine American Lifestyles: Who We Are and Where We're Going* (New York: Warner Books, 1983).

43. Ibid., p. 154.

44. Yovovich, "It's 1982—do you know what your values are?" p. M29. It might be noted that *integrateds,* because they were thought to be so small and not easily identified by computer, were not typically addressed in marketing strategies developed by using the VALS categories. See Mitchell, *Nine American Lifestyles,* p. 154. The Yankelovich Monitor and Claritas were modified over time. See Judith Graham, "New VALS 2 takes psychological route," *Advertising Age,* February 13, 1989, p. 24.

45. J. C. Louis, "It's anthropological! Research takes a 'cultural' bent," *Advertising Age,* January 14, 1985, p. 3.

46. See, for example, Diane Mermigas, "Nielsen on the button with new meter test," *Advertising Age,* February 7, 1983, p. 38; Verne Gay, "Nielsen loses its diary, ABC: Meter woes mount," *Advertising Age,* January 12, 1987, p. 3; Verne Gay, "Nets hold time to counter make-goods: Upfront children's TV rates jump 30%," *Advertising Age,* April 27, 1987, p. 2; and Joe Mandese, "TV ratings monopoly faces a changing future," *Advertising Age,* November 15, 1993, p. 24.

47. For example, Joseph Smith, "Let's realize our potential," *Advertising Age,* May 23, 1983, p. M12; Sonia Yuspeh, "Slamming syndicated data," *Advertising Age,* May 17, 1984, p. M16; and Gerald Schoenfeld, "A lost art," *Advertising Age,* February 22, 1982, p. M12.

48. Craig Reiss, "New audience data fuel erosion debate," *Advertising Age,* July 25, 1983, p. 6.

49. Maureen Christopher, "Cable tv: It's still in a swirl," *Advertising Age,* November 16, 1981, p. S1. Broadcasters carped that the 1980 cable ad estimates and 1981 cable ad projections exaggerated by including WTBS, since much of that station's revenues from national advertisers were generated as a result of its over-the-air audiences.

50. See "Interactive ads," *Information Week,* October 3, 1994, p. 25.

51. Interview, Roger Baron, director of market research, Foot Cone and Belding, Chicago, June 1994.

52. Interview, Bonnie Berest, executive director of media services, Publicis Bloom, June 1994.

53. Maureen Christopher and Bob Marich, "Cablecasters watch several channels," *Advertising Age,* May 12, 1980, p. 12.

54. Robert Coen, "Vast U.S. and worldwide ad expenditures expected," *Advertising Age,* November 13, 1980, p. 10.

55. Christopher, "Cable TV: It's still in a swirl," p. S22 (chart).

56. By April 1982, cable had penetrated to 37.2 percent of U.S. households, according to Nielsen. Using Nielsen data, the CAB added that while network affiliates reached 78 percent of all viewers through the day, in cable homes

they reached only 60 percent of all viewers. See Susan Spillman, "CAB: Advertisers must recognize two-tv universe," *Advertising Age,* April 11, 1983, p. 1.

57. [Editorial], "Waiting for cable," *Advertising Age,* October 5, 1981, p. 16.

58. [No author], "Net tv won't dominate: Ford boss outlines shift to 'rifle' media," *Advertising Age,* October 26, 1981, p. 1.

59. See, e.g., John D. Lane and Mary Jo Manning, "From static to success: A history," *Advertising Age,* November 18, 1981, p. S2.

60. Richard L. Gilbert, "Agencies may have a big say on content," *Advertising Age,* November 16, 1981, p. S16.

CHAPTER FOUR

1. Peter Franchese, "A symphony of demographic change," *Advertising Age,* November 9, 1988, p. S138.

2. Daniel Pope, *The Making of Modern Advertising* (New York: Basic Books, 1983), p. 139.

3. See, for example, *True Story,* "When *True Story* readers cook out, they cook out all out," *Advertising Age,* June 20, 1983, p. 20. See also *Handyman,* "Oh, do they need our magazine," *Advertising Age,* July 27, 1981, p. 26.

4. *Forbes,* "We're all created equal," *Advertising Age,* January 18, 1982, gatefold.

5. *Time,* "Bye-bye, buy buy," *Advertising Age,* June 21, 1982, p. 43. See also [No author], "Media moves," *Advertising Age,* June 14, 1982, p. 26.

6. Jesse Snyder, "Tracking trend setters helps marketers gear up," *Advertising Age,* June 21, 1984, p. 31. See also Dave Galanti, "American Express goes for the platinum," *Advertising Age,* August 23, 1984, p. 20; and [No author], "Affluent marketing," *Advertising Age,* May 9, 1985, sect. 2, p. S9.

7. Dave Galanti, "American Express goes for the platinum," p. 20; and Jesse Snyder, "Tracking trend setters helps marketers gear up," p. 31.

8. Galanti, "American Express goes for the platinum," p. 20

9. [No author], "Affluent marketing."

10. [No author], "Forum," *Advertising Age,* August 23, 1984, p. S20.

11. *Club Living* [ad], "How to sell to the rich." *Advertising Age,* November 2, 1981, p. 50. The theme was often that rich is good. *W,* a fashion monthly, confided to its readers knowledge that "our brandy is better, our clothes finer. . . . We have absolutely no guilt about our gilt." See *W* [ad], "Our readers get what they want," *Advertising Age,* July 27, 1981, p. S11.

12. *Newsweek,* "The rich get cheaper," *Advertising Age,* April 18, 1983, p. 4.

13. Alice Z. Cuneo, "Reaching the rich when wealth is a state of mind," *Advertising Age,* November 7, 1994, p. S16.

14. Cuneo, "Reaching the rich when wealth is a state of mind," p. S16.

15. Susan Spillman, "CAB: Advertisers must recognize two-tv universe," *Advertising Age,* April 11, 1983, p. 1.

16. Alvin Eicoff, "Would you buy from a catalog," *Advertising Age,* January 17, 1983, p. M14.

17. Clinton Walker, "Interactive ads," *Information Week,* October 3, 1994, p. 24.

18. Jane Weaver, "Net gain: advertising on the Internet computer network," *Inside Media,* June 13, 1994, p. 28. See also Betsy Frank, quoted in Stuart Elliot, "A study by four agencies paints a surprising portrait of interactive computer users," *New York Times,* September 25, 1995, p. D9.

19. Anonymous executive, quoted in Peter Ginsberg, *The Logic in the Numbers* (Philadelphia: M.A. Thesis, The Annenberg School for Communication, 1994), p. 75.

20. Greg Gattuso, "Lillian Vernon looks to the future," *Direct Marketing Magazine,* August 1994, p. 33.

21. Jann Wenner, quoted in Patrick Reilly, "Magazines beckon 'New Man,'" *Advertising Age,* April 17, 1989, p. 3.

22. B. G. Yovovich, "Pinning down the elusive man of men's magazines," *Advertising Age,* October 19, 1991, p. S26.

23. Charline Allen, "Radio listens to an increasingly female audience," *Advertising Age,* October 3, 1983, p. M32.

24. Ibid.

25. Jim Auchmutey, "Graphic changes charted in the middle class," *Advertising Age,* September 12, 1985, p. 15.

26. Janet Simons, "Agencies tearing out old labels," *Advertising Age,* October 4, 1984, p. M17.

27. [No author], "Marketers slighting many male 'settlers,'" *Advertising Age.* July 25, 1983, p. 34.

28. [No author], "C&W discovers new breed of husband," *Advertising Age,* November 10, 1980, p. 64.

29. Anthony Astrachan, "Magnifying changes in masculine marketplace," *Advertising Age,* October 4, 1984, p. 11.

30. Mary McCabe English, "Catering to different segments," *Advertising Age,* September 19, 1985, p. 15.

31. Eileen Brill, "Super marketers pursue the new consumers," *Advertising Age,* October 13, 1986, p. S4.

32. Ibid., p. 3.

33. *Ladies Home Journal.* "I don't have to play God anymore," *Advertising Age,* April 20, 1981, p. 89.

34. Astrachan, "Magnifying changes in masculine marketplace," p. 11.

35. Gary Belsky, "*Esquire, GQ* fashionably ahead," *Advertising Age,* April 18, 1988, p. S2.

36. Auchmutey, "Graphic changes charted in the middle class," p. 15.

37. Ibid.

38. Interview, Rena Bartos, president, the Rena Bartos Company, June 1994.

39. Lori Kesler, "Behind the wheel of a quiet revolution," *Advertising Age,* July 26, 1982, p. M11.

40. [No author], "Working women now more attractive—Y&R," *Advertising Age,* January 11, 1982, p. 76.

41. Faye Brookman, "Upscale tactics honed for mass market," *Advertising Age,* March 28, 1988, p. S14.

42. [No author], "Homemakers a happy breed," *Advertising Age,* March 16, 1981, p. 2.

43. Ibid.

44. Ibid.

45. Rena Bartos, *The Moving Target* (New York: Basic Books, 1982).

46. Auchmutey, "Graphic changes charted in the middle class," p. 17; and Neil Bennet and David Bloom, "Why fewer women marry," *Advertising Age,* January 12, 1987, p. 18.

47. Allen, "Radio listens to an increasingly female audience," p. M32.

48. Dennis McDougal, "There's a new Geraldo . . . sort of," *Los Angeles Times,* March 5, 1989; and Wayne Wally, "Female audience lifeblood of Lifetime," *Advertising Age,* April 11, 1988, p. S22.

49. Wally, "Female audience lifeblood of Lifetime," p. S22.

50. Ibid., p. M32; also Auchmutey, "Graphic changes charted in the middle class," p. 15; and Joanne Cleaver, "Lifestyle ads boost banks, insurers," *Advertising Age,* March 7, 1988, p. S8.

51. Wally, "Female audience lifeblood of Lifetime," *Advertising Age,* April 11, 1988, p. S22.

52. Cecelia Lentini, "Balancing act in women's magazines," *Advertising Age,* October 19, 1981, p. S62.

53. Sarah Stern, "Working to meet women's multiple roles," *Advertising Age,* October 3, 1985, p. 50.

54. Ibid.

55. "The so-called sweatless women I was afraid of all have the same questions and problems we all do"—such as divorce, baby sitters and men—said Lenore Hershey, former editor-in-chief of the *Ladies Home Journal,* in 1983. The quote is in Stuart Elliot, "At age 100, LHJ says it's still solid," *Advertising Age,* July 11, 1983, p. 14.

56. Adrienne Ward, "Sibling rivalry," *Advertising Age,* October 6, 1991, p. 38.

57. Scott Donaton, "*Redbook* narrows in on new look," *Advertising Age,* June 3, 1991, p. 1.

58. Terese Kauchak, "Dominant color? Try red," *Advertising Age,* October 6, 1991, p. 40. "They don't need the same information anymore. [Working mothers] used to be in the minority in the neighborhood; now they *are* the neighborhood."

59. Ward, "Sibling rivalry," p. 38.

60. Kauchak, "Dominant color? Try red," p. 40.

61. Ward, "Sibling rivalry," p. 38.

62. Pat Sloan, "*Good Housekeeping* sees trend," *Advertising Age,* October 17, 1988, p. 12.

63. *Good Housekeeping,* "The New Traditionalist," *Advertising Age,* August 22, 1988, p. 9.

64. Ibid.

65. Ibid.; see also Ward, "Sibling rivalry," p. 38.

66. Van Wallach, "New magazines take root in social climate," *Advertising Age,* November 10, 1986, p. S4; Lenore Skenazy, "Affluent, like masses, are flush with worries," *Advertising Age,* July 10, 1989, p. 55; See Peter Bart, "Rupert's raison d'etre," *Variety,* January 31, 1994, p. 5; [No author], "USA Network," *Advertising Age,* February 20, 1989, CABLE 16.

67. Taft Broadcasting Company (ad), "Shake hands with a fantasy," *Advertising Age,* January 2, 1978, p. 15; and Anita Busch, "Advertisers draw cartoons into endorsements," *Advertising Age,* June 9, 1986, p. S5.

68. Today, nobody seems quite sure why the forty-ninth year, and not the forty-eighth or fifty-second, was chosen as the cutoff for prime-time audience heaven. Peripheral hours might be for "children" (aged two—twelve), "teens" (aged thirteen—seventeen), or people fifty years or older. But "eighteen to forty-nine" became one of the phrases that network programmers, salespeople, and agency media planners learned to recite about prime time as they were socialized into the commercial television system.

69. Peter Franchese, "Women in work force boost economy," *Advertising Age,* September 3, 1984, p. 30; and [No author], "Graphic of baby boomer qualities," *Advertising Age,* October 18, 1984, p. 11. Another definition of the baby boom had it that they appeared between 1945 and 1959. In 1984, that would place them at fifty-six million strong. That represented 56.7 percent of the twenty-five to thirty-nine year olds or 24.2 percent of the U.S. population. See B. G. Yovovich, "Getting a reading on the baby boom," *Advertising Age,* October 18, 1984, p. 11.

70. Leo Shapiro and Dwight Bombach, "Young adults power economic engine," *Advertising Age,* August 5, 1985, p. 12.

71. [No author], "Graphic of baby boomer qualities," p. 11.

72. B. G. Yovovich, "Generation opens more doors for publishers," *Advertising Age,* October 18, 1984, p. 12.

73. Landon Jones, "Baby boomers can be an elusive bunch," *Advertising Age,* November 18, 1984, p. 16.

74. Ibid.

75. Yovovich, "Getting a reading on the baby boom," p. 11; and Janice Steinberg, "Soft touch a new age for medium," *Advertising Age,* August 31, 1987, p. S1.

76. [No author], "Consumer shock," *Advertising Age,* October 26, 1987, p. 1.

77. Ibid.

78. *Family Life* [ad], "Money used to be the most important thing in our wallets. Now it's the photographs," *Advertising Age,* November 1, 1993, pp. 20–21.

79. Franchese, "A symphony of demographic change," p. S138; Beth Bogart, "Word of mouth travels fastest," *Advertising Age,* February 6, 1989, p. S6.

80. Eileen Brill, "Super marketers pursue the new consumers," *Advertising Age,* October 13, 1986, p. S4.

81. William Robinson, "Promoting tag teens," *Advertising Age,* April 4, 1989, p. 60.

82. Nancy Coltun Webster, "Marketing to kids," *Advertising Age,* February 5, 1995, p. S1.

83. James McNeal, *Kids as Customers* (New York: Lexington Books, 1992), p. 6.

84. Ibid., p. 16.

85. Ibid., p. 16.

86. Cable Advertising Bureau, *Cable Network Profiles '94* (New York: Cable Advertising Bureau).

87. C.T., "Upscale moms groom the ultimate consumers," *Advertising Age,* September 12, 1985, p. 35.

88. Nielsen Media Research, as cited in Robert Famighetti (ed.), *The World Almanac and Book of Facts, 1995* (Chicago: Funk and Wagnalls, 1995), p. 312.

89. Webster, "Marketing to kids," p. S1.

90. Lynn Folse, "They're not getting older; they're getting bigger," *Advertising Age,* October 3, 1985, p. 44.

91. Patrician Strnad, "Age said key, not zip codes," *Advertising Age* October 18, 1984, p. 7; Peter Franchese, "Incomes had a very good year," *Advertising Age,* October 27, 1985, p. 62; Jon Lafayette and Lenore Skenazy, "How to

reach seniors? Be positive," *Advertising Age,* October 31, 1988, p. 12; and Adrienne Ward, "Senior-slanted media reap auto bounty: buying power of market wakes up carmakers," *Advertising Age,* July 24, 1989, p. S21.

92. Lafayette and Skenazy, "How to reach seniors? Be positive," p. 12.

93. Ann Clurman quoted in J. Fred MacDonald, *Advertising Age,* June 29, 1981, p. S2. See also Patrick Reilly, "Not-mature market: old is gold to publishers," *Advertising Age,* June 13, 1988, p. 3.

94. Ellen Norris, "Radio listens closely to mature market," *Advertising Age,* October 19, 1987, p. S2.

95. Interview with Jerry Ohlsten, director of marketing, Simmons Market Research, February 2, 1995.

96. Interview with Jerry Ohlsten, February 2, 1995.

97. The network's programming had traditionally "skewed old." When the number of households was the criterion for ratings success, that didn't matter much. However, as interest in audience segmentation led marketers increasingly to consider income, gender, and age as key criteria for ratings success, CBS found itself under challenge. Beginning in the mid-'80s, the network tried to make a virtue of its predicament.

Trying to defend the attraction of more older people than were drawn to NBC or ABC, CBS executives argued that an age cluster tilting toward fifty-four had more disposable income than the young end of the eighteen to forty-nine cluster. They contended further that the mature adult audience would bring stability to the broadcast networks at a time of fear over new media, since eighteen- to twenty-four- or eighteen- to thirty-four-year-olds were more likely than those aged thirty-five to forty-nine to desert the broadcast networks for cable programs. Advertisers and their agencies did not buy the arguments, however, and CBS began to bow to their interests. By 1995, CBS officials was trying furiously to mount programming designed to attract people at the lower end of the eighteen to forty-nine cluster. See, for example, Bill Carter, "Cable picks up viewers the networks cast adrift," *New York Times,* June 5, 1995, p. D7; and Bill Carter, "NBC grabs young adults from ABC," *New York Times,* November 28, 1994, p. D1.

98. Ani Hadijian, "While it will be hip to be old," *Fortune,* November 22, 1993, p. 86.

99. Ibid.

100. [No author], "Studies tell the story but dollars don't follow," *Advertising Age,* May 22, 1989, p. S4; and Laurie Freeman, "Teen buying power not just cosmetic," *Advertising Age,* September 12, 1989, p. 29.

101. Dan Cray, Tom Curry, and William McWhirter, "twentysomething," *Time,* July 16, 1990, p. 57.

102. Vincenzo James Petretti, *Tracking and analyzing the media discourse*

of Generation X (Philadelphia: M.A. thesis, Annenberg School for Communication: 1994), p. 68.

103. For a history of the term and its use, see Ibid.

104. B. W. Powe, "The forward spin to nowhere," the *Toronto Star*, August 22, 1992, p. H12.

105. Karen Ritchie, "Get ready for 'Generation X,'" *Advertising Age*, November 9, 1992, p. 21.

106. Scott Donaton, "The media wakes up to Generation X," *Advertising Age*, February 1, 1993, p. 17. See also Laura Zinn, "Move over, Boomers," *Business Week*, December 14, 1992, p. 79; and "The new generation gap," *Atlantic*, December 1992.

107. A prominent example was Jann Wenner, the publisher and founder of *Rolling Stone* magazine. His periodical was attempting to build an audience across the eighteen to forty-nine spectrum, and Wenner found the GenX-vs.-boomer talk anathema. In a 1993 article for *Advertising Age*, he questioned whether Xers and boomers were really that different and announced concern about what he said was the implicit negativity and hostility that marketers had poured into their notions of Generation X. In different tones, the letters *Ad Age* printed in reply disagreed with his fundamental proposition that there was no generational split. Karen Ritchie, in particular, wrote a withering missive suggesting that Wenner's claims reflected a misguided attempt by his magazine to reach too broad an age spectrum. "I applaud the altruism," she wrote sarcastically, "that, no doubt, motivates him to protect our young folks from crass and odious marketers who insist that young people today are not miniature baby boomers." See Karen Ritchie, "Boomers and GenX" [Letter], *Advertising Age*, October 25, 1993, p.30.

108. Jessica Kerwin, "Generation X-Force," *Village Voice*, August 24, 1993. p. 51.

109. [No author], "Generation X," *Direct*, January 1993, pp. 34–35; Michael Sansolo, "Riding the age wave," *Progressive Grocer*, June 1993, p. 83; and Alex Benady, "Faith in brands top faith in authority," *Marketing*, August 19, 1993, p. 13.

110. Laurie Freeman, "Advertising's mirror is cracked," *Advertising Age*, February 6, 1995, p. 30.

111. Stuart Elliot, "When the smoke clears, it's still Reynolds," *New York Times*, September 13, 1995, p. D1.

112. Laurie Freeman, "No tricking the media savvy," *Advertising Age*, February 6, 1995, p. 30.

113. Andy Meisler, "MTV's sister channel alters its pitch," *New York Times*, February 6, 1995, p, D6.

114. Michael Wilborn, "TV's football frenzy," *TV Guide,* September 3, 1994, p. F2.

115. J. Max Robins, Brian Lowry, and Jim Benson, "Nervous nets play sweeps for keeps," *Variety,* November 22, 1993, p. 1.

116. Hilary De Vries, "You gotta have friends: How NBC made a sitcom about Generation X that even your monther could love," *TV Guide,* January 28, 1995, p. 37.

117. Rivendell Marketing Company, "The gay market," *Advertising Age,* September 8, 1983, p. 15.

118. From 1978 through 1993, *Advertising Age* carried no more than forty-five ads and articles about them. Many of these were about the AIDS epidemic or "scandals" such as the disclosure of tennis star Billy Jean King's homosexuality that would scare national advertisers away from targeting gays. In 1980, in fact, *Advertising Age* stated flatly that national advertisers "other than book and record companies and a few liquor accounts shy away from being identified with homosexuals." See Leah Rozen, "National ads elude gay book," *Advertising Age,* December 29, 1980, p. 31.

119. Riccardo Davis, "Marketers game for gay events," *Advertising Age,* May 30, 1994, p. S1.

120. See Brett Chase, "Gay economy lures dollars of major advertisers," *Business Record,* August 8, 1994, p. 1; Lynn Berling-Manual, "Reaching the gay market," *Advertising Age,* March 26, 1984, p. M4; Gary Levin, "List-generating hot—to direct mail's delight," *Advertising Age,* May 30, 1994, p. S8; Jon Boorstein, "Strub, Nathan launch gay affinity card," *DM News,* June 20, 1994; and Karen De Witt, "Gay presence leads revival of declining neighborhoods," *New York Times,* September 6, 1994, p. A14. In late 1994, Strubco, a direct marketing firm that aimed at slices of the homosexual market, was even considering a mailing list with names of Jewish homosexuals, according to an interview with Charlie Connard, Strubco direct-marketing executive (December 17, 1994).

121. Nancy Coltun Webster, "Playing to gay segments opens doors to marketers," *Advertising Age,* May 30, 1984, p. S6. As mainstream beverage, liquor, fashion, and travel advertisers, in particular, continued to move onto the pages of gay/lesbian periodicals, the utility and differentiation of homosexuals even drew the attention of media giant Time Warner. The company in 1994 considered but abandoned a proposal for a magazine targeted at upscale gay men with the primary-community label *Tribe.* See Keith Kelly, "Healthcare fuels magazine growth: Mainstream advertisers latching on in numbers," *Advertising Age,* May 30, 1994, p. S4.

122. De Witt, "Gay presence leads revival of declining neighborhoods," p.

A14. Yankelovich did point out that gays and lesbians still had a far higher proportion of college graduates than the heterosexual population. And the publisher of the *Research Alert* newsletter repeated the idea that because gays "have no families, they have more discretionary income" than the public at large. See De Witt, "Gay presence leads revival of declining neighborhoods," p. A–14; [No author], "A portrait of the gay/lesbian market," *Research Alert,* September 2, 1994; and Cuneo, "Reaching the rich when wealth is a state of mind," p. S16.

123. Michael Wilke, "Simmons plans definitive survey of gay consumers," *Advertising Age,* February 19, 1996, p. 39.

124. Cuneo, "Reaching the rich when wealth is a state of mind," p. S16; and [No author], "Advertising spending in gay print publications," *Business Wire,* July 24, 1995.

125. See, for example, Larry Gutenberg, letter, *Advertising Age,* October 3, 1983, p. 72. In 1984, *Advertising Age* noted that "one segment that is not addressed in most gay-oriented research is lesbians. That is because women earn less and lesbians often have more traditional households, including children." See Berling-Manual, "Reaching the gay market," p. M4. Judging by the trade press, in the mid–1990s the emphasis was on finding marketable slices of young gay men. Even pictures told this story. While paying lip service to the phrase "gays and lesbians," all but one of the photos in ads for consultants, magazines, and direct-mail firms that were featured in *Advertising Age*'s special section were of young adult men.

126. De Witt, "Gay presence leads revival of declining neighborhoods," p. A14. The quote is by Dick Dadey: "As people exhibit individual acts of courage by coming out, we're finding out how diverse we are."

127. Interview with Byron Lewis, chairman and CEO of Uniworld, February 10, 1995.

128. Adrienne Ward Fawcett, "The battle for black accounts," *Advertising Age,* February 5, 1996, p. 14.

129. Shiela Gadsden, "Seeking the right tack in talking to blacks," *Advertising Age,* September 12, 1985, p. 18.

130. Ibid.

131. Martha Moore, "Black agencies seek recognition," *USA Today,* July 25, 1994, p. 3B.

132. B. G. Yovovich, "Marketing to blacks: The debate rages on," *Advertising Age,* November 29, 1982, p. M9.

133. Shiela Gadsden, "Blowing the whistle on media placement," *Advertising Age,* December 19, 1985, p. 26. See also Wally Tokarz, "Minority marketing looks to the '80s," *Advertising Age,* April 7, 1980, p. 1; and Hulin-Salkin, "Premise in minority media changes," *Advertising Age,* April 7, 1980, p. S2.

134. Interview with Byron Lewis, chairman and CEO of Uniworld, February 10, 1995.

135. Wally Tokarz, "Minority marketing looks to the '80s," p. 1; Ed Yardang Advertising [ad], "Suddenly, everyone's 'discovering' the Hispanic market," *Advertising Age,* April 7, 1980, p. S3; Jennifer Pendleton, "Growth in Hispanic population forecast," *Advertising Age,* August 2, 1982, p. 32.

136. Interview, Doug Darfield, vice president of research, Univision, February 9, 1995.

137. See Eileen Norris, "Piecing together fragmented research," *Advertising Age,* August 11, 1986, p. S28; Richard Edel, "Outdoor boards are growing in stature," *Advertising Age,* August 11, 1986, p. S2; Universion [ad], "Mucho Money: The Hispanic Market," *Advertising Age,* January 23, 1995, p. 34; and Jack Honomichl, "How to research the U.S. Hispanic market," *Advertising Age,* January 18, 1982, p. 22.

138. Carol Wright Hispanic [ad], "Hispanic mothers buy 17% more baby food than non-Hispanics," *Advertising Age,* June 7, 1982, p. 64; Carol Wright Hispanic [ad], "Hispanic females use 36% more eye-liner than non-Hispanics," *Advertising Age.* June 14, 1982, p. 52; and Christy Fisher, "Telcos lead Hispanic ad stampede," *Advertising Age.* January 25, 1995, p. 30.

139. For a history of the debate and the vested interests involved, see Michelle Klich, *The Hispanic Image: The Making of the Spanish-Speaking Audience* (Lafayette, Ind.: M.A. Thesis, Purdue University, 1988).

140. Interview with Shelly Cagner, press relations, Arbitron, February 15, 1995.

141. [No author], "Nielsen Hispanic Index," *Advertising Age,* October 26, 1992, p. 49. See also, Christy Fisher, "Ratings worth $40 million?" *Advertising Age,* January 24, 1994, p. S8.

142. Interview with Mark Rice, vice president, Network–New York Agencies, Nielsen Audience Measurement, February 1995.

143. Interview with Doug Darfield, vice president of research, Univision, February 1995.

144. Christy Fisher, "Younger Hispanics get the word," *Advertising Age,* January 25, 1995, p, 29.

145. Leon Wynter, "Reaching Hispanics across a racial and cultural divide," *Wall Street Journal,* February 15, 1995, B1.

146. Interview with Doug Darfield, February 9, 1995.

147. Eileen Brill, "Super marketers pursue the new consumers," *Advertising Age,* October 13, 1986, p. S4.

148. Wynter, "Reaching Hispanics across a racial and cultural divide," p. B1. There were strong doubts about racial and language commonality within

the U.S. Hispanic American population among regional marketers and Census takers. Through the years, as well, some worried that Hispanic Americans were being stigmatized by the image of "a people who speak only, or preferably, Spanish and who are unassimilated, non-acculturated and living in cultural self-segregation," to quote one letter writer to *Advertising Age*. The writer argued that such a portrait was "outmoded and hurtful" to the image of Hispanics in the United States. See Raul Chavarria, "Changing Hispanic market" [Letter], *Advertising Age*, February 6, 1995, p. 20.

149. See, for example, Jeanne Whalen, "Sears targets Asians," *Advertising Age*, October 10, 1994, p. 1; Leah Rickard and Jeanne Whalen, "Ethnic opportunities for retailers," *Advertising Age*, May 1, 1995, p. 1; and Robert J. Morais, "Reaching Asian-Americans not a one-dimensional task," *Advertising Age*, February 27, 1995, p. 18.

CHAPTER FIVE

1. [No author], "ANA eyes viewer 'cells,'" *Advertising Age*, October 6, 1980, p. 1.

2. [No author], "Consumer magazine paid circulation," *Advertising Age*, February 20, 1995, p. 34.

3. Interview with Hans Tennsma, design director, *Family Fun*, March 1995.

4. Ibid.

5. Interview with Brad Pallas, art director, *Woman's Day*, March 1995.

6. Ibid.

7. Though one might suspect the one-parent rule was enacted to welcome divorced parents to the magazine, the real reason is aesthetic: The art directors asserted that a photo with two parents and a child makes the cover unacceptably cluttered.

8. Interview with Laura Eisman, art director, *Family Life*, March 1995.

9. Interview with Hans Tennsma, design director, *Family Fun*, March 1995.

10. Inteview with Jay Guither, vice president in charge of new ventures, Arbitron, March 1995.

11. Interview with Tommy Hadges, president, Pollack Media Group, March 1995; and Ted Bolton, president, Bolton Research, March 1995.

12. Interview with Ted Bolton, March 1995.

13. See, for example, Cyndee Maxwell, "Kelly speaks out on 'The Alternative Radio Myth,'" *Radio and Records*, March 31, 1995, p. 57; also Andrew Page, "We are The Underground," *Welcomat: The Philadelphia Weekly / News, Arts & Opinion*, February 8, 1995, p. 1.

14. Interview with Jon Coleman, president, Coleman Research, March 1995.

15. Interviews with Jay Guither, March 1995; Russ Motla, program director, WDRE: The Underground Network, March 1995; Tommy Hadges, March 1995; Ted Bolton, March 1995; and Jon Coleman, March 1995.

16. Interview with Tommy Hadges, March 1995.

17. See Shawn Alexander, "Imaging the account profile," *Radio and Records,* March 31, 1995, p. 25.

18. Interview with Ted Bolton, March 1995.

19. Interview with Rich Dunray, interviewer, Irwin Research Services, March 1995.

20. Interview with Ted Bolton, March 1995.

21. Joe Mandese, "In new growth phase, cable feeding on itself," *Advertising Age,* March 27, 1995, p. S1.

22. Ibid.

23. Michael Wilke, "100 cabooses, two or three engines," *Advertising Age,* March 27, 1995, p. S4.

24. Mandese, "In new growth phase, cable feeding on itself," p. S1.

25. Wilke, "100 cabooses, two or three engines," p. S4.

26. Ibid.

27. Jefferson Graham, "'Bio' gets new lease on lives," *USA Today,* June 13, 1994, p. 3D.

28. Interview with Lee Masters, president and CEO of E! Entertainment Television, April 1995.

29. See William Spain, "Fishing for sales through cable," *Advertising Age,* March 27, 1995, p. S6.

30. Ibid.

31. The youthful Fox broadcast network sometimes signaled a divisive generational "attitude" to set itself apart from its more mass-oriented rivals in front of its core GenX audience. In 1995, a Fox print advertising campaign showed a comical elderly man with his pants hiked to his armpits. "Cool like them?" the ad asked, implying that the old guy viewed ABC, CBS, and NBC. An adjacent picture showed a handsome actor from *Melrose Place,* a Fox soap opera. "Or cool like us?" it asked rhetorically. See Anthony Ramirez, "Showtime is pushing for an image that is bold, innovative and edgy," *New York Times,* August 11, 1995, p. D5.

32. Interview with Dale Hopkins, marketing director, E! Entertainment Television, March 1995.

33. See David Kronke, "Kids think Beavis and Butt-head are cool . . .," *Los Angeles Times,* September 12, 1993, p. 73; and Joseph Turow, "Just boys or civilization destroyers?" *Los Angeles Times,* September 12, 1993, p. 73.

34. Subheading for Turow, "Just boys or civilization destroyers?" p. 73.

35. ESPN International, "A handful of guys . . ." *Advertising Age: International,* September 18, 1995, p. 112.

36. Comedy Central, "We're proud to say . . .," *Advertising Age,* April 3, 1995, p. S25.

37. *Advertising Age,* which often publishes multiple angry letters on a topic, published only one letter objecting to the ESPN ad after weeks of running it. Comedy Central's contribution didn't ignite any public anger at all.

38. Leslie Savan, "Niked lunch," *Village Voice,* September 6, 1994, p. 51.

39. Interview with Kevin Ampter, art director, Messner Vetere Berger McNamee Schmetterer / Euro RSCG, March 1995.

40. Jeffrey D. Zbar, "In diverse Hispanic world, image counts," *Advertising Age,* April 3, 1995, p. S18.

41. Gary Levin, "New media mean new methods," *Advertising Age,* June 20, 1994, p. 37.

42. Interview with Alan Klein, executive vice president, group creative director, Leo Burnett, March 1995.

43. Interview with Mark Abellara, copywriter, Messner Vetere Berger McNamee Schmetterer / Euro RSCG, March 1995.

44. Ibid.

45. Ibid.

46. Interview with Robert Arix, president, Capital Sports, June 1994.

47. Suzaine Lainson, "Effective event marketing," *Mediaweek,* September 27, 1993, p. 14.

48. Robyn Griggs, "Specializing in sponsorship," *Inside Media,* April 13, 1994, p. 20.

49. Ibid.

50. Interview with Jeff Milgram, president, Event Marketing Strategies, April 1995.

51. Lynda Drexheimer and Mike Reynolds, "Measuring sponsorships," *Inside Media,* November 17, 1993, p. 22.

52. Interview with Lisa Ukman, president, International Events Group, May 1995.

53. Ibid.

54. Kate Fitzgerald, "Sponsorquest," *Advertising Age,* April 10, 1995, p. 33.

55. Interview with Robert Arix, June 1994.

56. Ibid.

57. Robert McAllister, "Pace setters: the running and walking shoe market," *Footwear News,* November 7, 1994, via Nexis; see also Robert McAllister, "Avia's bold adventure," *Footwear News,* January 23, 1995, via Nexis.

58. McAllister, "Pace setters: the running and walking shoe market."

59. Ibid.

60. Jo McIntyre, "Avia scrambles to outdo rivals' races," *Advertising Age,* August 15, 1994, p. 27.

61. McAllister, "Pace setters: the running and walking shoe market."

62. Richard Brunelli, "The big event gets bigger," *Mediaweek,* August 16, 1993, p. 9. Also see Stephen Blacker, "Magazines' role in promotion," *Advertising Age,* June 20, 1994, p. 32.

63. *Advertising Age,* September 5, 1994, p. 5.

64. Deirdre Carmody, "Conde Nast to jump into cyberspace," *New York Times,* May 1, 1995, p. D10.

65. Melanie Warner, "Conde Nast's custom push," *Inside Media,* July 13, 1994, p. 1.

66. Wendy Marx, "Where the boys are, women aren't," *Advertising Age,* February 20, 1995, p. 12.

67. Keith Kelly, "Magazine of the year," *Advertising Age,* March 6, 1995, p. S1.

68. Ibid.

69. Michael Walsh, "Stats and demographics," a description of a talk in *How to Market on the Internet,* a conference brochure created by the Marketing Advisory Council, 1995, p. 4.

70. Michael Bower, "Frequently asked questions about marketing on the Internet," also in *How to Market on the Internet,* p. 2.

71. [No author], "InterViews," *Advertising Age,* March 13, 1995, p. S22.

72. Stuart Elliot, "The Internet is being used . . .," *New York Times,* April 24, 1994, p. D10.

73. See Debra Aho Williamson and Bradley Johnson, "Web ushers in next generation," *Advertising Age,* May 29, 1995, p. 13; and Keith J. Kelly, "'Net' finally snares Conde Nast," *Advertising Age,* March 6, 1995, p. S18.

74. Judy Black, quoted in Harry Berkowitz, "Marketers explore cyberspace," *Newsday,* April 10, 1995, p. CO2.

75. See Howard Reingold, *Virtual Communities* (Reading, Mass.: Addison Wesley, 1993).

76. Jeff Jensen, "Hackers revel in marketing hype," *Advertising Age,* September 11, 1995, p. 36.

77. Richard Saltzer, "Building communities on the Internet," a description of a talk in *How to Market on the Internet* (the Marketing Advisory Council brochure), p. 4.

78. Berkowitz, "Marketers explore cyberspace," p. CO2.

79. Robert Rossney, "Is it worth keeping all the information on the net?" *San Francisco Chronicle,* December 15, 1994, p. E4. Also see [No author],

"Some web sites do well, many flop. Why?" *Internet Business Report,* January 1995, p. 6.

80. Interview with Alexandra Jaffe, advertising/promotion manager, CBS Interactive, March 1995.

81. Berkowitz, "Marketers explore cyberspace," p. CO2.

82. Communication from Eric Blum, Modem Media's "tribemaster" for Zima's site, May 1995.

83. [No author], "Internet world—free Web directions offered," *Newsbytes News Network,* April 13, 1995, via Nexis.

84. Kim Cleland, "A gaggle of web guides vie for ads," *Advertising Age,* April 17, 1995, p. 16. Also, interview with Adam Curry, CEO, Onramp, April 1995; and Don Rogers, Account Executive, Modem Media, May 1995.

CHAPTER SIX

1. Murray Raphael, "Supermarketing yesterday, today and tomorrow," *Direct Marketing,* July 1994, pp. 18–20.

2. Michael Delman, quoted in Bradley Johnson, "In a milisecond, Microsoft boots up marketing database," *Advertising Age,* November 8, 1993, p. S6.

3. Rance Crain, "Power of advertising more like a myth," *Advertising Age,* January 1, 1994, p. 21.

4. Len Strazewski, "Non-profits learn long-term lesson," *Advertising Age,* July 27, 1987, p. S1.

5. [No author], "Direct marketing," *Advertising Age,* July 19, 1982, p. M27.

6. Hershell Gordon Lewis, "Are they seniors, old people, mature folks or what," *Direct Marketing,* June 1994, pp. 18–19.

7. [No author], "Direct marketing," *Advertising Age,* July 19, 1982, p. M27.

8. Stan Rapp and Tom Collins, *The Great Marketing Turnaround* (Englewood Cliffs, N. J.: Prentice Hall, 1990), p. 110.

9. [No author], "Direct marketing," *Advertising Age,* July 19, 1982, p. M27.

10. J. Fred MacDonald, "The clutter in the mailbox 'aint no junk,'" *Advertising Age,* January 17, 1983, p. M32.

11. Jo Anne Pagnetti, "Sales sprout from the seeds of segmentation," *Advertising Age,* January 17, 1983, p. M9.

12. MacDonald, "The clutter in the mailbox 'aint no junk,'" p. M32.

13. [No author], "Direct marketing flow chart," *Direct Marketing,* May 1985, p. 21; December 1987, p. 25; December 1990, p. 4; and March 1995, p. 4.

14. [No author], "Direct marketing flow chart," *Direct Marketing,* January 1986. p. 17; December 1991, p. 2; and March 1995, p. 4.

15. Robert Delay, "Direct marketing—'way beyond catalogs," *Advertising Age,* April 30, 1980, p. 188. In a 1990 book, Peter Winter reflected the new high-tech aspect of direct marketing with a definition that updated the 1982 version noted earlier. It described direct marketing as "the distribution of goods, services and information to targeted consumers through response advertising while keeping track of sales, interest and needs in a computer database." He was quoted in Rapp and Collins, *The Great Marketing Turnaround,* p. 46.

16. Rapp and Collins, *The Great Marketing Turnaround,* p. 110.

17. Don Peppers and Martha Rogers, *The One to One Future* (New York: Doubleday, 1993), pp. 314–15.

18. Ibid.

19. Ibid., p. 316.

20. Oscar Gandy, *The Panoptic Sort* (Boulder, Colo.: Westview Press, 1994), p. 90.

21. Ibid., pp. 90–94.

22. Warshawsky/Whitney [ad], "Segmentation + Selection = Success," *Direct Marketing,* December 1993, p. 29.

23. Gandy, *The Panoptic Sort,* p. 91.

24. Peppers and Rogers, *The One to One Future,* p. 105.

25. Interview with Barbara Dolan, client services director, Mowry Company, May 1995.

26. Gandy, *The Panoptic Sort,* pp. 90–91.

27. Interview with Barbara Dolan, May 1995.

28. Peppers and Rogers, *The One to One Future,* pp. v–vi.

29. Claude Johnson, "Winning back customers through database marketing," *Direct Marketing,* November 1994, pp. 36–37.

30. [No author], "Wunderman: 'Personalized' marketing will gain dominance," *Advertising Age,* October 25, 1993, p. S1.

31. Lester Wunderman, "New frontiers in direct marketing," *Direct Marketing,* December 1993, p. 29. See also Peter G. Miller, "Changing consumers spark mail's growth," *Advertising Age,* September 27, 1993, p. P4.

32. Peppers and Rogers, *The One to One Future,* pp. 37–38.

33. Rapp and Collins, *The Great Marketing Turnaround,* p. 96.

34. Ibid., p. 27.

35. Wunderman, "New frontiers in direct marketing," p. 29.

36. Ibid.

37. John Goodman, "Leveraging the customer database to your competitive advantage," *Direct Marketing,* December 1992, p. 26.

38. Peppers and Rogers, *The One to One Future,* p. 329.

39. James R. Rosenfeld, "In search of database marketing," *Direct,* March 1992, p. 65.

40. Cyndee Miller, "Rewards for the best customers," *Marketing News TM,* July 5, 1993, p. 1.

41. Quoted in Peter G. Miller, "Changing consumers spark mail's growth," p. P4.

42. Peppers and Rogers, *The One to One Future,* p. 65.

43. Quoted in Miller, "Changing consumers spark mail's growth," p. P4.

44. Don Peppers, "Digitizing desire, part two: How technology has changed marketing," *Forbes,* April 10, 1995, p. 76, via Nexis.

45. [No author], "Using databases to seek out the brand loyal shoppers," *Progressive Grocer,* February 1995, p. S10, via Nexis.

46. Personal communication from John Cummings, president, John Cummings and Associates, June 1995.

47. Quoted in Alice Z. Cuneo, "Savvy frequent-buyer plans built on loyal base," *Advertising Age,* March 20, 1995, p. S10. Also, interview with Gary Langstaff, president, Retail Resolve, June 1995.

48. Karen Burka, "Customer retention: real thing for Coke; Coca-Cola Co," *Direct,* January 1994, p. 1.

49. Ibid.

50. [No author], "Two-thirds of major retailers are using database marketing," *Advanced Promotion Technology Vision News,* January–February 1995, p. 3.

51. [No author], "Using databases to seek out the brand loyal shoppers," *Progressive Grocer,* February 1995, p. S10.

52. Laurie Freeman, "Direct contact key to building brands," *Advertising Age,* October 25, 1993, p. S2.

53. Sylvia Wieland Noaki, "Retailers get personal with customers," *Seattle Times,* March 24, 1995, p. E4. Sears, for example, intensified its bid for middle-class Hispanic Americans by creating a magazine targeted to them, *Nuestra Gente.* According to a representative of Sears' Hispanic ad agency, the merchandiser's executives decided to create the magazine when they realized that no Hispanic periodical signaled the middle-class Latino audience values Sears was trying to mirror. *Nuestra Gente* did that from front to back. But the magazine, which carried ads from companies other than Sears, clearly also had additional value as a name collecter. Sears distributed single copies throughout middle-class Hispanic American communities and offered free subscriptions inside. In that way the company built a database that reflected the kind of people that it wanted as its core Hispanic consumers. Interview with Gilda Bullon, account executive, Mendoza, Dillon & Asociados, March 1995.

54. Scott Greiper, "Advanced promotion technologies," S. G. Warburg Research, January 20, 1995, p. 8.

55. [No author], "Two-thirds of major retailers are using database marketing," p. 3.

56. Greiper, "Advanced Promotion Technologies," pp. 21–22.

57. See, for example, Larry Armstrong, "Coupon clippers, save your scissors," *Business Week,* June 20, 1994, p. 164; James McNair, "Food marketing goes high tech," *Miami Herald,* January 10, 1994, p. 7; Denise Zimmerman, "Supervalu tests system in Pittsburgh," *SN Supermarket News,* September 12, 1994, p. 35; and Gary Levin, "Supermarkets hold best purchase data," *Advertising Age,* October 17, 1994, p. 31.

58. Gandy, *The Panoptic Sort,* pp. 177–225.

59. Karl Dentino, "Taking privacy into our own hands," *Direct Marketing,* September 1994, p. 38; and GG and ES, "Map issued for Internet advertising," *Direct Intelligence,* September 1994, p. 5.

60. Peppers and Rogers, *The One to One Future,* p. 328.

61. Peppers, "Digitizing desire, part two: How technology has changed marketing," p. 76.

62. [No author], "Two-thirds of major retailers are using database marketing," p. 3.

63. Don E. Schultz, quoted in [No author], "Using databases to seek out the brand loyal shoppers," p. S10.

64. Communication with Anthony Lee, marketing development vice president, Spiegel Catalogs, June 5, 1995.

65. Cuneo, "Savvy frequent-buyer plans built on loyal base," p. S10.

66. Peppers and Rogers, *The One to One Future,* p. 108.

67. Leslie Wayne, "If it's Tuesday, this must be my family: Mega-travelers love their lot, despite the costs," *New York Times,* Sunday, May 14, 1995, sect. 3, p. 1.

68. Ibid.

69. Harold Brierley, "The art of relationship marketing," *Direct Marketing,* September 1994, p. 22, emphasis added.

70. Ibid.

71. Wayne, "If it's Tuesday, this must be my family," sect. 3, p. 12.

72. Interview with Barbara Dolan, May 1995.

73. Andrew Leckey, "Bank fees are on the rise," *Chicago Tribune,* May 18, 1995, p. 7.

74. Saul Hansell, "The bane of today's banks: Those educated consumers," *New York Times,* June 5, 1995, p. A1.

75. Maria Mooshill, "Bank's $3 teller fee has pros wondering," *Advertising Age,* May 15, 1995, p. 12C.

76. Hansell, "The bane of today's banks," p. A1; and interview with Jim Derosier, vice president, Mastercard International, May 1995.

77. Michael Hales, "Focusing on 15% of the pie," *Bank Marketing,* April 1995, p. 29.

78. Len Egol, "Quaker flirts with Direct—again," *Direct,* September 1993, p. 15.

79. Ibid. Also, interview with Marion Jacobson, brand manager, Gatorade Division, Quaker Oats Company, May 1995.

80. Rapp and Collins, *The Great Marketing Turnaround* p. 97.

81. Ibid.

82. Ibid., p. 98.

83. Quoted in "Chrysler's Cirrus takes on Japanese," *Advertising Age,* August 15, 1995, p. 45.

84. Deirdre Carmody, "Magazines go niche-hunting with custom-made sections," *New York Times,* June 26, 1995, p. D7.

85. Rapp and Collins, *The Great Marketing Turnaround,* p. 98.

86. Keith Kelly, "Detroit puts publishers back in the driver's seat," *Advertising Age,* October 24, 1994, p. 4.

87. Peppers and Rogers, *The One to One Future,* p. 235.

88. [No author], "Schwab expands lead in personal investment technology," *PR Newswire,* May 31, 1995.

89. [No author], "Individual to provide iNews personalized news service for The Microsoft Network," *Business Wire,* June 12, 1995.

CHAPTER SEVEN

1. Edwin Artzt, "The future of advertising," *Vital Speeches,* September 1, 1994 (delivered May 12, 1994), via Nexis.

2. Richard Rappaport, "Digitizing desire," part 1, *Forbes ASAP,* April 10, 1995, p. 66.

3. Donald Libby, "Cruising and vacuuming the Internet," *Internet Marketing News,* January 20, 1995, p. 7.

4. Artzt, "The future of advertising."

5. Dottie Enrico, "High-tech media may reshape ads," *USA Today,* March 13, 1995, p. 2B.

6. Artzt, "The future of advertising."

7. Ibid.

8. Ibid.

9. See, for example, Michael Williams, "Rupert's sporting life," *Variety,* July 23, 1995, p. 1.

10. Artzt, "The future of advertising."

11. See, for example, Maureen Christopher, "Cable clout: P&G." *Advertising Age,* June 23, 1980, p. 1; Maureen Christopher, "P&G slates cable ad hike," *Advertising Age,* December 12, 1983; Maureen Christopher, "Who's Who hardly better than Who Was," *Advertising Age,* November 12, 1984, p. 72; Steven Colford, "P&G ventures into video," *Advertising Age,* September 2, 1985, p. 6.

12. See, for example, Verne Gay, "Advertiser, affiliate objections growing, NBC, ABC take 15s," *Advertising Age,* October 7, 1985, p. 1; and Bernice Kanner, "S&S, C&W talks off; P&G may be reason," *Advertising Age,* February 4, 1980, p. 1.

13. Stuart Elliot, "From the company that invented the soap opera, a call to embrace new technology," *New York Times,* May 13, 1994, p. D16.

14. Conversation with Judy Black, senior partner and co-director of interactive development at Bozell, June 1995.

15. Interview with Suzanne Kaufman, executive vice president–director of new technologies at N. W. Ayer and Partners' Media Edge unit, June 1995.

16. Quoted in Allen Rosenshine, "Advertising's demise greatly exaggerated," *Advertising Age,* March 20, 1995, p. 15.

17. Ibid.

18. Rance Crain, "Artzt's call cause for agency concern," *Advertising Age,* March 20, 1995, p. 12.

19. Debra Aho Williamson, "The latest pitch: Interactive AOR," *Advertising Age,* January 30, 1995, p. 13.

20. Enrico, "High-tech media may reshape ads," p. 2B.

21. Scott Donaton and Pat Sloan, "Control new media: Artzt spurs advertisers to seek greater role in programming," *Advertising Age,* March 13, 1995, p. 1.

22. See Stan Rapp and Tom Collins, *The Great Marketing Turnaround* (Englewood Cliffs, N. J.: Prentice Hall, 1990).

23. Adrienne Ward Fawcett, "Special report: Brand forecast; interactive looms large in budgets," *Advertising Age,* October 3, 1994, p. S1.

24. [No author], "*Advertising Age*'s media future forum," *Advertising Age,* June 26, 1995, p. 10.

25. Ibid.

26. Wayne Friedman and Jane Weaver, "Calculating cyberspace," *Inside Media,* February 15, 1995, p. 1.

27. Ibid.

28. Wayne Friedman, "Cyberspace coalition," *Inside Media,* March 29, 1995, p. 5.

29. Ibid.

30. P&G executive Robert Herbold (representing CASIE), quoted in Steven W. Colford, "Mr. Herbold Goes to Washington," *Advertising Age,* July 18, 1994, p. 21.

31. Ibid.

32. Nick Donatiello, quoted in "Artzt enthusiastic about CASIE gains," *Advertising Age,* March 13, 1995, p. S24.

33. See Maureen Christopher "Cable Ad Bureau debut readied," *Advertising Age,* August 4, 1980, p. 58; Maureen Christopher, "Massive cable study set to roll," *Advertising Age,* February 9, 1981, p. 2; Colby Coates, "Arbitron plots path to ratings battle," *Advertising Age,* April 13, 1981, p. 3; Tom Bayer, "Advertisers urged to delve CATV depths," *Advertising Age,* July 6, 1981, p. 58; James Forkan, "TV raters explore 'unidentified' viewing," *Advertising Age,* November 2, 1981, p. 68; Maureen Christopher, "Cable TV: It's still in a swirl," *Advertising Age,* November 16, 1981, p. S1; James Forkan, "New president unsure of metering: ESPN balks at Nielsen," *Advertising Age,* February 8, 1982, p. 2; Susan Spillman, "Nielsen to compare 6 methods: Test ways to measure cable," *Advertising Age,* March 1, 1982, p. 3; [Editorial], "Cable at the crossroads," *Advertising Age,* March 1, 1982, p. 6; Hugh Beville, Jr., "Cable data: another view," *Advertising Age,* March 1, 1982, p. M36; Maureen Christopher, "Cable ties to Madison Avenue," *Advertising Age,* March 9, 1981, p. 73; Colby Coates, "ESPN signs up for Nielsens," *Advertising Age,* June 7, 1982, p. 1; Sarah Stiasen, "With data, if you've got them, flaunt them," *Advertising Age,* November 15, 1982, p. M22; Susan Spillman, "Tracking cable no easy task, test finds," *Advertising Age,* March 7, 1983, p. 34; Jack Meyers, "[Cable] Networks stake survival on ad revenues," *Advertising Age,* May 31, 1984, p. M30; and Len Strazewski, "As milestones fall, cable carries more weight," *Advertising Age,* November 30, 1987, p. S7.

34. Friedman and Weaver, "Calculating cyberspace," p. 1.

35. Joe Mandese, "'Clickstreams' in Cyberspace," *Advertising Age,* March 20, 1995, p. 18.

36. Friedman and Weaver, "Calculating cyberspace," p. 1.

37. Lester Wunderman, "New frontiers in direct marketing," *Direct Marketing,* December 1993, p. 28.

38. Redgate Communications, "Will new technology change the marketing rules?" *Direct Marketing,* October 1994, p. 14. The article is an excerpt of the firm's paper "New Rules. New Media."

39. Ibid.

40. Donald Libby, "Cruising and vacuuming the Internet," p. 7.

41. Interview with Suzanne Kaufman, executive vice president–director of new technologies at N. W. Ayer and Partners' Media Edge unit, June 1995.

42. Don Peppers and Martha Rogers, *The One to One Future* (New York: Doubleday, 1993), p. 377.

43. On the consolidation of list firms, see Eileen Norris, "Databased marketing sets enticing bait," *Advertising Age,* November 11, 1988, p. S10.

44. Andrew Susman, "New media and brand reformation," *Advertising Age,* August 8, 1994, p. 18.

45. Wunderman, "New frontiers in direct marketing," p. 29.

46. See, for example, Judith Lockwood, "Dialing for dollars: Video dial tone," *Convergence,* May 1995, p. 19; and David Smith, "Reinventing business in the inforcosm," *Convergence,* May 1995, p. 34.

47. [No author], "Interactive television pioneers," *Direct Marketing,* October 1994, p. 19.

48. See, for example, Christine Blank, "Taking a slow road in Orlando," *Advertising Age,* June 26, 1995, p. 24. See also Fawcett, "Special Report: Brand forecast; interactive looms large in budgets," p. S1; and Richard Purcell, "Anything you want—virtually," *Convergence,* May 1995, p. 5.

49. See, for example, Keith Kelly and Joe Mandese, "TV ads set record, $1B still unspent," *Advertising Age,* June 12, 1995, p. 1; R. Craig Endicott, "Special report; The ad age 300: Gleeful magazines make most of rebound," *Advertising Age,* June 12, 1995, p. S1; and Martin Peters, "Blockbuster set to face the music," *Variety,* May 22, 1995, p. 1.

50. Martin Peers, "Cable turns the tables on broadcast tv," *Variety,* September 17, 1995, p. 1.

51. See [Editorial], "Get ready for '97," *Advertising Age,* June 19, 1995, p. 21.

52. Tom Rogers, quoted in Rappaport, "Digitizing desire," p. 66.

53. See Lindsey Kelly, "Interactive TV's rough road: cable, telecom companies inching toward viable systems," *Advertising Age,* March 13, 1995, p. S12; and Artzt, "The future of advertising."

54. Quoted in Rappaport, "Digitizing desire," p. 66.

55. Michael Schrage, "Bob Herbold," *Mediaweek,* February 6, 1995, p. IQ8.

56. Stuart Elliot, "The Internet is being used because, as an executive says, everyone wants a connection to what's new," *New York Times,* April 24, 1995, p. D10.

57. Deborah Aho, "P&G backs words with action," *Advertising Age,* May 23, 1994, p. 14.

58. Peppers and Rogers, *The One to One Future,* p. 83.

59. Raymond Serafin, "Even Lamborghini must think marketing," *Advertising Age,* May 1, 1995, p. 4.

CHAPTER EIGHT

1. Peter Brimelow, *Alien Nation* (New York: Random House, 1995); Michael Lind, *The Next American Nation* (New York: Free Press, 1995); Douglas Massey and Nancy Denton, *American Apartheid: Segregation and the Making of the Underclass* (Cambridge: Harvard University Press, 1993); and Arthur Meir Schlesinger, Jr., *The Disuniting of America* (New York: Norton, 1992).

2. See, as an example, John McCormick et al., "The Overclass," *Newsweek,* July 31, 1995, p. 33.

3. The *Dallas Morning News* article put the percentage at one-third, while a piece in *Roll Call,* a newspaper aimed at Congress, said some estimates were closer to two-thirds. See David Dillon, "Security for sale," *Dallas Morning News,* June 19, 1994, p. 1A; and Morton Kondrake, "Instead of 100,000 cops why not ask for a million?" *Roll Call,* April 18, 1994.

4. Dillon, "Security for sale," p. 1A.

5. U.C.L.A. planning director John Friedman, quoted by Dillon in "Security for sale."

6. Michael Goodboe, vice president of Wackenhut, quoted in William Booth, "When no place seems 'safe' anymore," *Washington Post,* January 3. 1995, p. A1.

7. Quoted in Dillon, "Security for sale," p. 1A.

8. Ibid.

9. Quoted in J. Linn Allen, "Tragic blindness to think city's problems can be left behind," *Chicago Tribune,* September 11, 1994, Perspection Section, p. 1.

10. Massey and Denton, *American Apartheid.*

INDEX

Naisbitt, John, 43, 49, 128
National Decision Systems, 131
National Inquirer, 196
National Parks, 93
NBA (National Basketball Association), 116
NBA Hot Shots, 116
NBA Plus, 153
NBC, 24, 26, 49, 50–52, 159, 180, 191
Negroponte, Nicholas, 10, 118, 192
Netscape, 123
New Rules, 43
news, 3, 4, 6, 7, 9, 10, 38, 52, 53, 76, 89, 92, 93, 94, 99, 125, 151, 154–55, 158, 161, 178, 179, 180, 187, 189, 190, 191, 192–93, 196, 197, 199
newsletters, 82
newspapers, 3, 4, 8, 9, 10, 12, 13, 14, 22, 27, 53, 56, 59, 65, 93, 111, 133, 151, 178, 187, 168, 174, 187
Newsweek, 58, 122
New Traditionalist woman, 68
New Yorker, 29, 30, 154, 196
New York Times, 150, 152
NFL (National Football League), 153
Nick at Nite, 9
Nickelodeon, 5, 72–73, 105, 114, 186
Nielsen, xii, xiii, 25–26, 47–49, 87–88, 102–3, 129
Nimeh, George, xiv
Nintendo, 77
Nissan, 153
Northwestern University, 166
Nueman, Russ, xiv
N. W. Ayer and Partners, 58, 163

Ogilvy and Mather, 61
Ohlsten, Jerry, xiii
OK Cola, 78
on-demand programming, 178
Onramp, 122, 164
on-site marketing, 64, 110
Oprah, 79
Orlando, 179
Ostrow, Joseph, xiii
outdoor advertising, 14, 55, 64. *See also* billboards

package goods, 96–97, 140, 142–44, 158, 181
Paddock, Barbara, xiii
Pallas, Brad, xiii, 96
Palmer, Volney, 22
Palmolive, 14
Pampers, 157
Paramount, 52
Parents, 95
parents, 40, 42, 68, 69, 70–73, 97–99, 100, 106, 152, 175, 200
Pathfinder, 116
pay-cable, 12, 51, 157
pay-per-view, 157, 160, 189
Pennsylvania, 195
People, 9, 153
People Meter, 48, 73, 170
Pepsi, 133, 182
Pertschuk, Michael, 18
Petretti, Vincenzo, xiv
pharmaceuticals, 64, 77, 140
Philadelphia, 99, 153
Philip Morris, 14, 142, 152
Phoenix, 45, 143, 194
photography, 21, 93–94, 97–98, 107, 116
physicians, 61
Pike's Peak Ascent, 114